Time Out

SHORTLIST

Barcelona
2008

WHAT'S NEW | WHAT'S ON | WHAT'S BEST

www.timeout.com/barcelona

Contents

Barcelona by Area

Essentials

Published by Time Out Guides Ltd
Universal House
251 Tottenham Court Road
London W1T 7AB
Tel: + 44 (0)20 7813 3000
Fax: + 44 (0)20 7813 6001
Email: guides@timeout.com
www.timeout.com

Managing Director Peter Fiennes
Editorial Director Ruth Jarvis
Deputy Series Editor Dominic Earle
Business Manager Gareth Garner
Editorial Manager Holly Pick
Accountant Ija Krasnikova

Time Out Guides is a wholly owned subsidiary of Time Out Group Ltd.

© **Time Out Group Ltd**
Chairman Tony Elliott
Financial Director Richard Waterlow
Time Out Magazine Ltd MD David Pepper
Group General Manager/Director Nichola Coulthard
Managing Director, Time Out International Cathy Runciman
Time Out Communications Ltd MD David Pepper
Production Director Mark Lamond
Group Marketing Director John Luck
Group Art Director John Oakey
Group IT Director Simon Chappell

Time Out and the Time Out logo are trademarks of Time Out Group Ltd.

This edition first published in Great Britain in 2007 by Ebury Publishing
A Random House Group Company
Company information can be found on www.randomhouse.co.uk
10 9 8 7 6 5 4 3 2 1

For further distribution details, see www.timeout.com

ISBN 13: 978184670 0224
ISBN 10: 1-84670-022-1

A CIP catalogue record for this book is available from the British Library

Printed and bound by Firmengruppe APPL, aprinta druck, Wemding, Germany

The Random House Group Limited makes every effort to ensure that the papers used in
our books are made from trees that have been legally sourced from well-managed and
credibly certified forests. Our paper procurement policy can be found on
www.randomhouse.co.uk

Barcelona Shortlist

The **Time Out Barcelona Shortlist 2008** is one of a new series of guides that draws on Time Out's background as a magazine publisher to keep you current with what's going on in town. As well as Barcelona's key sights and the best of its eating, drinking and leisure options, it picks out the most exciting venues to have opened in the last year and gives a full calendar of events from September 2007 to December 2008. It also includes features on the important news, trends and openings, all compiled by locally based editors and writers. Whether you're visiting for the first time in your life or the first time this year, you'll find the *Time Out Barcelona Shortlist* contains all you need to know, in a format that is both portable and easy to use.

The guide divides central Barcelona into seven areas, each containing listings for Sights & Museums, Eating & Drinking, Shopping, Nightlife and Arts & Leisure, and maps pinpointing their locations. At the front of the book are chapters rounding up these scenes city-wide, and giving a shortlist of our overall picks. We include itineraries for days out, plus essentials such as transport information and hotels.

Our listings give phone numbers as dialled within Spain. From abroad, use your country's exit code followed by 34 (the country code for Spain) and the number given.

We have noted price categories by using one to four euro signs (**€-€€€€**), representing budget, moderate, expensive and luxury. Major credit cards are accepted unless otherwise stated. We also indicate when a venue is NEW, and give Event highlights.

All our listings are double-checked, but businesses do sometimes close or change their hours or prices, so it's always a good idea to call a venue before visiting. While every effort has been made to ensure accuracy, the publishers cannot accept responsibility for any errors that this guide may contain.

Venues are marked on the maps using symbols numbered according to their order within the chapter and colour-coded as follows:

- ❶ Sights & Museums
- ❶ Eating & Drinking
- ❶ Shopping
- ❶ Nightlife
- ❶ Arts & Leisure

Map key	
Major sight or landmark	
Hospital or college	
Railway station	
Park	
River	
Carretera	
Main road	
Main road tunnel	
Pedestrian road	
Airport	✈
Church	✚
Metro station, FGC station	Ⓜ ⍉
Area name	EIXAMPLE

Time Out Barcelona Shortlist 2008

EDITORIAL

Editor Sally Davies
Copy Editors Edoardo Albert,
  Simon Coppock, Ros Sales
Researchers John O'Donovan,
  Alx Phillips, Roberto Rama,
  Dylan Simanowitz
Proofreader Gill Harvey

DESIGN

Art Director Scott Moore
Art Editor Pinelope Kourmouzoglou
Senior Designer Henry Elphick
Graphic Designer Gemma Doyle
Junior Graphic Designer Kei Ishimaru
Digital Imaging Simon Foster, Tessa Kar
Ad Make-up Jodi Sher
Picture Editor Jael Marschner
Deputy Picture Editor Tracey Kerrigan
Picture Researcher Helen McFarland

ADVERTISING

Sales Director/Sponsorship Mark Phillips
International Sales Manager Fred Durman
International Sales Consultant
  Ross Canadé
International Sales Executive
  Charlie Sokol
Advertising Sales Time Out (Barcelona)
  Creative Media Group
Advertising Assistant Kate Staddon

MARKETING

Marketing Manager Yvonne Poon
**Sales & Marketing Director, North
America** Lisa Levinson
Marketing Designer Anthony Huggins

PRODUCTION

Production Manager Brendan McKeown
Production Co-ordinator Caroline Bradford
Production Controller Susan Whittaker

CONTRIBUTORS

This guide was researched and written by Sally Davies and Nadia Feddo, with additional contributions from Jonathan Bennett, Guillermo González, Alx Phillips and Tara Stevens.

PHOTOGRAPHY

Photography by Natalie Pecht, except: pages 7, 13, 33, 43, 47, 49, 62, 68, 78, 81, 105, 114, 167 Karl Blackwell; pages 8, 19, 23, 45, 50, 98, 133, 157 Olivia Rutherford; page 35 Ros Ribas; page 38 Albert Casanovas; page 130 Greg Gladman.

The following image was provided by the featured establishment/artist: page 95.

Cover photograph: La Pedrera (Casa Milà), Credit: © AM Corporation / Alamy.

MAPS

JS Graphics (john@jsgraphics.co.uk).

Thanks to Jordi Artal, Greg Gladman and Lorena Martínez.

About Time Out

Founded in 1968, Time Out has expanded from humble London beginnings into the leading resource for those wanting to know what's happening in the world's greatest cities. As well as our influential what's-on weeklies in London, New York and Chicago, we publish more than a dozen other listings magazines in cities as varied as Beijing and Mumbai. The magazines established Time Out's trademark style: sharp writing, informed reviewing and bang up-to-date inside knowledge of every scene.

Time Out made the natural leap into travel guides in the 1980s with the City Guide series, which now extends to over 50 destinations around the world. Written and researched by expert local writers and generously illustrated with original photography, the full-size guides cover a larger area than our Shortlist guides and include many more venue reviews, along with additional background features and a full set of maps.

Throughout this rapid growth, the company has remained proudly independent, still owned by Tony Elliott nearly four decades after he started Time Out London as a single fold-out sheet of A5 paper. This independence extends to the editorial content of all our publications, this Shortlist included. No establishment has been featured because it has advertised, and no payment has influenced any of our reviews. And, for our critics, there's definitely no such thing as a free lunch: all restaurants and bars are visited and reviewed anonymously, and Time Out always picks up the bill.
For more about the company, see www.timeout.com.

Don't Miss
2008

Casa Batlló p11

Sights & Museums

With the opening of two new museums, 2007 was a bumper year for Barcelona sights; fears that the city might 'do a Prague' and fall prey to the tourist fatigue that generally follows a few years in the limelight seem unfounded. Though both museums – the Museu Olímpic i de l'Esport (p116) and the Museu de la Música (p126) – are in fact revamps (and relocations), someone out there did the sums and they add up to very healthy visitor numbers. Certainly the babel of languages on the streets in summer and the ever-lengthening queue for the Museu Picasso would seem to attest to the city's enduring popularity.

Contrary to what those holding a determined vigil along the Carrer Montcada might believe, packing comfy shoes and drawing up a checklist of unmissable sights is not what a weekend in Barcelona is all about. Yes, Gaudí was here, and Picasso, but their fingerprints are all over the city and the fun lies in seeking out their lesser-known work. (For a little help tracking down some of Picassos, see the walk on p44.)

With a couple of exceptions, such as the excellent Fundació Joan Miró (p113), or the odd gem of an exhibition at the CaixaForum (p112), Barcelona is a city to savour from the street. Even its best-known museums, such as the Picasso (p74) or the MACBA (p88), are really more notable for their stunning buildings than their holdings. A trip around the inside of the Sagrada Familia (p129) is nothing compared to contemplating the excesses of its façade, while the huddle of medieval streets around the cathedral (p56) is as intriguing to explore as its tourist-thronged interior. We do not, however, suggest you extend this approach to Barcelona's most-visited sight, the Nou Camp football stadium (p152), which looks exactly like a football stadium.

Barrio by barrio

The Old City, centred around the cathedral, is made up of the scruffy **Raval**, the **Barri Gòtic** and the **Born**, and is flanked by the **Montjuïc** hill to the west and the newly cool **Poblenou** area to the east. Fanning out above this are the grid-like streets of the **Eixample**, almost subsuming the former village of **Gràcia**.

Cutting straight through the Old City are La Rambla and Via Laietana. **La Rambla**, once a seasonal riverbed that formed the western limit of the 13th-century city, is now a tree-lined boulevard dividing the medieval buildings and cathedral of the Barri Gòtic from the Raval, home to the MACBA and the CCCB (p88). **Via Laietana**, driven through in the 19th century to bring light and air to the slums, is the boundary between the Barri Gòtic, and Sant Pere and the achingly trendy Born, where you'll find the stunning Palau de la Música Catalana (p76), the Museu Picasso and the Parc de la Ciutadella (p77). Between these two thoroughfares is the **Plaça Sant Jaume**, the heart of the city ever since it was the centre of the Roman fort from which Barcelona grew.

With the demolition of the medieval walls in 1854, the open fields beyond the choleric city were a blank canvas for urban planners,

S H O R T L I S T

Best newcomers
- Museu de la Música (p126)
- Museu Olímpic i de l'Esport (p116)

Best temporary exhibitions
- CaixaForum (p112)
- CCCB (p88)
- Fundació Joan Miró (p113)

Gaudí's greatest
- Casa Batlló (p123)
- Palau Güell (p70)
- Park Güell (p144)
- La Pedrera (p127)
- Sagrada Família (p129)

Oddball museums
- Museu de Carrosses Fúnebres (p126)
- Museu del Calçat (p56)
- Museu del Perfum (p127)
- Museu Frederic Marès (p57)

Gorgeously florid buildings
- Casa Batlló (p123)
- Hospital de la Santa Creu i Sant Pau (p126)
- Palau de la Música Catalana (p74)

Let us pray
- Cathedral (p56)
- Sagrada Família (p129)
- Sant Pau del Camp (p94)
- Santa Maria del Mar (p77)

Best for kids
- L'Aquàrium (p108)
- CosmoCaixa (p155)
- Museu de la Xocolata (p74)
- Zoo de Barcelona (p77)

Prettiest parks
- Jardí Botànic (p113)
- Parc de la Ciutadella (p77)
- Park Güell (p144)

Best views
- Park Güell (p144)
- Sagrada Família spires (p129)
- Telefèric de Montjuïc (p116)
- Torre de Collserola (p153)

Palau de la Música Catalana p9

architects and sculptors. The Eixample, with its gridiron layout, is a showcase for the greatest works of Modernisme, including the Sagrada Familia, Hospital de Sant Pau, Casa Batlló and La Pedrera. When the only traffic was the clip-clopping horse and cart, these whimsical flights of architectural fancy must have been still more impressive; nowadays the Eixample can be noisy and polluted, as almost every road carries four lanes of traffic. Beyond lies the **Park Güell**, with Gaudí's emblematic dragon.

Getting around

Public transport is cheap and generally excellent in Barcelona, but there is little call for the short-term visitor to use it. The Old City is easily traversed on foot, as is the Passeig de Gràcia – although trips to sights such as the Park Güell or the Sagrada Familia are a tedious hike on a hot day. For a map of the metro, see the back flap.

The city council runs walking tours on various themes (Picasso, Modernisme, Gourmet and Gothic) at weekends and occasional other days. These tours start in the underground tourist office in Plaça Catalunya. The Gothic tour concentrates on the history and buildings of the Old City, while the Picasso visits the artist's haunts and ends with a visit to the Picasso Museum (entry is included in the price). The Modernisme tour is a circuit of the 'Golden Square' in the Eixample, taking in Gaudí's Casa Batlló and La Pedrera, and the Gourmet tour includes 13 stops in some of the city's emblematic cafés, food shops and markets. Tours take 90 minutes to two hours, excluding the museum trip. For more information, see www.barcelonaturisme.com.

A fun and eco-friendly way to get around the city (and to head to the beach) is to hire a bright yellow Trixi rickshaw. Running 11am to 8pm, April to September, and costing €10 per half hour, they can be hailed on the street or booked on 93 310 13 79 and www.trixi.com. Cycling has also seen a boost with the council's new Bicing scheme (see box p62). For other bike hire, see p180.

There are two tourist buses seen all over town: the orange Barcelona Tours (93 317 64 54, www.barcelonatours.es, €19-€12) and the white Bus Turistic (www.barcelonaturisme.com, €18-€11). The former is less frequent but less popular, meaning you won't have to queue, while the latter gives a book of discounts for various attractions. Both visit many of the same sights and cost much the same.

Tickets

As well as those given with the Bus Turístic passes, a range of discount passes exists. The Articket (www.articketbcn.com, €20) gives free entry to seven museums and art galleries over three months: Fundació Miró, MACBA, the MNAC, Espai Gaudí-La Pedrera, the Fundació Tàpies, the CCCB and the Museu Picasso. The ticket is available from participating venues and tourist offices.

The Barcelona Card (€23-€30) gives two to five days of unlimited transport on the metro and buses, as well as discounts on the airport bus and cable cars, reduced entry to a wide variety of museums and attractions, and discounts at several restaurants, bars and shops. The card is sold at tourist offices, the airport and various participating venues.

A word of warning

Barcelona's reputation for muggings is not completely without justification, though robbery involving violence is rare. Bag-snatching and pickpocketing are rife, however, especially in the Old City, on the beach and on public transport. Leave whatever you can in your hotel, keep your wallet in your front pocket, wear backpacks on the front and be wary of anyone trying to clean something off your shoulder or sell you a posy or a newspaper.

Sagrada Família p9

Wushu p15

WHAT'S BEST
Eating & Drinking

If the last couple of years are anything to go by, the days of throwaway restaurant trends may well be numbered. First off we had the doomed, multitasking resto-clubs – not in a sophisticated 1920s dinner-dance sense, but rather lame efforts involving airline food until midnight, when the tables would be cleared to create a dancefloor in a manner uncomfortably reminiscent of the village-hall disco. Then we had the restaurant that, inexplicably, only served dishes made from eggs, and there was Camper shoes' foray into the dining scene with Foodball, which served food in – yes – balls. Its closure in 2007 was seen as a victory for good sense by almost everyone in Barcelona.

One rather more welcome trend that has risen to take the place of these fly-by-nights is a return to basics, done well and with prime ingredients at centre stage. Albert Adrià, brother and erstwhile pastry chef to the celebrated Ferran at El Bulli, opened tapas bar Inopia (p132) with a view to re-establishing old favourites, such as ham croquettes or *patatas bravas*, but using excellent quality produce. Chef Carles Abellan of Comerç 24 (p80) also learnt his art in the legendary kitchens of El Bulli, but like Albert has eschewed the fanciful in his new

CULLERA
de BOIX

RESTAURANT

Rda. Sant Pere, 24 BCN · Tel. 93 268 79 82
info@culleradeboix.com · www.culleradeboix.com

tapas venture Tapa Ç24 (p134). His *ensaladilla*, croquettes and lentil stew also come at a price, but taste exactly as classic tapas should – and so rarely do.

Elsewhere, ethnic cooking was given a boost with the opening of the excellent Wushu (p83), a pan-Asian restaurant with an alumnus of Sydney's Neil Perry wielding the woks. Vietnamese restaurant Hanoi has opened a new branch (p132) in response to enormous demand, and new restaurant Icho (p151) pulls off a curious marriage of Japanese and Spanish cuisine with aplomb.

Drink up

One of the first words in Spanish uttered by many visitors is *cerveza* – but few know that it applies only to bottled beer. If you want draught beer, ask for a *caña*, which is a small measure; only a true tourist would ask for a *jarra*, which is closer to a pint. Recently there has been a welcome comeback for Moritz beer, brewed in Barcelona and infinitely superior to the ubiquitous Estrella. Shandy (*clara*) is also popular, untainted by the stigma it has in the UK.

Catalan wines are gaining ground over Rioja and Albariño, even internationally, and it's worth looking out for the local DOs Priorat, Montsant, Toro and Costers del Segre, as well as the commonplace Penedès. Most wine drunk here is red (*negre/tinto*), apart from the many many cavas, running from *semi-sec* (which is 'half-dry', but actually pretty sweet) to *brut nature* (very dry).

Spanish coffee is strong and generally excellent. The three basic types are *solo* (also known simply as *café*), a small strong black coffee; *cortado*, the same but with a little milk, and *café*

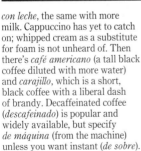

Saüc

con leche, the same with more milk. Cappuccino has yet to catch on; whipped cream as a substitute for foam is not unheard of. Then there's *café americano* (a tall black coffee diluted with more water) and *carajillo*, which is a short, black coffee with a liberal dash of brandy. Decaffeinated coffee (*descafeinado*) is popular and widely available, but specify *de máquina* (from the machine) unless you want instant (*de sobre*).

Tea is pretty poor and generally best avoided. If you can't live without it, ask for cold milk on the side (*'leche fría aparte'*) or run the risk of getting a glass of hot milk and a teabag. Basic herbal teas, such as chamomile (*manzanilla*), limeflower (*tila*) and mint (*menta*), are common.

Tapas tips

Tapas are not an especially Catalan concept, and with a few exceptions (such as those at Inopia, Tapa Ç24 or Quimet i Quimet, p120), they are a pale imitation of those found elsewhere in Spain. The Andalucian custom of giving a free tapa, or just a saucer of crisps and nuts, is almost unheard of.

What has caught on big time in Barcelona are *pintxo* bars – their Basque origin means that the word is always given in Euskera – such as Euskal Extea (p80). A *pintxo* (be careful not to confuse it with the Spanish term *pincho*, which simply refers to a very small tapa) consists of some ingenious culinary combination on a small slice of bread. Platters of them are usually brought out at particular times, often around 1pm and again at 8pm. *Pintxos* come impaled on toothpicks, which you keep on your plate so that the barman can tally them up at the end. The Brits hold the worst reputation for abusing this eminently civilised system by 'forgetting' to hand over all their toothpicks.

Without a decent grasp of the language, tapas bars can be quite intimidating unless you know exactly what you want. Don't be afraid to seek guidance, but some of the more standard offerings will include *tortilla* (potato omelette), *patatas bravas* (fried potatoes in a spicy red sauce and garlic mayonnaise), *ensaladilla* (Russian salad), *pinchos morunos* (small pork skewers), *champiñones al ajillo* (mushrooms fried in garlic), *gambas al ajillo* (prawns and garlic), *mejillones a la marinera* (mussels in a tomato and onion sauce), *chocos* (squid fried in batter), *almejas al vapor* (steamed clams with garlic and parsley), *pulpo* (octopus) and *pimientos del padrón* (little green peppers, one or two of which will kick like an angry mule).

How it's done

In bars, unless they're very busy or you're sitting outside, you won't usually be required to pay until you leave. If you have trouble attracting a waiter's attention, a loud but polite '*oiga*' or, in Catalan, '*escolti*' is acceptable. On the vexed question of throwing detritus on the floor (cigarette ends, paper napkins, olive pits and so on), it's safest to keep an eye on what the locals are doing.

In restaurants, lunch starts around 2pm and goes on until roughly 3.30pm or 4pm; dinner is served from about 9pm until 11.30pm or midnight. Some restaurants open earlier in the evening, but arriving before 9.30 or 10pm generally means you'll be dining alone or in the company of foreign tourists. Reserving a table is generally a good idea: not only on Friday and Saturday nights, but also on Sunday evenings and Monday lunchtimes, when few restaurants are open. Many also close for lengthy holidays, including about a week over Easter, and the month of August. We have listed closures of more than a week wherever we can, but restaurants are fickle, particularly on the issue of summer holidays, so call to check.

Money matters

Eating out in Barcelona is not as cheap as it used to be, but low mark-ups on wines keep the cost relatively reasonable for northern Europeans and Americans. All but the upmarket restaurants are required by law to serve an economical fixed-price *menú del día* (*menú* is not to be confused with the menu, which is *la carta*) at lunchtime; this usually consists of a starter, main course, dessert, bread and something to drink. The idea is to provide cheaper meals for the workers, but while it can be a real bargain, it is not by any means a taster menu or a showcase for the chef's greatest hits; rather, they're a healthier version of what in other countries might amount to a snatched lunchtime sandwich.

Laws governing the issue of prices are routinely flouted, but, legally, menus must declare if the seven per cent IVA (VAT) is included in prices or not (it rarely is), and also if there is a cover charge (generally expressed as a charge for bread). Catalans and the Spanish in general, tend to tip little, but tourists should let their conscience decide.

Maremàgnum p21

Shopping

Barcelona's high streets offer many of the same chains and labels as other large European cities. But it's at the small scale that the city really shines as a shopping destination: the indie art galleries of the upper Raval; the traditional artesans and antique shops of the Barri Gòtic; the quirky jewellery workshops of Gràcia or the hip fashion boutiques in the Born.

Shops in Barcelona match their context so neatly that they can almost seem to be part of a giant themed architectural park. The Eixample's expansive boulevards and Modernista architecture complement its wealth of upmarket designer furniture, fashion and homeware stores, while the Old City's narrow streets and restored medieval spaces are home to a jumble of small craft shops, antiques dealers and specialist outlets, selling anything from religious candles to carnival masks and anchovy-flavoured bonbons.

Marketing

Traditional local markets have maintained a key position on Barcelona's shopping list although they have had to move with the times. Many of the old rough-and-ready warehouse-style buildings have been seriously sexed up after the Ajuntament pumped over €50 million into revamping them. The new generation of markets, particularly the more central ones such as Santa Caterina or Barceloneta, are arguably more

important as pieces of high-profile architecture acting as catalysts for urban redevelopment than as support for small shopkeepers. In an attempt to fuse modern and traditional approaches to shopping, the modernised markets tend to hold far fewer actual stalls than before, with more space turned over to supermarkets, restaurants and even performance spaces. Not everyone is happy about this new direction, especially when it was revealed that the recently rebuilt Barceloneta market had been designed for future 'flexibility', with the possibility of being turned into a mall or leisure centre.

The ring thing

In the architectural equivalent of keyhole surgery, Richard Rogers is overseeing the project of inserting a vast commercial and entertainment centre into the neo-Mudéjar shell of the Las Arenas bullring on Plaça d'Espanya. The centre is due to open in 2008 and should fill the glaring shopping vacuum between the Sants neighbourhood and Montjuïc. Plans are also afoot for Barcelona's other bullring, the Modernista-style El Monumental, which is currently losing so much money that closure seems almost inevitable. One of the more popular suggestions is to convert it into a new home for the historic Bellcaire flea market (more popularly known as Els Encants Vells), which is soon to be made homeless due to large-scale remodelling at Glòries.

The best possible taste

As a newly crowned gastro capital, Barcelona is designing itself into its own navel with an ever-growing range of shops that present food as modern art. For classy chocolates in classier packaging, head to Bubó (p83), Chocolat Factory (p136), Escribà (p72) and Enric Rovira

Boqueria p21

SALAONS

(p151). Retro sweet shop chic is the order of the day at Papabubble (p66), whose USP is that the candy is cooked, stretched and rolled out right in front of you, while the newly opened Demasié (p84) proves that even biscuits can be cool.

For a kitchen cupboard makeover of sleekly packaged global groceries, head to the brand new Delishop (p136); for the more traditional aesthetic of local foodie classics, get your bagged nuts and coffee from toasting house Casa Gispert (p84), hanging herbs from Herboristeria del Rei (p65) and well-sourced artisan cheeses from Formatgeria La Seu (p65). Even golden oldies like the Vila Viniteca wine shop (p85) have moved with the times, opening a stylish taster café next door and taking wine out of the fusty *bodegas* and into young and funky surroundings.

Flash-in-the-pan fashion

The success of urban fashion fair BREAD & butter has created a buzz, throwing the spotlight on Barcelona's fashion scene, particularly the indie labels. This translates into a rash of tiny boutiques packed with unusual designs and posing of catwalk-like intensity in fashion hotspots such as C/Avinyó in the Barri Gòtic, the MACBA area in the Raval, C/Verdi in Gràcia and the Born.

Barcelona is especially strong in the arena of adventurous streetwear, helped along by the city's prestigious fashion schools churning out young designers. The most famous of them all is Custo Barcelona, but for far more affordable and fresh one-offs from the BAU Escola de Disseny head to the boutiques along C/Avinyó in the Barri Gòtic. For a good selection of interesting designers who are established but not annoyingly ubiquitous, try boutiques like Tribu (p66), On Land (p85) and Giménez y Zuazo (p92).

Open for business

Most small independent stores still open 10am-2pm and 5-8pm Monday to Saturday, but more shops are adopting a European timetable and staying open through the siesta period. Don't be surprised to see many shutters down on Saturday afternoons, especially in summer. Many shops close for at least two weeks in August. Except for the run up to Christmas, Sunday opening is still limited to shops in tourist zones such as La Rambla and the Maremàgnum. Many newspaper kiosks, bakeries and flower stalls are open Sunday mornings and the majority of convenience stores stay open all day. The newer markets, such as Barceloneta and Santa Caterina, also have extended opening hours and now open until 8.30pm Tuesday to Friday.

Shop tactics

Sales (*rebaixes* or *rebajas*) run from 7 January to mid February, and again during July and August. Tourist offices stock free Shopping Guide booklets, with a map and advice on everything from how to get your VAT refund to using the Barcelona Shopping Line bus.

Money matters

Cheap shopping in Barcelona is a thing of the past, although items that are significantly less pricey here than abroad include olive oil, cured ham, Spanish wines and home-grown designs like Zara (p67), Mango (p136) and Camper (p135). Bargaining should only be attempted at the Els Encants flea-market or when haggling over Barça strips on La Rambla; in shops, prices are fixed. As long as you're spending over €10 or so, all but the most cobwebby of places now accept major credit cards. Very few have installed chip-and-pin machines, but you will be required to show some form of picture ID.

Camper p21

La Paloma

WHAT'S BEST
Nightlife

I t's fair to say the last few years have not been especially kind to Barcelona's nightlife scene. Vociferous neighbourhood campaigns and a couple of mayors keen to be seen as giving the city back to its residents have resulted in a raft of closures and a dearth of exciting new venues.

The news is not all bad, however. In a city with more DJs than palm trees, many bars and restaurants have employed laptop turntablists to conjure up beats from bytes to enhance the eating and drinking experience. This stems partly from the current impossibility of securing an 'entertainment licence' – which allows a venue to charge an admission fee and stay open until the early hours. These combinations sometimes result in a certain

personality disorder, yet if done well, can make for a unique night.

By and large, the aforementioned laptops have all but replaced traditional live acts, now on the endangered species list thanks to the council's relentless pursuit of unlicensed music venues. The city-wide clampdown on late-night noise has resulted in the closure of over 80 bars in two years and continues to this day, counting classics such as London Bar and Kentucky among its latest victims. Even La Paloma (p93), which has outlasted civil war and a dictatorship, is having trouble surviving the wrath of its neighbours, who continue to hang signs reading '*¡Salón de baile, si! ¡Discoteca, no!*' ('Dancehall, yes! Club, no!) from their balconies during the various temporary closures that they have managed to bring about, pending improvements to soundproofing and crowd dispersal methods.

Moving out

But while the authorities seem intent on pursuing classic venues, they do support the non-traditional venues outside the city centre. Clubs like BeCool (p157) survive, hassle-free, by being in the middle of the financial district, far from nagging neighbours. At the port and far from the earshot of sleeping citizens, Mondo (p108) and Sugar (p108) spice up the otherwise lifeless Maremàgnum and the World Trade Center respectively. While last year saw the demise of legendary Café Royale, this year new and improved Suite Royale (p103) replaces it in a soundproofed basement in Barceloneta. Taxpayers finally seem to be getting some of their money's worth from the über-expensive multifunctional public square in Poblenou called the Fòrum. All of the major festivals except for Sónar have moved there: Primavera Sound, Wintercase, Summercase and BAM, as well as a Movistar tent hosting the occasional concert. The metro and bus lines have even extended their weekend operating hours to address the growing demand for late-night transport to the 'burbs.

Moving up

Still far from being New York or Paris, Barcelona has recently had a much needed shot of sophistication in the arm. Cocktail bars are popping up everywhere in a city that only a few years ago didn't know a cosmopolitan from a Manhattan, and whose most complicated drink involved ice, gin and tonic. New bars like Xix (p135), Club Mix (p85)

SHORTLIST

Best new kids on the block
- Club Mix (p85)
- Diobar (p85)
- Mondo (p108)
- Suite Royale (p103)

Best for the grown and sexy
- CDLC (p102)
- Elephant (p158)
- Mondo (p108)

Best for big-time bands
- Bikini (p151)
- Razzmatazz (p160)
- Sala Apolo (p121)

Best for small-time bands
- BeCool (p157)
- Sidecar Factory Club (p69)

Best for disco divas
- Arena (p137)
- Metro (p139)
- Salvation (p139)

Best for dancing 'til dawn
- BeCool (p157)
- Club Catwalk (p109)
- Razzmatazz/Loft (p160)
- La Terrrazza (p119)

Best for chilling
- Maumau (p121)
- Spiritual Café (p97)

Best for swingin' hepcats
- Harlem Jazz Club (p67)
- Jamboree (p67)
- Suite Royale (p103)

Best for bohemians
- Bar Pastis (p97)
- Marsella (p96)
- Tinta Roja (p121)

Best gilded dancehalls
- Luz de Gas (p138)
- La Paloma (p93)
- Sala Apolo (p121)

Best under the stars
- La Caseta del Migdia (p117)
- Danzatoria (p138)
- La Terrrazza (p119)

Fellini p25

and Omm Hotel (p175) strive to outdo each other's cocktail menus to entice the uptown crowd.

An emerging business trend in Barcelona seems to be the nightlife tour guide who doubles as a public relations firm, like Lo Mejor De Barcelona (www.lomejorde barcelona.com) or Night Barcelona (www.nightbarcelona.com), who organise nights about town to A-list parties. Musically, as everywhere, lounge is the new rock 'n' roll, and new clubs like Club Mix, Diobar (p85), and Suite Royale (p103) favour jazz funk and rare groove over four-to-the-floor house beats, which still reign supreme in La Terrrazza (p119) and Discothèque (p118).

Concerts

Barcelona tends to have musical scenes rather than any big emblematic bands. Jazz, indie, *rock català* and electronica are all well represented and local names to look out for at festivals such as BAM, Primavera Sound and Sónar include indie rockers Unfinished Sympathy, electro-popper Iris and 12Twelve, an unclassifiable quartet bringing together free jazz,

psychedelia and cosmic krautrock. Where Barcelona has had most international success is with *mestizaje* – a blend of influences including rock, flamenco, rai, hip hop, and various South American, Asian and African styles. Joining the *mestizaje* top draws of Ojos de Brujo and the Raval's 08001 are Dumballa Canalla, who fuse Catalan and gypsy folk into an electric vaudevillian performance.

The main venue for international names (as well as hotly tipped unknowns and local musicians) is the multi-faceted industrial space Razzmatazz, which has recently hosted everything from Arctic Monkeys, !!! and LCD Soundsystem to where-are-they-now bands like Marillion. Moving into fallback position, the mall-like Bikini still nets some top-notch international names and plenty of local stars. For weirder and less well-known acts, the old dancehalls Sala Apolo and Luz de Gas host several concerts a week. Global superstars perform in Montjuïc's sports stadiums or at the sprawling Fòrum, where even 44,000 people at Primavera Sound can't seem to fill the space.

L'Auditori

Arts & Leisure

At times it can seem as though Barcelona's cultural movers and shakers plough so much energy into its many festivals that there is not a great deal left to sustain the city's arts scene during the rest of the year. Classical music is perhaps an exception to this, and it has been given a fillip recently thanks to the efforts of L'Auditori (p139), which, within the space of a year, has opened a new 600-seater auditorium, installed the Museu de la Música (p126) and also overhauled its programming policy in the hope of attracting a new, younger audience.

Elsewhere, big brash theatrical productions still reign supreme, though the dance scene continues to be popular, while cinema thrives as never before.

Film

Things looked a little bleak for the independent filmgoer after the closing down of the much-loved Cine Maldà and Cine Ambigú and the end of the outdoor summer cinema, Cine Sin Techo, but a couple of years on, things are picking up again. The Cine Maldà (p69) has reopened ostensibly as a Bollywood cinema, but between the whirling saris and heavily kohled eyelids of its headline programme, you can usually find the latest release from David Lynch, Michael Winterbottom or Michel Gondry.

Cine Ambigú (p140), meanwhile, has relocated uptown. The sterile confines of the Casablanca-Gràcia cinema may not have the charm of the tatty old Apolo dance-hall

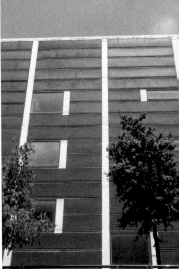

where these film nights were previously held, but the seats are considerably more comfortable.

Meanwhile, Barcelona's popularity as a film location has never been greater. In 2006, *Perfume* turned some of the city's more atmospheric *plazas* into medieval market scenes (enraging neighbours as the displays of offal attracted a plague of rodents), while Woody Allen was next to sign up. He was due to shoot his latest Scarlett Johansson vehicle, *Midnight in Barcelona*, here in summer 2007.

For undubbed, subtitled films, look for the letters 'VO' (*versió original*) in listings.

Performing arts

Thanks, in part, to linguistic censorship under Franco, Catalan theatre has traditionally been very physical and reliant on spectacle – something that has aided its international success, most notably in the case of La Fura dels Baus.

Theatre is cliquey everywhere, of course, but in Catalonia it often seems that the same coterie of directors and performers gets all the work. Little of this is in English, but sometimes groups such as Cheek by Jowl (who recently performed *The Changeling* here) are invited. Look out too for low-key productions by the local English-speaking group Black Custard.

Classical music fares rather better in Barcelona, though the emphasis is on local composers: look out for excellent concert cycles at the Palau de la Música (p76) and L'Auditori. In the world of opera Barcelona has its own *enfant terrible*, Calixto Bieito, who is renowned for his wildly polemical interpretations of *Hamlet* and *Don Giovanni*, and more recently his staging of Michel Houellebecq's *Platform*. Look out, too, for another local genius, Carles Santos, who composes, directs and performs in surreal operatic-cum-theatrical performances that combine sex, psychology and sopranos.

Although the city has many thriving contemporary dance companies, there are few major dance venues, and most companies spend a large amount of their time touring. Performers such as Pina Bausch and the Compañía Nacional de Danza (directed by the revered Nacho Duato) have played to sell-out crowds in the Teatre Nacional and the Liceu, while the Teatre Nacional has a resident company led by Sol Picó, and the Teatre Lliure hosts quite a lot of new work. However, it's generally difficult for companies to find big audiences.

Innovative ensembles such as Sol Picó and Mar Gómez usually run a new show every year, as do emblematic, influential companies such as Metros, Mudances and Gelabert-Azzopardi.

Festivals

The Festival del Grec (p40), which takes place from June to August, is the mother of all Barcelona festivals, attracting musicians, dance troupes and actors from all over the world; its open-air venues are magical on a summer night. The Marató de l'Espectacle (p40) is in June, with two nights of non-stop micro performances. Dies de Dansa (p40) offers three days of national and international dance in June and July, in sites such as the Port, the CCCB or the MACBA. Several music festivals are staged, the foremost of which are the Festival de Música Antiga (p39) and the Nous Sons (p37) festival of contemporary music, both in spring. In summer, the focus moves. Various museums hold small outdoor concerts and there are weekly events in several city parks, particularly as part of July's Clàssics als Parcs season (p40).

Family fun

Boys will be boys and will be entranced by a trip to the Nou Camp stadium (p152), either for a match or a tour of the grounds and museum. Other kid-friendly attractions include the IMAX cinema (p108), L'Aquàrium (p108), the zoo (p77), the Font Màgica de Montjuïc (p112) and trips on the cable car (p116). Even the local museums are feeling the pull of small, sticky hands on the purse strings and provide an ever-growing choice of kids' activities, from making chocolate figurines at the Museu de la Xocolata (p74) to blowing giant paint bubbles at CosmoCaixa (p155). There's also the beach, of course, and La Rambla (p69), with its entertainers, artists and living statues, although the pet stalls are finally being moved on at some point in 2007.

hello sushi
food, drink & loun...

...In the historic centre of Barcelona you can enjoy award-winning sushi and hot dishes of traditional Japonese cuisine. We invite you to try our thematic midday and evening menus based on Mediterranean & Japonese fusion specially prepared with fresh products from the Boqueria market. Here you can also have a drink in an urban atmosphere with a Zen touch...

Tues - Sun 12.30pm - 16.3...
& 20.00pm - 01.00pm

tel.93 412 08 30
Junta de comerc st.
metro Liceu-Raval

www.hello-sushi.co...

Santa Eulàlia p37

The following are the pick of the annual events that happen in Barcelona, as well as major one-off events. Further information and exact dates can be found nearer the time from flyers and seasonal guides available from tourist offices (p185). For gay and lesbian events, look out for free magazines such as *Nois* and *Shanguide*.

Dates highlighted in **bold** are public holidays.

September 2007

4-25
Festival L'Hora del Jazz
Various venues
www.amjm.org
Festival of local jazz acts, with free daytime concerts.

11 Diada Nacional de Catalunya
All over Barcelona
Flags and marches affirm cultural identity on Catalan National Day.

13-17 **Festival Asia**
Various venues
www.casaasia.es/festival
Shows, music, workshops and stalls from 17 Asian countries.

15 **Weekend Dance**
Parc del Fòrum, Poblenou
www.weekendance.es
New electronic dance festival, featuring Massive Attack and Faithless.

15-16 **Hipnotik**
CCCB (p88)
www.cccb.org
www.hipnotikfestival.com
A two-day festival that celebrates everything hip hop.

21-24 **Barcelona Arts de Carrer**
Various venues
www.artsdecarrer.org
Street performance festival.

21-23 **Mostra de Vins i
Caves de Catalunya**
Moll d'Espanya, Port Vell
Tasting fair, at which you can sample
the local wines and cavas.

21-23 **Barcelona Acció Musical
(BAM)**
Various venues
www.bam.es
Around 40 concerts, mostly from local
acts, and many free.

21-24 **Festes de la Mercè**
All over Barcelona
www.bcn.es
Barcelona's biggest, brightest festival
with fire-running, human castles,
giants, concerts, an airshow, fireworks
on the beach and more.

24 **La Mercè**

26-30 **Festa Major
de la Barceloneta**
All over Barceloneta
www.cascantic.net
Festival fever fills the fishing quarter.

October 2007

4-28 **LEM Festival**
Various venues, Gràcia
www.gracia-territori.com
Festival of multimedia art and experimental electronica.

12 **Dia de la Hispanitat**

20-21 **Caminada Internacional
de Barcelona**
www.euro-senders.com/internacional
The International Walk is conducted
along several different routes of a variety of lengths.

Late Oct **Festival de
Tardor Ribermúsica**
Various venues, Born
www.ribermusica.org
Over 100 free music performances are
held in squares, churches, bars and
even shops.

25-28 **Art Futura**
Mercat de les Flors (p121)
www.artfutura.org
Digital and cyber art festival.

25-25 Nov **Festival of
Pocket Opera**
Various venues
www.festivaloperabutxaca.org
Small-scale contemporary opera. This
year's featured countries are Belgium
and England.

31-1 Nov **La Castanyada**
All over Barcelona
All Saints' Day and the evening before
are celebrated with piles of *castanyes*
(roast chestnuts).

25-1 Nov **In-Edit Beefeater
Festival**
Cine Rex, Gran Via 463 & Aribau
Club, Gran Via 565-567
www.in-edit.beefeater.es
Cinema festival of musical documen-
taries that range from jazz to flamenco.

November 2007

Ongoing Festival of Pocket Opera
(see Oct); La Castanyada (see
Oct); In-Edit Beefeater Festival
(see Oct)

Nov **Wintercase Barcelona**
Sala Razzmatazz 1, C/Almogàvers
122, Poblenou
www.wintercase.com
Big-name indie bands.

1 **Tots Sants (All Saints' Day)**

16-24 **L'Alternativa**
CCCB (p88)
www.alternativa.cccb.org
Indie cinema festival.

26-10 Jan **BAC!**
CCCB (p88) & other venues
*www.cccb.org, www.lasanta.org,
www.bacfestival.com*
Contemporary art festival.

Nov-Dec **Els Grans del Gospel**
Various venues
www.the-project.net
A three-week festival of international
gospel music.

Festival del Grec p40

Nov-July **AvuiMúsica**
Various venues
www.accompositors.com
Contemporary music cycle.

Nov/Dec **Festival Internacional de Jazz de Barcelona**
Various venues
www.theproject.es
Jazz from bebop to big band.

December 2007

Ongoing Els Grans del Gospel (see Nov), AvuiMúsica (see Nov), Festival Internacional de Jazz de Barcelona (see Nov), BAC! (see Nov)

1-24 **Fair of Sant Eloi**
C/Argenteria, Born
Christmas street fair for artisans, with live music playing from 6-8pm.

1-24 **Fira de Santa Llúcia**
Pla de la Seu & Avda de la Catedral, Barri Gòtic
www.bcn.es/nadal
Fira de Santa Llúcia is a Christmas market with trees, decorations and nativity-scene figures.

6 **Día de la Constitución**

8 **La Immaculada**

Mid Dec **Resfest**
Mercat de les Flors (p121)
www.resfest.com
Four-day festival showcasing innovative film, music, art, design, fashion and technology.

13 Dec-9 Mar **Festival Mil·lenni de Barcelona**
Palau de la Música Catalana (p74)
www.festivalmillenni.com
An annual series of music, dance and spoken word performances.

14-16 **Drap Art**
CCCB (p88)
www.drapart.org
This international creative recycling festival comprises concerts, performances, workshops and a Christmas market of recycled goods.

Late Dec **BAF (Belles Arts Festival)**
Sala Apolo (p121)
One day avant-garde, non-commercial art and performance with music and DJs until dawn.

25 **Nadal (Christmas Day)**

26 **Sant Esteve (Boxing Day)**

28 **Día dels Inocents**
Local version of April Fool's Day, with paper figures attached to the backs of unsuspecting victims.

31 **Cap d'Any (New Year's Eve)**
Swill Cava and eat a grape for every chime of the clock at midnight. Wear red underwear for good luck.

January 2008

Ongoing BAC! (see Nov), AvuiMúsica (see Nov), Festival Mil·lenni de Barcelona (see Dec)

1 **Any Nou (New Year's Day)**

5 **Cavalcada dels Reis**
All over Barcelona
www.bcn.es/nadal
The three kings (Melchior, Gaspar and Balthasar) head a grand parade around town from 5-9pm.

6 **Reis Mags (Three Kings)**

Mid Jan-Mar **Tradicionàrius**
Various locations, mainly in Gràcia
www.tradicionarius.com
Cycle of concert performances of traditional and popular Catalan music.

17 **Festa dels Tres Tombs**
Around Mercat Sant Antoni & Raval
Neighbourhood festival celebrating St Anthony's day.

25-26 **Sa Pobla a Gràcia**
Gràcia, around Plaça Diamant
www.bcn.es
Two days of festivities drawn from Mallorcan folk culture.

February 2008

Ongoing AvuiMúsica (see Nov),
Festival Mil·lenni de Barcelona
(see Dec), Tradicionàrius
(see Jan)

2-6 **Carnestoltes (Carnival)**
All over Barcelona
www.bcn.es
King Carnestoltes leads the fancy dress
parades and street parties before being
burned on Ash Wednesday.

9-13 **Santa Eulàlia**
All over Barcelona
www.bcn.es
Blowout winter festival in honour of
Santa Eulàlia, co-patron saint of
the city and a particular favourite of
children. Expect many kids' activities.

Feb-Mar **Xcèntric Film Festival**
CCCB (p88)
www.cccb.org/xcentric
Avant-garde festival showcasing short
films and videos.

Late Feb **Minifestival de Música
Independent de Barcelona**
C/Teide 20, Nou Barris
www.minifestival.net
An eclectic range of indie sounds from
around the world.

Late Feb-mid Mar **Barcelona
Visual Sound**
Various venues
www.bcnvisualsound.org
Showcase for untried film talent covering shorts, documentaries, animation
and web design.

March 2008

Ongoing AvuiMúsica (see Nov),
Festival Mil·lenni de Barcelona
(see Dec), Tradicionàrius (see
Jan), Xcèntric Film Festival
(see Feb), Barcelona Visual
Sound (see Feb)

Mar-June **Festival Guitarra**
Various venues
www.theproject.net
Guitar festival spanning everything
from flamenco to jazz.

2 **Marató Barcelona**
Starts & finishes at Plaça
de Espanya
www.maratobarcelona.com
City marathon.

3 **Festes de Sant
Medir de Gràcia**
Gràcia
www.santmedir.org
Decorated horse-drawn carts shower
the crowds with blessed boiled sweets.

Mid Mar **Nous Sons – Músiques
Contemporànies**
L'Auditori (p139) & CCCB (p88)
www.auditori.org
International contemporary music at
the week-long New Sounds festival.

14-18 **El Feile**
Various venues
www.elfeile.com
Irish festival of music, dance and
stand-up comedy for Saint Patrick's.

17-23 **Setmana Santa
(Holy Week)**
Palm fronds are blessed at the cathedral on Palm Sunday, and children
receive elaborate chocolate creations.

21 **Divendres Sant (Good Friday)**

24 **Dilluns de Pasqua
(Easter Monday)**

April 2008

Ongoing AvuiMúsica (see Nov),
Festival Guitarra (see Mar)

23 **Sant Jordi**
La Rambla & all over Barcelona
Feast day of Sant Jordi (St George), the
patron saint of Catalonia. Couples
exchange gifts of red roses and books.

24 Apr-3 May **BAFF Barcelona
Asian Film Festival**
Various venues
www.baff-bcn.org
Digital cinema, non-commercial films
and anime from Asia.

Late Apr **Dia de la Terra**
Passeig Lluis Companys, Born
www.diadelaterra.org
One-day eco-festival.

Dies de Dansa p40

Late Apr-early May **Feria de Abril de Catalunya**
Fòrum area
www.fecac.com
Satellite of Seville's famous fair with decorated marquees, manzanilla sherry and flamenco.

30 Apr-21 May **Festival de Música Antiga**
L'Auditori (p139)
www.auditori.org
Cycle of ancient music.

May 2008

Ongoing AvuiMúsica (see Nov), Festival Guitarra (see Mar), BAFF Barcelona Asian Film Festival (see Apr), Feria de Abril de Catalunya (see Apr), Festival de Música Antiga (see Apr)

1 **Dia del Treball (May Day)**
Various venues
Mass demonstrations across town, led by trade unionists.

Early May **Festival Internacional de Poesia**
All over Barcelona
www.bcn.es/barcelonapoesia
Week-long city-wide poetry festival, with readings in English.

4 **La Cursa del Corte Inglés**
All over Barcelona
www.elcorteingles.com
Over 50,000 participants attempt the seven-mile race.

11 **Sant Ponç**
C/Hospital, Raval
www.bcn.es
Street market of herbs, honey and candied fruit to celebrate the day of Saint Ponç, patron saint of herbalists.

18 **Dia Internacional dels Museus**
All over Barcelona
http://icom.museum/imd.html
www.museus2008.cat
Free entrance to the city's museums.

Mid May **Festa Major de Nou Barris**
Nou Barris

www.bcn.es
Neighbourhood festival famous for outstanding flamenco.

12 **Segona Pascua (Whitsun)**

20-24 May **Festival de Flamenco de Ciutat Vella**
CCCB (p88) & other venues
www.tallerdemusics.com
The Old City Flamenco Festival, with concerts, films and children's activities.

22-20 June **Festival de Música Creativa i Jazz de Ciutat Vella**
All over Old City
www.bcn.es/agenda
The Old City Festival of Creative Music and Jazz hosts performances at small intimate venues.

23-25 **L'Ou com Balla**
Cathedral cloisters & other venues
www.bcn.es/icub
Corpus Christi processions and the unusual L'Ou Com Balla – for which hollowed-out eggs have a dance on specially decorated fountains.

Late May **La Tamborinada**
Parc de la Ciutadella, Born
www.fundaciolaroda.net
A one-day festival of concerts, workshops and circus performances, with the events aimed at children.

Late May-early June **Loop Festival**
Various venues
www.loop-barcelona.com
Experimental video art festival.

Late May-early June
Primavera Sound
Fòrum area
www.primaverasound.com
Excellent big-name three-day music festival with a record fair and Soundtrack Film Festival on the side.

June 2008

Ongoing AvuiMúsica (see Nov), Festival Guitarra (see Mar), Festival de Música Creativa i Jazz de Ciutat Vella (see May), Loop Festival (see May), Primavera Sound (see May)

June-July **De Cajón**
Various venues
www.theproject.es
Series of top-class flamenco concerts.

Early June **Festa dels Cors
de la Barceloneta**
Barceloneta
www.bcn.es
Choirs sing and parade on Saturday
morning and Monday afternoon.

4-7 June **Mostra Sonora i Visual**
Convent Sant Agustí, C/Comerç,
Sant Pere
www.conventagusti.com
Experimental electronica concerts, DJs,
VJs, installations and video art.

6, 7 **Marató de l'Espectacle**
Mercat de les Flors (p121)
www.marato.com
Anarchic performance marathon, over
two nights, with pieces lasting from
three seconds to ten minutes.

Mid June **Sónar**
Various venues
www.sonar.es
The Festival of Advanced Music and
Multimedia Art, which encompasses
electronic music, urban art and media
technologies.

18-21 **Festa de la Música**
All over Barcelona
www.bcn.cat/festadelamusica
Free international music festival with
amateur musicians from 100 countries
playing in the streets.

21 **Gran Trobada d'Havaneres**
Passeig Joan de Borbó,
Barcelona
www.bcn.es/icub
Sea shanties with fireworks and *cremat*
(flaming spiced rum).

June-Aug **Festival del Grec**
Various venues
www.bcn.es/grec
Two-month spree of dance, music and
theatre all over the city.

23-24 **Sant Joan**
All over Barcelona
Summer solstice means cava, all-night
bonfires and fireworks.

July 2008

Ongoing AvuiMúsica (see
Nov), De Cajón (see June),
Festival del Grec (see June)

July **Festival Internacional
de Percussió**
L'Auditori (p139)
www.auditori.org
International percussion festival.

4-6 July **Dies de Dansa**
Various venues
www.marato.com
Dance performances in public spaces
dotted around the city.

Mid July **Festa Major
del Raval**
Raval
www.bcn.es/icub
Over three days, events include giants,
a fleamarket, children's workshops and
free concerts on the Rambla del Raval.

July **Clàssics als Parcs**
Various venues
www.bcn.es/parcsijardin
Free alfresco classical music, played
by a variety of young performers in
Barcelona's parks.

Mid July **Downtown
Reggae Festival**
Jardins de les Tres Ximeneies,
Poble Sec
www.nyahbingicrew.com
A free Jamaican music festival puts on
dancehall reggae from 5pm-2am.

Mid July **Summercase**
Parc del Fòrum
www.summercase.com
A weekend-long music festival that
pulls in big indie names.

Late July **B-estival**
Poble Espanyol (p116)
www.b-estival.com
Ten days of blues, soul, R&B and more
in a 'festival of rhythm'.

Late July-early Sept
Mas i Mas Festival
Various venues
www.masimas.com
The best of Latin music in Barcelona.

August 2008

Ongoing Festival del Grec
(see June), Mas i Mas
Festival (see July)

Every Wed **Summer Nights at CaixaForum**
CaixaForum (p112)
www.fundacio.lacaixa.es
All exhibitions are open until midnight with music, films and other activities.

Every Wed & Fri
Jazz in Ciutadella Park
Parc de la Ciutadella, Born
www.bcn.es/parcsijardins
Free 10pm shows from jazz trios and quartets in front of the fountain.

Every Tue-Thur **Gandules**
CCCB (p88)
www.cccb.org
A series of outdoor films screened to the deckchair-strewn patio of the CCCB.

12-16 **Festa de Sant Roc**
Barri Gòtic
www.bcn.es
The Barri Gòtic's party with parades, fireworks, traditional street games and fire-running.

15 L'Assumció (Assumption Day)

Late Aug **Festa Major de Gràcia**
Gràcia
www.festamajordegracia.org
A best-dressed street competition, along with giants and human castles.

Late Aug **Festa Major de Sants**
Sants
www.festamajordesants.org
Traditional neighbourhood festival with street parties, concerts and fire-running.

September 2008

Ongoing Mas i Mas Festival
(see July)

Sept **Festival L'Hora del Jazz**
See above Sept 2007.

11 Diada Nacional de Catalunya
See above Sept 2007.

Fair play

As a well-established sporting and gay capital, Barcelona should be the perfect host for the 12th annual EuroGames (24-28 July 2008, www.euro games.info). The four-day event, the 'Gay Olympics', is governed by the European Gay & Lesbian Sports Championships Federation (EGLSF) and is Europe's largest athletics event for lesbian, gay, bisexual and transgender people.

The goal is for equal male and female representation in each of the 27 sporting disciplines, particularly sports such as football where the vast majority of applicants are male. Half the spaces are for women and childcare is provided.

The real municipal catnip, however, is that the games will attract up to 7,000 participants and 35,000 visitors to the city; sure enough, the Ajuntament, the Generalitat and Barcelona Turisme have been generous in funding the event.

The majority of the sporting events will be held on Montjuïc and the inauguration ceremony will be held on 24 July in the Palau Sant Jordi. A slew of parallel cultural and tourist-related activities will include a 'village' set up in Avda Reina Maria Cristina, offering sporting workshops and activities, along with conferences, concerts, theatre and cinema. At night, the action moves to the 'Gaixample' area of the Eixample with plenty of chill-out zones and meeting points for Europe's athletes. The Fòrum is set to host the closing party.

Mid Sept **Festival Asia**
See above Sept 2007.

Late Sept **Barcelona
Acció Musical (BAM)**
See above Sept 2007.

Late Sept **Barcelona
Arts de Carrer**
See above Sept 2007.

Late Sept **Mostra de
Vins i Caves de Catalunya**
See above Sept 2007.

Late Sept
Festes de la Mercè
See above Sept 2007.

24 **La Mercè**

Late Sept **Festa Major
de la Barceloneta**
See above Sept 2007.

October 2008

Oct **LEM Festival**
See above Oct 2007.

12 **Dia de la Hispanitat**

Late Oct **Caminada Internacional
de Barcelona**
See above Oct 2007.

Late Oct **Festival de
Tardor Ribermúsica**
See above Oct 2007.

Late Oct **Art Futura**
See above Oct 2007.

Late Oct-early Nov
In-Edit Beefeater Festival
See above Oct 2007.

Late Oct-late Nov
Festival of Pocket Opera
See above Oct 2007.

31-1 Nov **La Castanyada**
See above Oct 2007.

November 2008

Ongoing Festival of Pocket Opera
(see Oct); La Castanyada (see
Oct); In-Edit Beefeater Festival
(see Oct)

Nov **Wintercase Barcelona**
See above Nov 2007.

1 **Tots Sants (All Saints' Day)**

Nov **L'Alternativa**
See above Nov 2007.

Nov-Dec **Els Grans del Gospel**
See above Nov 2007.

Nov-July **AvuiMúsica**
See above Nov 2007.

Late Nov-Jan **BAC!**
See above Nov 2007.

Nov/Dec **Festival International
de Jazz de Barcelona**
See above Nov 2007.

December 2008

Ongoing Els Grans del Gospel
(see Nov), AvuiMúsica (see Nov),
Festival de Jazz de Barcelona
(see Nov), BAC! (see Nov)

1-24 Dec **Fair of Sant Eloi**
See above Dec 2007.

1-24 **Fira de Santa Llúcia**
See above Dec 2007.

6 **Día de la Constitución**

8 **La Immaculada**

Mid Dec **Resfest**
See above Dec 2007.

Mid Dec **Drap Art**
See above Dec 2007.

Mid Dec-Mar **Festival Mil·lenni
de Barcelona**
See above Dec 2007.

Late Dec **Bellas Artes
Festival (BAF)**
See above Dec 2007.

25 **Nadal (Christmas Day)**

26 **Sant Esteve (Boxing Day)**

28 **Día dels Inocents**
See above Dec 2007.

31 **Cap d'Any (New Year's Eve)**
See above Dec 2007.

Itineraries

Picasso Museum p46

Picasso's Barcelona

'Barcelona, beautiful and bright', was how Picasso remembered the city where he spent his formative years. He arrived just before his 14th birthday and the seven years he spent here were to be a huge influence on his work, most directly the Blue Period, although Barcelona continued to feature heavily even in his later paintings, when he had not been back for many years.

A tour of Picasso's Barcelona is a full-day itinerary; to trace his time in the city in roughly chronological order, start where the Born meets Barceloneta by the Pla del Palau. When Picasso and his family first arrived in the city in the autumn of 1895, they lived here, at C/Reina Cristina 3, on the corner of C/Llauder.

Just over the road, at C/Consolat de Mar 2, is La Llotja, the old stock exchange that housed the art school where Picasso's father worked as a tutor. At just 15 years old, Picasso breezed through the entrance exam and shone as a student of realist painter Antoni Caba.

From here, cross over Via Laietana to C/Mercè 3, the next Picasso family home, now destroyed. While still living with his parents, Picasso also rented a series of studios which often doubled up as overnight accommodation; his first, which he shared with his fellow art student and lifelong friend, Manuel Pallares, was almost next door on C/Plata 4. In the 1890s, the whole harbour area was a red-light district filled with drunks, sailors and beggars, and Picasso soon developed a fascination with the low life around him. On the right, the once notorious C/Avinyó was lined with brothels and inspired his Cubist masterpiece, *Les Demoiselles D'Avignon* (1907).

Continue along C/Mercè and cross over La Rambla to another of Picasso's bedsit-studios at C/Nou de la Rambla 10, which at the time was next door to his favourite sleazy cabaret venue, the Edén Concert. At this point Picasso was living in great poverty and had to resort to burning some of his work to keep warm. His Blue Period (1901-1904) reflects this period of personal hardship and the poverty he witnessed around him: two famous examples include the *Old Guitarist* (1903) and *Life* (1903). This particular studio also happened to be directly opposite Gaudí's newly built Palau Güell. While Picasso was no great fan of Gaudí, art critic Robert Hughes and artist Ellsworth Kelly both suggest that the bright colours

and fragmented mosaics of the terrace chimneys might have sown the seeds of Picasso's Cubism, developed several years later.

Back on La Rambla, walk up towards Plaça Catalunya; turn right up C/Cardenal Casañas and then turn left at C/Petritxol. The Sala Parès gallery at no.5 was a meeting point for the fin-de-siècle Barcelona set, hosting debates and concerts, and also exhibited the work of the young Picasso in 1901 along with that of Ramon Casas.

At the top of C/Petritxol turn right on C/Portaferrissa and up the broad shopping avenue of Portal de l'Àngel. About halfway up on the right is C/Montsió, where, at no.3, is the most famous symbol of Picasso's days in Barcelona: Els Quatre Gats (p60).

Luxuriantly designed by Catalan Modernista architect Puig i Cadafalch, this tavern was inspired by Le Chat Noir in Montmartre and run by the decidedly eccentric art lover, Pere Romeu. It was the hub of bohemian

ITINERARIES

Els Quatre Gats

Barcelona with political debates, poetry readings, music recitals and, of course, countless art exhibitions. From 1899 to the time he left, almost all of Picasso's closest friends were members of the circle he met here, including the writer and artist Carles Casagemas whose suicide in 1901 also coloured the doleful Blue Period. Picasso even designed the menu illustration, which is still used today (the original is displayed in the Museu Picasso) and held his first exhibition here in February 1900 at the age of 19, featuring his portraits of many of the café's prominent habitués. If you stop here for lunch, come as early as possible to beat the queues of tourists; the place is no gastro temple but does serve decent Catalan favourites and has a reasonable set lunch for €12.80 (the menu is posted daily online).

After lunch head back down Portal de l'Àngel; on the corner of Plaça Nova, opposite the cathedral, is the Col·legi d'Arquitectes (Architect's Association). Its façade is decorated with a graffiti-style triptych of Catalan folk scenes, from a design drawn by Picasso while in exile in the 1950s and sculpted by Norwegian Carl Nesjar in 1961. Known as the *Three Friezes of the Mediterranean*, the section on C/Capellans celebrates the Senyera (Catalan flag); the section facing Plaça Nova depicts the *gegants* (giant figures that head traditional processions) and the section facing C/Arcs depicts dancing children. Ask inside to be directed to two interior friezes depicting a *sardana* dance and a wall of arches.

Then it's time to head over to the Born for an afternoon at the Picasso Museum (p74), which is expanding in 2007-08 to accommodate its 1.2 million visitors a year. A converted old orphanage on C/Flassaders, newly inaugurated in May 2007, will open on to Plaça Jaume Sabartés, named after Picasso's lifelong Barcelona friend and personal secretary. This addition will also create a pedestrian thoroughfare and a new back patio, which will be named after Raimon Noguera, another good Barcelona friend of Picasso's.

Refresh with a coffee and snack in the luxurious new museum café, which was taken over in autumn 2006 by the Hotel Arts. It's an airy space with stone arches and squishy sofas serving up light dishes such as brie panini, rosemary focaccia or scallop and grapefruit salad from a menu with good-resolution titles like Today I Feel Like a Sandwich, or Today I Will Take Care of Myself With a Delicious Salad.

Finish off with a stroll down C/Princesa to the Ciutadella park. Just down Passeig Picassso from the entrance stands Antoni Tàpies' 1981 centenary monument, *Homage to Picasso*. Commissioned by the Ajuntament, the water-covered glass cube and its contents quickly fell prey to mould and graffiti, but the sculpture was recently renovated by Pere Casanovas in time for the Year of Picasso 2006. The sculpture within the cube is an assemblage of Modernista period furniture cut through by white iron beams and draped cloth. This reflects the importance of industry and the working-class rebellion against wealthy Catalan society during Picasso's time in Barcelona. Quotations by Picasso decorate the bottom of the sculpture, notably one stressing the social function of art, which Tàpies took for his own: 'A painting is not intended to decorate a drawing room but is instead a weapon of attack and defence against the enemy.'

Caelum p48

The Jewish Quarter

Barcelona is a seriously *goyische* place these days. The current lack of Jewish presence on the streets makes it hard to believe that Jews thrived here for over a thousand years and, before the 14th-century pogroms, made up over 15 per cent of Barcelona's population. The city is now enjoying some of the first signs of Hebraic regeneration in over 500 years with a recent influx of Ashkenazi Jews from Argentina, newly established synagogues, study centres such as the Chabad Lubavitch (www.chabadbarcelona.org) and even the Jewish Film Festival (www.fcjbarcelona.org).

The best place to start a half-day tour of Jewish Barcelona is the Call (from the Hebrew word *kahal*, which means community or congregation), a tiny patch of narrow medieval streets to the west of the cathedral. Despite heavy taxes and few civil rights the Jews prospered here; by the 13th century, the Call held over 4,000 inhabitants and was regarded as one of the most religious and learned Sephardic Jewish communities. Beginning at Plaça Sant Jaume, head west down C/Call, once the Call's main street and where the ghetto gates at either end were locked at night. The first street to your right is C/Sant Honorat, where the water fountains were located; the second is C/Sant Domènec del Call, once the religious heart of the Call, with the main synagogue, kosher slaughter-houses and schools; the third street is the Call's western boundary of C/Arc de Sant Ramon, where there was once a Jewish women's school.

The Christianised street names are the result of the vicious pogrom of 1391 when the Call passed into the hands of the king, inhabitants were murdered or forced to convert to Catholicism and emblematic buildings were decorated with Catholic effigies.

Double back to C/Sant Domènec del Call, and walk halfway up to C/Marlet, where at No.5 part of the main synagogue still survives, now known as the Shlomo Ben Adret (93 317 07 90, www.calldebarcelona.org, admission €2). With foundations dating back to the first century AD, it is one of the oldest synagogues in Europe, but after the pogrom it fell into obscurity. These two small, semi-subterranean rooms were being used as an electrical supplies warehouse when a chance investigation revealed their identity. The Call Association of Barcelona restored the space and it reopened in 2002 as a museum and working synagogue, and was finally consecrated in 2006. The main room, to the left of the entrance, has a Max Iaffa stained-glass window featuring the Star of David and 12 stones to commemorate the tribes of Israel, a large collection of Judaic pewter and the huge iron menorah by Mallorcan artist Ferran Aguiló.

Coming out of the synagogue, head a few steps west towards C/Arc de Sant Ramon, where an eye-level engraving in Hebrew renders homage to Rabbi Samuel Ha-Sardi who lived here in the seventh century. In a bid to draw more attention to the area's history, the Ajuntament is renovating various buildings and creating a series of information plaques in Catalan, Spanish and English – these should be in place by 2008.

Head left, back down on to C/Call and turn right on to C/Banys Nous (New Baths street), where there are two hidden *mikvot* (Jewish ritual baths). The men's *mikveh* is at the back of S'Oliver furniture shop (at No.10), where the well-preserved arches are dramatically lit in sulphurous yellow tones and tower over the bed frames and wooden coffee tables below. Where C/Banys Nous meets C/Palla is the café Caelum (p64) with the women's *mikveh* in its basement; descend to enjoy some sticky traditional treats of ironic provenance: the Catholic monasteries of Spain.

Walk back down C/Banys Nous to C/Ferran; at No.30 is the church of Sant Jaume, once the synagogue of the Call Menor, an extension of the overflowing Jewish quarter. The only visible traces of this neighbourhood's Jewish past are a few faint niches over the doorways where *mezuzot* once hung, containing a rolled-up prayer.

Follow C/Ferran past Plaça Sant Jaume and down C/Llibreteria, turning left onto C/Verguer to reach the Plaça del Rei. Here, in the Museu d'Història de la Ciutat (p56), are Jewish tombstones, most of which were unceremoniously recycled as building materials after the pogrom: near the exit of the subterranean walk, Hebrew inscriptions are visible on the foundations of the 15th-century Palau del Lloctinent.

The Jewish necropolis itself lies across town on Montjuïc ('Jewish mountain'), named after one of the oldest and largest Jewish cemeteries in Europe, dating from the ninth century. To get there, head back down C/Ferran to La Rambla and take the metro from Liceu to Paral·lel followed by the funicular and the cable car.

Some of the tombstones are housed in the neighbouring Museu Militar (p116) but in 2001, over 500 more were discovered during construction on the mountain. Despite lobbying from local Jewish communities, there is no monument commemorating the site's historic importance and the Ajuntament is about to build visitor facilities directly over the burial grounds.

Barcelona Head

Street Art

Since time immemorial, high design and grand architectural gestures have formed a part of Barcelona's urban planning, most famously when the vast neighbourhood of the Eixample ('Extension') was created to relieve the overcrowding of what is now the Old City. Gaudí and the other Modernista architects were given free rein to create and embellish buildings so fantastical as to provide the perfect counterpoint to the grid-like layout of the streets. A more recent example might be the Born's Mercat Santa Caterina; old, leaking and thoroughly shabby, it was completely overhauled and given a kaleidoscopic undulating roof, which has succeeded in lightening the mood of an entire district, attracting a slew of new shops and businesses in the process.

But what to do when the bricks and mortar have already been in place for centuries? This was the dilemma facing city planners when it was decided that Barceloneta and the shoreline should be spruced up for the 1992 Olympics. The answer lay in street art, most of which can be enjoyed in a half-day stroll, perhaps with a break for lunch at one of the neighbourhood's many fish restaurants.

The most instantly recognisable piece commissioned at this time, and as emblematic of modern-day Barcelona as the dragon in Park Güell was in its day, is Roy Lichtenstein's pop art **Barcelona Head**, at the junction of Passeig Colom and Via Laietana. This brazen, comic and colourful sculpture features Lichtenstein's trademark use of Benday dots, only here as ceramic plates in homage to Gaudí's broken-tile technique.

After the irresistible gaiety of this piece, Ulrich Rückreim's sombre **Four Wedges** in the nearby Pla de Palau is harder to love and slightly puzzling. It consists of two groups of two almost-identical stout granite wedges that, despite locals linking them to the four bars of the Catalan flag, are meant to represent nothing but their own purity and strength.

Heading towards the port from here, the next sculpture, Lothar Baumgarten's **Wind Rose**, is best seen from above – and the Museu d'Història de Catalunya (p104) provides the perfect vantage point. Take the lift to the top floor where a practically unknown café boasts the biggest terrace and some of the best views in all of Barcelona. Place an order for coffee and then scrutinise the pavement far below and you'll see giant bronze letters forming words in all directions. These are the names of the Catalan winds – *tramuntana*, *llevant*, *xaloc*, *migjorn*, *ponent*, *garbí*, *mestral* and *gregal* – positioned according to the direction from which they blow.

Descending to street level, head up Passeig Joan de Borbó, stepping over *gregal* and *llevant* as you go, and halfway up you'll come across Italian artist Mario Merz's line of pink neon numbers under glass, set into the pavement. This piece, **Growing in Appearance**, is more noticeable by night, and 15 years of beach-going traffic have left some of the numbers the worse for wear, but keen-eyed mathematicians will make out the Fibonacci sequence.

Continue along this stretch to the Plaça del Mar at the end for one of the most unsettling of this group of sculptures, Juan Muñoz's **A Room Where It Always Rains**. A slatted bronze cage reminiscent of the Umbracle ('shade house') in the

Parc de l'Estació del Nord

Parc de la Ciutadella, it nods to Pirandello's *Six Characters in Search of an Author*, the expressionless figures within sharing a space but disconnected, conferring an unshakeable air of melancholy on the whole. The original idea was that 'rain' should indeed fall continuously through the bars, but problems with the recycling of the water and leaf fall from above had not been resolved by the time of the sculptor's untimely death in 2001.

Next up, and a little further along the beach, is Rebecca Horn's celebrated **Wounded Star**. This towering stack of rusted cubes is a homage to the fishermen's shacks and *xiringuitos* – makeshift seafood bars – that once filled this stretch of the shore but were torn down in the 1980s to make way for Barcelona's new beach. It's still the essential seaside meeting place – 'We're by the cubes!' is shouted into a hundred mobiles an hour – but is another to have fallen into disrepair, the nautical instruments contained within no longer lit up at night.

This area bristles with old-school seafood restaurants for an outdoor lunch, or you can grab a wrap at nearby La Piadina (p102) on the way to the next sculpture on C/Almirall Cervera, Jannis Kounellis' **Roman Scales**. These also recall the *barrio*'s maritime trading history; six scales hanging from a vertical 18-metre (60-foot) iron beam, each supporting sacks of coffee. The piece initially met with resistance from local residents, but its strength and harmony with its surroundings have become much better appreciated in recent years.

With the exception of *Barcelona Head*, all the sculptures named above are part of a group of pieces commissioned by curator Gloria Moure and collectively known as *Configuracions Urbanes*. The last

two are a ten-minute walk away, in the Born district. The first is Jaume Plensa's **Born**, on the *passeig* of the same name. Comprising a large iron trunk sitting atop one of the stone benches that line the promenade, and several cast-iron cannon balls bearing apparently random letters below and around them, it's an unobtrusive but thought-provoking work, attracting double takes from passers-by – those who notice at all.

The same can be said of James Turrell's **Deuce Coop**, a short walk from here along C/Comerç. Housed in the entrance to the former Convent Sant Agustí at no.23, it takes the form of a light sculpture and is the most magical of all the pieces, with an almost spiritual quality, particularly late at night, when it's viewed through the slats of the solid iron doors. Different architectural elements are illuminated with coloured lights, the door ringed in a neon glow.

All these sculptures make up a tiny part of the 50 or so pieces commissioned in the 1980s as part of the city's grand revamping, and just so happen to be conveniently close to one another. With a few more hours to spare, however, it's also worth visiting **Fallen Sky**, Beverly Pepper's azure land sculptures in the Parc de l'Estació del Nord (p127); Frank Gehry's glittering bronze **Fish** in front of the Hotel Arts (p173), and **Eduardo Chillida's sculptures** in the Plaça del Rei and the Parc de la Creueta del Coll (p158). Most fun of all, though, and certainly worth the metro ride out to Montbau, is Claes Oldenburg's **Matches**. This huge pop art matchbook is one of the city's best-loved and most-photographed pieces, the striking of the flame evoking the lighting of the Olympic torch over on Montjuïc, when the fun began in earnest.

Ready for take off?

Choose one of the coolest scooters in town and discover the fantastic city of Barcelona for yourself. Feel different from a tourist! Keep cool and do your thing, drive yourself or book one of our guided tours such as "the best views of Barcelona" or a fantastic and funny beach tour.

MotoLoco Barcelona › Phone +34 932 213 452 › www.motoloco.es

rent a scooter – feel the city like a loca

Barcelona by Area

La Rambla p69

Barri Gòtic & La Rambla

Barri Gòtic

An almost perfectly preserved time capsule, the Gothic Quarter is an unmissable part of town for any visitor. History is written in stone as Roman ruins rub shoulders with medieval palaces and great Gothic buildings, such as the **cathedral**.

One of the grander clusters of buildings from the Middle Ages has as its heart the **Plaça del Rei**, where you'll find the former royal palace (**Palau Reial**). The complex houses the **Museu d'Història de la Ciutat** and some of Barcelona's most historically significant buildings: the **chapel of Santa Àgata** and the 16th-century watchtower (**Mirador del Rei**

Martí). Parts of the palace are believed to date back to the tenth century, and there have been many additions to it since, notably the 14th-century Saló del Tinell, a medieval banqueting hall. It is here that Ferdinand and Isabella are said to have received Columbus on his return from America.

For the last 2,000 years, however, the heart of the city has been Plaça Sant Jaume, where the main Roman axes used to run. The **Temple of Augustus** stood where these streets met, and four of its columns can still be seen in C/Pietat. The square now contains the stolid neo-classical façade of the municipal government (**Ajuntament**) and the Renaissance seat of the Catalan

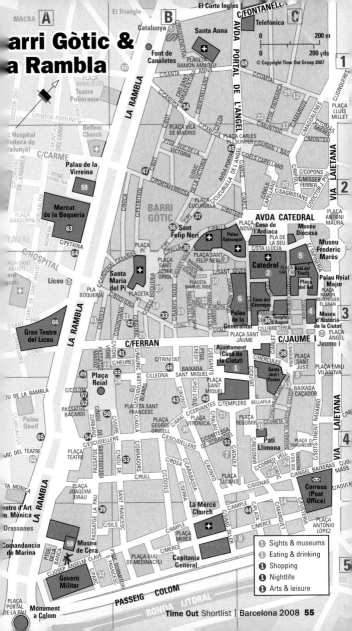

arri Gòtic &
a Rambla

MACBA **A**   **B**   El Corte Inglés   C/FONTANELL   **C**

Telefònica

0   200 m
0   200 yds

© Copyright Time Out Group 2007

Santa Anna

BARRI GÒTIC

AVDA CATEDRAL

Catedral

Palau de la Virreina **59**

Mercat de la Boqueria **63**

Santa Maria del Pi

Gran Teatre del Liceu **66**

Sant Felip Neri **56**

Palau Episcopal

Museu Diocesà

Museu Frederic Marès

Palau Reial Major

Museu d'Història de la Ciutat

Palau de la Generalitat

Ajuntament (Casa de la Ciutat)

Plaça Reial

Sants Just i Pastor

Pati Limona

La Mercè Church

Correus (Post Office)

Museu de Cera

Govern Militar

Capitania General

Monument a Colom

PASSEIG DE COLOM

RONDA LITORAL

<table>
<tr><td>❶</td><td>Sights & museums</td></tr>
<tr><td>❶</td><td>Eating & drinking</td></tr>
<tr><td>❶</td><td>Shopping</td></tr>
<tr><td>❶</td><td>Nightlife</td></tr>
<tr><td>❶</td><td>Arts & leisure</td></tr>
</table>

Plaça Felip Neri

regional government (**Palau de la Generalitat**), which stand opposite each other.

Sights & museums

Ajuntament (City Hall)

Plaça Sant Jaume (93 402 70 00/ special visits 93 402 73 64/www.bcn.es). Metro Jaume I or Liceu. **Open** *Office* 8.30am-2.30pm Mon-Fri. *Visits* 10am-1.30pm Sun. **Admission** free. **Map** p55 C3 ❶

The centrepiece and oldest part of the Casa de la Ciutat is the dignified 15th-century Saló de Cent, which is flanked by the semicircular Saló de la Reina Regent and the Saló de Cròniques, spectacularly painted with murals by Josep Maria Sert. On Sundays there are guided tours every 20 minutes.

Cathedral

Pla de la Seu (93 315 15 54/www. catedralbcn.org). Metro Jaume I. **Open** *Combined ticket* 1.30-4.30pm daily. *Church* 8am-12.45pm, 5-7.30pm Mon-Fri; 8am-12.45pm, 5-6pm Sat; 8-9am, 5-6pm Sun. *Cloister* 9am-12.30pm, 5-7pm daily. *Museum* 10am-1pm, 5.15-7pm daily. **Admission** *Combined ticket* €4. *Church & cloister* free. *Museum* €1. *Lift to roof* €2. *Choir* €1.50. No credit cards. **Map** p55 C3 ❷

The building is predominantly Gothic, save for the Romanesque chapel of Santa Llúcia to the right of the main façade. The cathedral museum, in the 17th-century chapter house, has paintings and sculptures, including works by the Gothic masters Jaume Huguet, Bernat Martorell and Bartolomé Bermejo. Santa Eulàlia, patron saint of Barcelona, lies in the dramatically lit crypt in an alabaster tomb carved with scenes from her martyrdom. To one side, there's a lift to the roof; take it for a magnificent view of the Old City.

Museu del Calçat (Shoe Museum)

Plaça Sant Felip Neri 5 (93 301 45 33). Metro Jaume I. **Open** 11am-2pm Tue-Sun. **Admission** €2.50; free under-7s. No credit cards. **Map** p55 B2 ❸

One of only three such collections in the world, this tiny footwear museum details the cobbler's craft from Roman times to the present day. Embroidered slippers from the Arabic world, 17th-

Museu Frederic Marès

century musketeers' boots and delicately hand-painted 18th-century party shoes are all highlights.

Museu d'Història de la Ciutat

Plaça del Rei 1 (93 315 11 11/www. museuhistoria.bcn.es). Metro Jaume I. **Open** *June-Sept* 10am-8pm Tue-Sat; 10am-3pm Sun. *Oct-May* 10am-2pm, 4-8pm Tue-Sat; 10am-3pm Sun. *Guided tours* by appointment. **Admission** *Permanent exhibitions* €4; €2.50 reductions; free under-16s. *Temporary exhibitions* varies. *Both* free 4-8pm 1st Sat of mth. No credit cards. **Map** p55 C3 ❹

Stretching from the Plaça del Rei to the cathedral are 4,000sq m of subterranean Roman excavations, including streets, villas and storage vats for oil and wine, which were discovered by accident in the late 1920s when a whole swathe of the Gothic Quarter was upended to make way for the central avenue of Via Laietana. The whole underground labyrinth can be visited as part of the City History Museum. The admission fee also gives you access to the Santa Àgata chapel and

the Saló del Tinell, at least when there's no temporary exhibition. This majestic room (1370) began life as the seat of the Catalan parliament and was converted in the 18th century into a heavy baroque church, which was dismantled in 1934. Tickets for the museum are also valid for the monastery at Pedralbes (p156).

Museu Frederic Marès

Plaça Sant Iu 5-6 (93 310 58 00/ www.museumares.bcn.es). Metro Jaume I. **Open** 10am-7pm Tue-Sat; 10am-3pm Sun. **Admission** €3; €1.50 reductions; free under-16s. Free 3-7pm Wed, 1st Sun of mth. **Guided tours** noon Sun. No credit cards. **Map** p55 C3 ❺

One of the city's most varied and charming museums, where the kaleidoscope of objects reflects sculptor and collector Frederic Marès' wide-ranging interests and his indulgently tolerated kleptomania as he 'borrowed' many items from his wealthy friends. The ground floor contains an array of Romanesque crucifixes, virgins and saints, while the first floor takes sculpture up to the 20th century. The base-

Plaça Reial

ment contains remains from ecclesiastical buildings dating back to Roman times: on the second floor is the 'Gentlemen's Room', stuffed with walking sticks, smoking equipment, and opera glasses, while the charming 'Ladies' Room' has fans, sewing scissors, nutcrackers and perfume flasks. Event highlights Barcelona at the time of artist Santiago Rusiñol in text and images (until 30 December 2007).

Palau de la Generalitat

Plaça Sant Jaume (93 402 46 17). Metro Jaume I. **Guided tours** every 30mins 10.30am-1.30pm 2nd & 4th Sun of mth; also 9.30am-1pm, 4-7pm Mon, Fri by appointment. **Admission** free. **Map** p55 C3 ⑥

Like the Ajuntament, the Generalitat has a Gothic side entrance on C/Bisbe, with a beautiful relief of St George (Sant Jordi), patron saint of Catalonia, made by Pere Johan in 1418. Inside, the finest features are the first-floor Pati de Tarongers ('Orange Tree Patio') and the magnificent 15th-century chapel.

Eating & drinking

Bar Bodega Teo

C/Ataulf 18 (93 315 11 59). Metro Drassanes or Jaume I. **Open** 9.30am-3pm, 5pm-2am Mon-Thur; 9.30am-3pm, 5pm-3am Fri, Sat. **Bar**. **Map** p55 B4 ⑦
An old *bodega* by day, with wine stored in huge oak barrels. At night young foreigners and *barcelonins* sip Moscow Mules amid the eclectic decor – fairy lights, futuristic insect lamps, a backlit panel of an expressive Mandarin duck and a blaze of stargazer lilies on the bar.

Bar Celta

C/Mercè 16 (93 315 00 06). Metro Drassanes. **Open** noon-midnight Tue-Sun. €. **Tapas**. **Map** p55 C5 ⑧
A bright and noisy Galician tapas bar, Bar Celta specialises in food from the region, such as *lacón con grelos* (boiled gammon with turnip tops) and good seafood – try the *navajas* (razor clams) or the *pulpo* (octopus) – and crisp Albariño wine served in traditional white ceramic bowls.

Cafè de l'Acadèmia

C/Lledó 1 (93 319 82 53). Metro Jaume I. **Open** 9am-noon, 1.30-5pm, 8.45-1am Mon-Fri. Closed 3wks Aug. €€€. **Catalan**. **Map** p55 C3 ⑨
Enjoy a power breakfast among the suits from the nearby town hall, bask in the sunshine over lunch at one of the tables outside on the evocative little Plaça Sant Just, or take a date for an alfresco candlelit dinner. The creative Catalan classics include home-made pasta (try shrimp and garlic), risotto with duck foie, guineafowl with a tiny tarte tatin and lots of duck.

Čaj Chai

C/Sant Domènec del Call 12 (mobile 610 334 712). Metro Jaume I. **Open** 3-10pm daily. No credit cards. **Tearoom**. **Map** p55 B3 ⑩
One for serious drinkers of the brown stuff, Čaj Chai is based on a Prague tearoom. Serenity reigns and First Flush Darjeeling is approached with the reverence usually afforded to a Château d'Yquem. A range of leaves come with tasting notes giving suggestions for maximum enjoyment.

Can Culleretes

C/Quintana 5 (93 317 30 22). Metro Liceu. **Open** 1.30-4pm, 9-11pm Tue-Sat; 1.30-4pm Sun. Closed July. €€. **Catalan**. **Map** p55 B3 ⑪
The rambling dining rooms at the 'house of teaspoons' have been packing them in since 1786, and show no signs of slowing. The secret to the place's longevity is straightforward: honest, hearty cooking and decent wine at the lowest possible prices. Expect sticky boar stew, pork with prunes and dates, goose with apples, partridge escabeche and superbly fresh seafood.

Cervecería Taller de Tapas

NEW *C/Comtal 28 (93 481 62 33/ www.tallerdetapas.com).* **Open** 8.30am-midnight Mon-Thur; 8.30am-1am Fri, Sat; noon-midnight Sun. **Beer/tapas**. **Map** p55 ⑫
A new venture from the people behind Taller de Tapas (p63), and still serving tapas, but this time with an emphasis

on beers from around the world. The list provides a refreshing alternative to Estrella, with Argentinian Quilmes, Brazilian Brahma (this one, admittedly, via Luton), Bass Pale Ale, Leffe and Hoegaarden, among others.

Ginger

C/Palma de Sant Just 1 (93 310 53 09). Metro Jaume I. **Open** 7pm-2.30am Tue-Thur; 7pm-3am Fri, Sat. Closed 2wks Aug. €€. **Tapas/cocktails**. Map p55 C4 ⑬
Ginger manages to be all things to all punters: swish cocktail bar; purveyor of fine tapas and excellent wines, and, above all, a superbly relaxing place to chat and listen to music. Be warned, it's no secret among the expat crowd.

Goa

C/Ample 46 (93 310 15 22). Metro Jaume I. **Open** 1-5pm, 7pm-midnight daily. €€. **Indian**. Map p55 C4 ⑭
If you're from Brick Lane, Bradford or Bangalore it might not be for you, but Goa is pretty good by local Indian restaurant standards. The pilau rice is underwhelming but naan comes fresh and hot, the rogan josh and chicken jalfrezi will warm the cockles of your heart and veggie accompaniments such as aloo palak are especially tasty.

La Granja

C/Banys Nous 4 (93 302 69 75). Metro Liceu. **Open** *June-Sept* 9.30am-2pm, 4-9pm Mon-Fri; 9.30am-2pm, 5-9pm Sat; 5-10pm Sun. *Oct-May* 9.30am-2.30pm, 5-9pm Mon-Sat; 5-10pm Sun. Closed 2wks Aug. €. No credit cards.
Tearoom. Map p55 B3 ⑮
There are a number of these old *granjes* (milk bars, often specialising in hot chocolate) around town, but this is one of the loveliest, with handsome antique fittings and its very own section of Roman wall at the back. You can stand your spoon in the chocolate, and it won't be to all tastes.

Matsuri

Plaça Regomir 1 (93 268 15 35). Metro Jaume I. **Open** 1.30-3.30pm, 8.30-11.30pm Mon-Fri; 8.30pm-midnight Sat. €€. **Asian**. Map p55 C4 ⑯

The trickling fountain, wooden carvings and wall-hung candles are saved from Asian cliché by the occidental lounge soundtrack. Reasonably priced tom yam soup, sushi, pad thai and other Southeast Asian favourites top the list, while less predictable choices include a zingy mango and prawn salad, and a rich, earthy red curry with chicken and aubergine.

Mercè Vins

C/Amargós 1 (93 302 60 56). Metro Plaça Catalunya. **Open** 8am-5pm Mon-Fri. €. **Catalan**. Map p55 C2 ⑰
With green beams, buttercup walls and fresh flowers, few places are as cosy as Mercè Vins. The standard of cooking varies a bit, but occasionally a pumpkin soup or inventive salad might appear, before sausages with garlicky sautéed potatoes. Dessert regulars are flat, sweet *coca* bread with a glass of muscatel, chocolate flan or figgy pudding.

Mesón Jesús

C/Cecs de la Boqueria 4 (93 317 46 98). Metro Jaume I or Liceu. **Open** 1-4pm, 8-11pm Mon-Fri. Closed Aug-early Sept. €€. **Spanish**. Map p55 B3 ⑱
The feel is authentic Castilian, with gingham tablecloths, oak barrels, cartwheels and pitchforks hung around the walls, while the waitresses are incessantly cheerful. The dishes are reliably good and inexpensive to boot – try the sautéed green beans with ham to start, then superb grilled prawns or a tasty fish stew.

Milk

C/Gignas 21 (93 268 09 22/www.milkbarcelona.com). Metro Jaume I. **Open** 6.30pm-3am Mon-Sat; noon-3am Sun. €€. **Fusion/cocktails**. Map p55 C4 ⑲
Milk's candlelit, low-key baroque look, charming service and loungey music make it an ideal location for that first date. Cocktails are a speciality, as is good solid home-made bistro grub, ranging from Caesar salad to fish and chips. A decent brunch is served on Sundays too.

Neri Restaurante

NEW *C/Sant Sever 5 (93 304 06 55/www.hotelneri.com). Metro Jaume I.*
Open 1.30-3.30pm, 8.30-11pm daily.
€€€€. **Catalan**. Map p55 20
Chef Jordi Ruiz cooks with a quiet assurance in tune with the Gothic arches and crushed velvet of his dining room, creating a perfect, tiny lamb Wellington to start; later there are cannelloni stuffed with wild mushrooms, or a fillet of hake on creamed parsnip with apricots and haricot beans.

Peimong

C/Templers 6-10 (93 318 28 73). Metro Jaume I. **Open** 1-4pm, 8-11.30pm Tue-Sat; 1-4pm Sun. **€€**. **Peruvian**. Map p55 B4 21
Peimong wins no prizes for design, but makes up for its rather unforgiving and overlit interior with some tasty South American dishes. Start with stuffed corn tamales, and then move on to *ceviche*, *pato en aji* (duck with a spicy sauce and rice) or the satisfying *lomo saltado* – pork fried with onions, tomatoes and coriander.

Els Quatre Gats

C/Montsió 3 bis (93 302 41 40/www. 4gats.com). Metro Catalunya. **Open** *Restaurant* 1pm-1am daily. *Café* 8am-2am daily. **€€€**. **Bar/Catalan**. Map p55 C1 22
This Modernista classic, which was frequented by Picasso and other luminaries of the period, nowadays caters mainly to tourists. The inevitable consequences include higher prices, so-so food and, worst of all, the house musicians. The place is still dazzling in its design, however, so avoid the worst excesses of touristification and come at lunchtime for a reasonably priced and varied *menú*. And that way you spare yourself 'Bésame Mucho'.

Les Quinze Nits

Plaça Reial 6 (93 317 30 75). Metro Liceu. **Open** 1-3.45pm, 8.30-11.30pm daily. **€€**. **Catalan**. Map p55 A3 23
Top of many tourists' dining agenda, with a queue stretching halfway across the Plaça Reial, the Quinze Nits man-

Shunka p63

ages all this with distinctly so-so food. The secret? Combining fast-food speed and prices with striking spaces, smart table linen and soft lighting. Diners get to feel special, eat local dishes and come away with nary a dent in their wallets. Order simply and a reasonable meal can still be had.
Other locations: La Fonda, C/Escudellers 10 (93 301 75 15).

El Salón

NEW *C/Hostal d'en Sol 6-8 (93 315 21 59). Metro Jaume I.* **Open** 1.30-4 pm; 8.30-11.30pm Mon-Sat. **€€**.
Mediterranean. Map p55 C4 24
Under new ownership, El Salón has retained its faintly bohemian style. Prices have come down a notch, and the dishes have become a little simpler – creamed carrot soup, lamb brochettes, tuna with ginger and brown rice, *botifarra* and beans, and ice-cream made with Galician Arzoa-Ulloa cheese to finish – but this remains one of the more charming places to eat in the Barri Gòtic.

BARCELONA BY AREA

Two wheels good

Barcelona gets on its bike and goes green.

In March 2007, photos of Mayor Jordi Hereu awkwardly straddling a bicycle filled the papers: Bicing had arrived. Barcelona's municipal bike-lending service (www.bicing.com, 902 31 55 31) is part of the 'greening' of the city, a scheme designed to encourage residents to make short trips by bicycle and to reduce the number of cars on the street.

Slightly less idealistic than the White Bikes project in Amsterdam in 1968, in which bicycles were left lying around for all to use, abuse and steal, Barcelona's are 'smart' cycles, with a tracking system and a register of users. Bicing is operated by a company that manages similar systems in Scandinavia, and which has been awarded a 10-year contract.

The new project began with just 200 bikes at 14 central parking spots but the aim is to have 3,000 bikes distributed over more than 100 parking stations by the end of 2007.

These points are located by metro and bus stations, shopping centres and major sights in the city centre. Users simply go online or to the office at Plaça Carles Pi i Sunyer 8, in the Barri Gòtic, and buy a personal, nontransferable card (€24 a year or €1 a week). This is swiped to release a bike from the parking system, giving the cyclist 30 minutes to get to their destination and drop off the bike in an available parking slot. Should no space be available, an electronic screen indicates the nearest bike-park with a free bay. The first half hour is free, after which there is a surcharge of 30ç per 30 minutes up to a maximum of two hours; there is no limit to the number of sessions in one day. The bikes are available from 5am to midnight Sunday to Thursday and 24 hours on Friday and Saturday. If the project proves a success with local residents, there are plans to make it more accessible to tourists.

Schilling

*C/Ferran 23 (93 317 67 87). Metro
Liceu.* **Open** *Sept-July* 10am-3am Mon-
Sat; noon-2.30am Sun. *Aug* 5pm-3am
daily. **Café. Map** p55 B3 ㉕

Schilling's airy, smart interior and
position smack in the centre of the Old
City make it Barcelona's meeting place
par excellence (not to mention the city's
number one spot for budding travel
writers to scribble in their journals),
but the aloofness of the staff can
become tiring.

Shunka

*C/Sagristans 5 (93 412 49 91). Metro
Jaume I.* **Open** 1.30-3.30pm, 8.30-
11.30pm Tue-Fri; 2-4pm, 8.30-11.30pm
Sat, Sun. Closed Aug. **€€€.
Japanese. Map** p55 C2 ㉖

Shunka is one of the better Japanese
restaurants in town, and a favourite
haunt of Catalan superchef Ferran
Adrià. Reserve for the best seats in the
house at the counter and watch the chefs
create decent-sized portions of prawn
and vegetable tempura, superb maki
rolls and extremely good nigiri-zushi.

Taller de Tapas

*Plaça Sant Josep Oriol 9 (93 301 80
20). Metro Liceu.* **Open** noon-midnight
Mon-Thur, Sun; noon-1am Fri, Sat. **€€.
Tapas. Map** p55 B3 ㉗

The more successful the three branch-
es (see also Cerveseria Taller de Tapas,
p59) of this tourist-oriented tapas bar
become, the more frequently quality
control is inclined to dip. At its best, it's
an easy, multilingual environment in
which to try tapas, from razor clams to
locally picked wild mushrooms, but at
worst the service can be hurried and
unhelpful, and dishes patchy.

Taxidermista

*Plaça Reial 8 (93 412 45 36). Metro
Liceu.* **Open** 1.30-4pm, 8.30pm-12.30am
Tue-Sun. Closed 3wks Jan. **€€€.
Mediterranean. Map** p55 B4 ㉘

When this place was a taxidermist's
shop, Dalí famously ordered 200,000
ants, a tiger, a lion and a rhinoceros.
Nowadays those who leave here
stuffed are generally tourists, though

this has not affected standards, which
remain reasonably high. À la carte
offerings include foie gras with quince
jelly and a sherry reduction; langoustine ravioli with seafood sauce; steak
tartare; and some slightly misjudged
fusion elements, such as wok-fried
spaghetti with vegetables. The lunch
menú is excellent, with two- or three-
course deals.

Tokyo

*C/Comtal 20 (93 317 61 80). Metro
Catalunya.* **Open** 1.30-4pm, 8-11pm
Mon-Sat. **€€€. Japanese. Map** p55
C1 ㉙

Resist the suggestion that there is no
menú, for this is the way to eat here. A
zingy little salad is followed by a
mountain of prawn and vegetable tempura, and a platter of maki rolls, nigiri
and a bowl of miso soup. It's a simple,
cosy space, with a reassuring Japanese
presence. À la carte, the speciality is
edomae (hand-rolled nigiri-zushi), but
the meat and veg sukiyaki cooked at
your table is also good.

La Verònica

*C/Avinyó 30 (93 412 11 22). Metro
Liceu.* **Open** *Sept-July* 7pm-1am Mon-
Thur; 7pm-1.30am Fri; 12.30pm-1.30am
Sat, Sun. *Aug* 7.30pm-1am Mon-Thur;
7.30pm-1.30am Fri; 1.30-7.30pm Sat,
Sun. Closed 2wks Feb. **€€. Pizzeria.
Map** p55 C1 ㉚

La Verònica's shortcomings (its huge
popularity among young foreigners,
the minuscule spacing between tables)
are all but hidden at night, when candles add a cosy glow to the red, orange
and yellow paintwork. Its pizzas are
crisp, thin and healthy, and come with
such toppings as smoked salmon, or
apple, gorgonzola and mozzarella.
Salads include the Nabocondensor, a
colourful tumble of parsnip, cucumber
and apple, and there is a short but reli-
able wine list.

La Vinateria del Call

*C/Sant Domènec del Call 9 (93 302 60
92). Metro Jaume I or Liceu.* **Open**
8.30pm-1am Mon-Sat; 8.30pm-midnight
Sun. **€€. Tapas. Map** p55 ㉛

La Vinateria's narrow entrance, furnished with dark wood and dusty bottles, has something of the Dickensian tavern about it, but once you're inside there's a varied music selection, from flamenco to rai, and lively multilingual staff. The wine list and range of hams and cheeses are outstanding; try the *cecina de ciervo* – wafer-thin slices of cured venison – and finish with homemade fig ice-cream.

Xeroga

C/Parc 1 (93 412 62 75). Metro Drassanes. **Open** 1-5pm, 8pm-midnight daily. **€€. Chilean. Map** p55 A5 **32**

A Chilean restaurant with a good-natured South American vibe, Xeroga has walls that are hung with bright oil paintings, a gold-stitched sombrero and a cracked and burnished guitar. On offer are various empanadas (*pino* is the classic option – meat, olives, egg and raisin), ceviche, *mariscal* (shellfish and hake in a fish broth) and a mighty *bife a lo pobre* – a trucker's breakfast of thin steak, two fried eggs and a stack of chips.

Shopping

Almacenes del Pilar

C/Boqueria 43 (93 317 79 84/www. almacenesdelpilar.com). Metro Liceu. **Open** 9.30am-2pm, 4-8pm Mon-Sat. Closed 2wks Aug. **Map** p55 B3 **33**

At Almacenes del Pilar there's an extensive array of fabrics and accessories for traditional Spanish costumes, on display in a shambolic interior that dates back to 1886. As you make your way through bolts of material, you'll find richly hued brocades, lace *mantillas* and the high combs over which they are worn, along with fringed, hand-embroidered pure silk *mantones de manila* (shawls) and colourful wooden fans.

Le Boudoir

C/Canuda 21 (93 302 52 81/www. leboudoir.net). Metro Catalunya. **Open** *Sept-July* 10.30am-8.30pm Mon-Fri; 10am-9pm Sat. *Aug* 11am-9pm Mon-Sat. **Map** p55 B1 **34**

Sensuality abounds in Barcelona's classy answer to Agent Provocateur. Sexy lingerie comes with designer labels (and prices to match), the swimwear is certainly not for shrinking violets and fluffy kitten-heeled mules have not been made with practicality in mind.

Caelum

C/Palla 8 (93 302 69 93). Metro Liceu. **Open** 5-8.30pm Mon; 10.30am-8.30pm Tue-Thur; 10.30am-midnight Fri, Sat; 11.30am-9pm Sun. Closed 2wks Aug. **Map** p55 B2 **35**

Spain's nuns and monks have a naughty sideline in traditional sweets, including candied saints' bones, sugared egg yolks and drinkable goodies such as eucalyptus and orange liqueur, all of which are beautifully packaged. There's also a taster café downstairs, which is on the site of some medieval Jewish thermal baths.

Cereria Subirá

Baixada de Llibreteria 7 (93 315 26 06). Metro Jaume I. **Open** *Jan-July, Sept-Nov* 9am-1.30pm, 4-7.30pm Mon-Fri; 9am-1.30pm Sat. *Aug* 9am-1.30pm, 4-7.30pm Mon-Fri. *Dec* 9am-1.30pm, 4-7.30pm Mon-Sat. **Map** p55 C3 **36**

The interior, which dates back to 1761, is extraordinary, with grand swirling mint-green, gilt-adorned balustrades and torch-wielding maidens, but the range of candles is also impressive. The varieties include simple votive candles, scented and novelty wax creations and tapered classics.

Drap

C/Pi 14 (93 318 14 87/www. ample24.com/drap). Metro Liceu. **Open** 9.30am-1.30pm, 4.30-8.30pm Mon-Fri; 10am-1.30pm, 5-8.30pm Sat. **Map** p55 B2 **37**

The enthusiastic staff at Drap are happy to show you the astonishingly artistic Lilliputian wares on offer: tiny versions of everything to fully furnish the world's best-equipped dolls' houses: from mini saucepans bubbling on mini ovens to miniature dogs in tiny dog baskets.

El Ingenio p66

Formatgeria La Seu

C/Dagueria 16 (93 412 65 48/www. formatgerialaseu.com). Metro Jaume I. **Open** 10am-2pm, 5-8pm Tue-Fri; 10am-3pm, 5-8pm Sat. Closed Aug. No credit cards. **Map** p55 C3 ⑱

Formatgeria La Seu stocks a delectable range of Spanish farmhouse olive oils and cheeses, among them a fierce *tou dels til·lers* and a blackcurranty *picón* from Cantabria. On Saturdays, from noon to 3pm, there is a sit-down cheese and oil tasting for €5.85, but you can wash down three cheeses with a glass of wine anytime for €2.40.

La Gauche Divine

NEW *Passatge de la Pau 7 (93 301 61 25/www.lagauchedivine.com). Metro Drassanes.* **Open** 5-8.30pm Mon; 11am-2.30pm, 5-8.30pm Tue-Sat. **Map** p55 ⑲

Tucked away in the sidestreets running off C/Ample, La Gauche Divine enlivens the clothes shopping experience with art exhibitions, video projections and DJ sets. It has a laid-back friendly vibe that belies the serious quality of its collection: this includes elegant tailoring from Ailanto, and complex, ambitiously constructed pieces from the young and talented Txell Miras.

Gotham

C/Cervantes 7 (93 412 46 47/www. gotham-bcn.com). Metro Jaume I. **Open** *Sept-July* 11am-2pm, 5-8pm Mon-Fri; 11am-2pm Sat. *Aug* 11am-2pm, 5-8pm Mon-Fri. Closed 2wks end Aug. **Map** p55 B4 ⑳

Fab 1950s ashtrays in avocado green, some bubble TV sets, teak sideboards, coat stands that look like molecular models… Take a trip down nostalgia lane with Gotham's classic retro furniture from the 1930s, '50s, '60s and '70s in warm cartoon colours.

Herboristeria del Rei

C/Vidre 1 (93 318 05 12). Metro Liceu. **Open** 10am-2pm, 5-8pm Tue-Sat. Closed 1-2wks Aug. **Map** p55 B3 ㉑

Designed by a theatre set designer in the 1860s, the shop's intricate wooden shelving hides myriad herbs and infusions, ointments and unguents for health and beauty. Its more up-to-date stock includes vegetarian foods, organic olive oils and mueslis.

El Ingenio

*C/Rauric 6 (93 317 71 38/www.
el-ingenio.com). Metro Liceu.* **Open**
11am-1.30pm, 4.15-8pm Mon-Fri; 10
am-2pm, 5-8.30pm Sat. **Map** p55 B3 ㊷
At once enchanting and disturbing, El
Ingenio's handcrafted toys, tricks and
costumes are reminders of a pre-digital world where people made their own
entertainment. Its cabinets are full of
practical jokes and curious toys; its fascinating workshop produces the oversized heads and garish costumes used
in Barcelona's traditional festivities
during carnival and the Mercé festival
in September.

Loft Avignon

*C/Avinyó 22 (93 301 24 20). Metro
Jaume I or Liceu.* **Open** 10.30am-
8.30pm Mon-Sat. **Map** p55 B4 ㊸
A smörgåsbord of top international
designers is on the menu at this purveyor of high-end informal fashion for
men and women. Think Diesel Style
Lab, Indian Rose, Vivienne Westwood
and Ungaro, with a gentle sprinkling
of Bikkemberg.
Other locations: C/Boters 8 (93 301 37
95); C/Boters 15 (93 412 59 10).

Papabubble

*C/Ample 28 (93 268 86 25/www.
papabubble.com). Metro Barceloneta
or Drassanes.* **Open** 10am-2pm, 4-8pm
Tue-Sat; 11am-7pm Sun. Closed Aug.
Map p55 C5 ㊹
Crowds of children are lured by the
sugary wafts floating into the street at
sweet-making time. You can watch the
Aussie owners create their kaleidoscopic humbugs before your eyes in
flavours both usual (orange, mint) and
unusual (lavender, passion fruit). The
adults are served by a recent venture
into obscene lolly territory.

Planelles Donat

*Portal de l'Àngel 7, Barri Gòtic (93 317
29 26). Metro Catalunya.* **Open** 10am-
10pm Mon-Sat. Closed Jan-Mar. **Map**
p55 ㊺
Turrón is Catalunya's traditional
sweet treat eaten at Christmas. It comes
in two types: the nougat-like *turrón de*

La Rambla p69

Alicante and grainy *turrón de Jijona*,
which is rather like marzipan. You can
try both, along with dusty *'polvorones'*
(crumbly marzipan-like sweets), ice-
cream and refreshing *horchata* (tiger
nut milk) here and at its nearby ice-
cream parlour (Portal de l'Àngel 25).

Tribu

*C/Avinyó 12 (93 318 65 10). Metro
Jaume I or Liceu.* **Open** *June-Sept*
11am-2.30pm, 4.30-8.30pm Mon-Fri;
11am-8.30pm Sat. *Oct-May* 11am-
2.30pm, 4.30-8.30pm Mon-Sat. **Map**
p55 B3 ㊻
One of the countless clued-up fashion
platforms in town, providing international and homegrown casual labels
such as Jocomomola, Nolita, Diesel and
Freesoul. Don't miss the designer trainers at the back.

Women's Secret

*C/Portaferrissa 7-9 (93 318 92
42/www.womensecret.com). Metro
Liceu.* **Open** 10am-9pm Mon-Sat.
Map p55 B2 ㊼

What's the secret? It seems to be that women rather wear underwear that's cute, colourful and comfortable than fussy, itchy bits of black nylon string. There are some sexy pieces here, but mostly it's versatile strap bras, cool cotton Japanesey wrap-around PJs and a funky line of skimpy shorts, miniskirts and vest tops in cartoonish stylings.

Zara

Avda Portal de l'Àngel 32-34 (93 301 08 98/www.zara.com). Metro Catalunya. **Open** 10am-9pm Mon-Sat. **Map** p55 C1 ❽

Zara's recipe for success has won over the world, but items are cheaper on its home turf. Well-executed, affordable copies of catwalk styles appear on the rails in a fashion heartbeat. The women's section is the front runner, but the men's and children's sections cover good ground too. The introduction of the 'Zara Home' department has also been a success.

Nightlife

Barcelona Pipa Club

Plaça Reial 3, pral (93 302 47 32/www.bpipaclub.com). Metro Liceu. **Open** 11pm-4am daily. **Admission** free. No credit cards. **Map** p55 A3 ❽

Once up some stairs and through a door, the chaos of the Plaça Reial below could not seem further away. Indeed, it feels less Barcelona, more Baker Street boozer circa 1900. Dusty wood, heavy curtains and cabinets full of antique pipes preserve a sedate atmosphere and, when it's not sectioned off for members' use, a small pool table sees a fair bit of action.

Club 13

Plaça Reial 13 (93 412 43 27). Metro Liceu. **Open** *Apr-Oct* 2pm-2.30am Mon-Thur, Sun; 2pm-3am Fri, Sat. *Nov-Mar* 6pm-2.30am Mon-Thur, Sun; 6pm-3am Fri, Sat. **Admission** free. **Map** p55 A4 ❺⓿

This glam little nightspot adds a touch of class to grungy Plaça Reial, what with its glittering chandeliers and

posh-nosh restaurant. Red flock wallpaper, exposed bricks in the cellar and black leather sofas downstairs make an ideal backdrop for smooth grooves from R&B to nu breaks via hip hop.

Harlem Jazz Club

C/Comtessa de Sobradiel 8 (93 310 07 55). Metro Jaume I. **Open** 8pm-4am Tue-Thur, Sun; 8pm-5am Fri, Sat. *Gigs* 10.30pm, midnight Tue-Thur, Sun; 11.30pm, 1am Fri, Sat. Closed 2wks Aug. **Admission** free Mon-Thur; €5 (incl 1 drink) Fri-Sun. No credit cards. **Map** p55 B4 ❺❶

For a time, the gig looked over for this Barcelona institution, but it's managed to come back bigger and stronger than ever, remodelled and, as a nod to the times, with a DJ booth. Live music is still what it does best, and it's a regular hangout for scruffy musicians, serious music buffs and students. Jazz, klezmer and flamenco fusion all get a run in a venue that holds no musical prejudices whatsoever.

Jamboree

Plaça Reial 17 (93 319 17 89/www. masimas.com). Metro Liceu. **Open** *Gigs* 8-11pm daily. *Club* 12.30pm-5.30am daily. **Admission** €6-€9. **Map** p55 A4 ❺❷

Every night Jamboree hosts jazz, Latin or blues gigs by mainly Spanish groups; when they're over the beards wander off and the beatbox comes out. On Mondays, particularly, the outrageously popular What the Fuck (WTF) jazz jam session is crammed with a young and local crowd waiting for the funk/hip hop night that follows. Note: you have to pay separately for the club.

La Macarena

C/Nou de Sant Francesc 5 (no phone/www.macarenaclub.com). Metro Drassanes. **Open** 11.30pm-4.30am Mon-Thur, Sun; 11.30pm-5.30am Fri, Sat. **Admission** free before 1.30am; €5 afterwards. **No credit cards. Map** p55 B4 ❺❸

Not a centre for embarrassing synchronised arm movements performed to cheesy pop tunes, but a completely

Testing times for statues

Now even street performers have to pass muster.

On any street but La Rambla, being a human statue is the last refuge of the talentless. If you can't play the guitar or draw a caricature, you can always paint yourself silver and stand very still until somebody throws you a coin.

Now even this career option is under threat, since the Ajuntament imposed artistic quality controls as part of their campaign to clean up Barcelona's main thoroughfare. Councillors promised to 'root out those who are not up to standard', although it was never clear how they planned to judge whether someone should have the privilege of dressing up like a paella for eight hours a day.

Instead the Ajuntament simply introduced new regulations in January 2007 that have halved the number of statues. The rules specify that a statue must wear home-made costumes and make up, not masks or shop-bought outfits, which automatically expels

the panhandlers shuffling around in moth-eaten Bart Simpson suits. Further rules prohibit statues from using street furniture or trees as props; they cannot take up a space larger than one by one-and-a-half metres; they cannot oblige the public to pay nor request a minimum fee in exchange for posing for a photo; they must avoid all expressions of violence and must not use any animals.

In addition, the statues are now limited to just 20 designated posing spots clustered around C/Bonsuccés, C/Portaferrissa, the Liceu and C/Nou de la Rambla. Those deemed unworthy of the 'statue' label are classified as 'artistas diversas' and banished to the purgatory of the Rambla de Santa Mònica down by the Columbus monument. This is the quietest and least profitable part of the Rambla, and it serves as a repository for acts which don't cut the mustard.

soundproofed cosy little dance space/bar with a kicking sound system that will pound away electro, minimal and house beats until the early hours. Guest house DJs Brett Johnson and Vincenzo have shared the decks with local talent, usually a day before or after a bigger gig elsewhere.

New York

C/Escudellers 5 (93 318 87 30). Metro Drassanes or Liceu. **Open** midnight-5am Thur-Sat. **Admission** (incl 1 drink) €5 with flyer and before 2am, €10 without. No credit cards. **Map** p55 A4 **54**

After a facelift and a change of management, this ancient former brothel-turned-rock-club is now indulging Spain's obsession for Depeche Mode and other newly trendy '80s sounds, alongside floppy-haired party fare from the likes of Franz Ferdinand, The Strokes et al. A long hallway bar leads on to the main dancefloor, where fairground figures leer from the stage and wallflowers gaze from the mezzanine.

Sidecar Factory Club

Plaça Reial 7 (93 302 15 86/www. sidecarfactoryclub.com). Metro Liceu. **Open** 6pm-4.30am Tue-Thur, Sun; 6pm-5am Fri, Sat. *Gigs* (Oct-July) 10.30pm Tue-Sat. **Admission** €4-€7. *Gigs* €5-€10. No credit cards. **Map** p55 B3 **55**

Sidecar still has all the ballsy attitude of the spit 'n' sawdust rock club that it once was and, while the gigs and weekend's rock-pop extravaganza continue to pack in the local indie kids and Interrailers, the programming has thankfully diversified considerably to include breakbeat on Wednesdays and Brazilian tunes on Tuesdays.

Arts & leisure

Cine Maldá

NEW *C/Pi 5 (93 481 37 04/www. cinemalda.com). Metro Liceu.* No credit cards. **Map** p55 **56**

In 2007 the much-lamented rep cinema, Cine Maldá, reopened its doors on a Bollywood tip. This means that, along-side nearly new indie films (last season's David Lynch and so on), there will be subcontinental movies of all stripes, and those that straddle the east/west divide like *Monsoon Wedding* and *East is East*.

Los Tarantos

Plaça Reial 17 (93 319 27 89/www. masimas.com). Metro Liceu. **Open** *Flamenco show* 8.30-11.30pm daily. **Admission** €6. **Map** p55 A4 **57**

This flamenco *tablao* has presented many top stars over the years. It now caters mainly to the tourist trade, but avoids the fripperies of some coach-party venues. Now under new ownership, prices have gone down, but the performers are less experienced. After 11.30pm Los Tarantos and Jamboree (p67) combine, but you have to pay again to join the jamboree.

La Rambla

This mile-long boulevard is one of the most famous promenades in the world. The identikit souvenir shops, pickpockets and surging crowds of tourists have driven away many of the locals who used to come here to play chess or have political debates, but despite a fall in fortunes, it remains the first port of call for visitors to the city. The human statues, fortune-tellers, card sharps, puppeteers, dancers and musicians might be infuriating to anyone late for work, but for those with a seat at a pavement café, it's not far short of pure theatre.

The Rambla is divided into five parts. First comes the **Font de Canaletes** drinking fountain; if you drink from it, goes the legend, you'll return to Barcelona. Here, too, is where Barça fans converge in order to celebrate their team's increasingly frequent triumphs. Next comes perhaps the best-loved section of the boulevard, known as **Rambla de les Flors** for its line of magnificent flower stalls, open into the night. To the right is the **Palau de la Virreina** exhibition and cultural information centre, and the superb Boqueria market. A little further is the **Pla de l'Os** (or **Pla de la Boqueria**), the centrepoint of the Rambla, with a pavement **mosaic** created in 1976 by Joan Miró. On the left, where more streets run off into the Barri Gòtic, is the extraordinary **Bruno Quadros** building (1883), with umbrellas on the wall and a single Chinese dragon protruding over the street.

The lower half of the Rambla is initially more restrained, flowing between the sober façade of the **Liceu** opera house and the more *fin-de-siècle* (architecturally and atmospherically) **Cafè de l'Opera**. On the right is C/Nou de la Rambla (where you'll find Gaudí's neo-Gothic **Palau Güell**); the broad promenade then widens into the **Rambla de Santa Mònica**, long a popular haunt of prostitutes.

Sights & museums

Museu de Cera

Ptge de la Banca 7 (93 317 26 49/www. museocerabcn.com). Metro Drassanes. **Open** *Mid July-mid Sept* 10am-10pm daily. *Mid Sept-mid July* 10am-1.30pm, 4-7.30pm Mon-Fri; 11am-2pm, 4.30-8.30pm Sat, Sun. **Admission** €7.30; €4.50 children; free under-5s. No credit cards. **Map** p55 A5 ⑤⑨

This is a wax museum that belongs to the so-bad-it's-good school of entertainment. Expect the savvy Playstation generation to be notably underwhelmed by clumsy renderings of Gaudí and Lady Di jumbled in with Frankenstein, neanderthals and ET (mysteriously perched atop the Millennium Falcon).

Palau de la Virreina

La Rambla 99 (93 301 77 75/www. bcn.es/cultura). Metro Liceu. **Open** 11am-2pm, 4-8pm Tue-Sat; 11am-3pm Sun. **Admission** €3; €1.50 reductions;

free under-16s. No credit cards.
Map p55 A2 ⑤⑨

The Virreina houses the city cultural department, and has lots of information on events and shows, but also boasts strong programming in its two distinct exhibition spaces. Upstairs is dedicated to one-off exhibitions, with the downstairs gallery focused on historical and contemporary photography.

Eating & drinking

Boadas

C/Tallers 1 (93 318 95 92). Metro Catalunya. **Open** *Sept-June* noon-2am Mon-Thur; noon-3am Fri, Sat. *July, Aug* noon-3pm, 6pm-2am Mon-Thur; noon-3pm, 6pm-3am Fri, Sat. No credit cards. **Cocktail bar**. **Map** p55 B1 ⑥⑩

Set up in 1933 by Miguel Boadas, born to Catalan parents in Havana (where he became the first barman at the legendary La Floridita), this classic cocktail bar has changed little since Ernest Hemingway used to come here. In a move to deter the hordes of rubbernecking tourists, there is now an exacting dress code.

Café de l'Opera

La Rambla 74 (93 317 75 85). Metro Liceu. **Open** 8.30am-2.15am Mon-Thur; 8.30am-2.45am Fri-Sun. No credit cards. **Café**. **Map** p55 A3 ⑥①

Cast-iron pillars, etched mirrors and bucolic murals create an air of fading grandeur now incongruous among the fast-food joints and souvenir shops. A reasonable selection of tapas is served by attentive bow-tied waiters. Given the atmosphere (and the quality of the competition), there's no better place for a coffee on La Rambla.

Kiosko de la Cazalla

NEW *C/Arc del Teatre (93 301 50 56). Metro Drassanes.* **Open** 10am-2am Tue, Wed, Sun; 10am-3am Thur-Sat. No credit cards. **Bar**. **Map** p55 ⑥②

Recently reopened after seven years boarded up, this emblematic hole-in-the-wall bar set in to the arch at the entrance of C/Arc del Teatre was for most of the last century a firm

Bruno Quadros

favourite of bullfighters and flamenco dancers, prostitutes and sailors. Little has changed since it first raised its hatch in 1912, and the tipple of choice is still the *cazalla*, an aniseedy firewater to warm the cockles.

Shopping

La Boqueria

La Rambla 89 (93 318 25 84/www. boqueria.info). Metro Liceu. **Open** 8am-8.30pm Mon-Sat. **Map** p55 A2 ⑬

Barcelona's most central food market outstrips all the rest. Visitors and residents alike never tire of wandering the hectic, colourful aisles and ogling the gory spectacle of tripe and sheep heads, the flailing pincers of live crabs and crayfish, bins of nuts, tubs of aromatic olives, and sacks of herbs and spices. Packed under an impressive vaulted glass and iron structure, the succession of stalls are a cacophony of buying and selling – each one brimming with local produce. Don't miss Llorenç Petràs's woodland stall of mushrooms and insect goodies, at the back. If it all makes you hungry, there are some great places to eat incomparably fresh food, if you can hack the noise and are prepared to pull up a stool at a frenzied bar.

However, be sure to steer clear of the conspicuous stalls near the front, as their neatly stacked picture-perfect piles of fruit, mounds of sweets, candied fruit and nuts, and ready-to-eat fruit salads are designed to ensnare tourists and have the prices to match. The Barcelona authorities seem to have cottoned on to the market's potential as tourist attraction and are capitalising on it with a range of Boqueria merchandise, available from a stall near the entrance.

Escribà

La Rambla 83 (93 301 60 27/www. escriba.es). Metro Urgell. **Open** 8.30am-9pm daily. **Map** p55 A3 ⑭

Antoni Escribà, who was known as the 'Mozart of Chocolate', died in 2004, but happily his legacy lives on. His team produces jaw-dropping confectionary creations for the Easter displays, from a hulking chocolate Grand Canyon to a life-size model of Michelangelo's *David*. Smaller, though less delectable, miracles include cherry liqueur encased in red chocolate lips.

Nightlife

Club Fellini

C/La Rambla 27 (93 272 49 80/www. clubfellini.com). Metro Liceu. **Open** midnight-5am Mon-Sat. **Admission** free before 1.30am, €6 before 3am, €9 afterwards Mon-Thur. €9-€12 Fri, Sat. No credit cards. **Map** p55 A4 ⑮

Due to its location on the Rambla, Fellini has had to work pretty hard to earn kudos with Barcelona's more discerning club-goers. However, thanks to some manically determined flyering and imaginative programming, it's managed to establish itself as pretty much the most talked-about new club in town. The monthly polysexual Puticlub parties are relatively mixed and lots of fun, and the last Thursday of the month is the semi-legendary Mond Club, with everyone from The Glimmers to Freelance Hellraiser playing dancey rock and rocky dance for a muso crowd.

Arts & leisure

Gran Teatre del Liceu

La Rambla 51-59 (93 485 99 13/tickets 902 53 33 35/www.liceubarcelona.com). Metro Liceu. **Map** p55 A3 ⑯

The Liceu has gone from strength to strength of late, steadily increasing the number of performances but still often selling out. The flames that swept away an outdated, rickety structure a decade ago cleared the decks for a fine new opera house. By comparison with the restrained façade, the 2,340-seat auditorium is an impressively elegant, classical affair of red plush, gold leaf and ornate carvings, but the mod cons include seat-back subtitles in various languages that complement the Catalan surtitles above the stage.

Parc de la Ciutadella

Born & Sant Pere

The Born has been the commercial hub of Barcelona since medieval times, but these days it trades in designer duds and haircuts rather than fish and vegetables. The food stores clustered around the old market have become fashionable bars and restaurants, full of the designers and photographers who now populate the area. Not quite as impeccably groomed, but catching up fast, is the neighbouring district of Sant Pere. With its dazzling new **Santa Caterina market** and freshly designed central avenue, it is gradually regaining some of the glory that it enjoyed during the Golden Age, when it was a favourite residential area of the city's merchant elite.

South of here, **C/Montcada**, one of the unmissable streets of old Barcelona, leads into the handsome **Passeig del Born**. C/Montcada is lined with medieval merchants' mansions, the greatest of which house museums. Both districts together, demarcated to the east by the **Parc de la Ciutadella** and to the west by Via Laietana, are still sometimes referred to as La Ribera ('the waterfront'), a name that recalls the time before permanent quays were built, when the shore reached much further inland and the area was contained within a 13th-century wall.

Sights & museums

Museu Barbier-Mueller d'Art Precolombí

C/Montcada 14, Born (93 310 45 16/ www.barbier-mueller.ch). Metro Jaume I. **Open** 11am-7pm Tue-Fri; 10am-7pm Sat; 10am-3pm Sun. **Admission** €3; €1.50 reductions; free under-16s. Free 1st Sun of mth. **Map** p75 B4 ①

Located in the 15th-century Palau Nadal, this world-class collection of pre-Columbian art includes frequently changing selections of masks, textiles, jewellery and sculpture, with pieces dating from as far back as the second millennium BC and running up to the early 16th century (showing just how loosely the term 'pre-Columbian' can be used). The holdings focus solely on the Americas, representing most of the styles that can be found among the ancient cultures of Meso-America, Central America, Andean America and the Amazon region.

Museu de Ciències Naturals de la Ciutadella

Passeig Picasso, Parc de la Ciutadella, Born (93 319 69 12/www.bcn.cat/ museuciencies). Metro Arc de Triomf. **Open** 10am-2pm Tue, Wed, Fri-Sun; 10am-6pm Thur. **Admission** *All exhibitions & Jardí Botànic* €4.20; €2.70 reductions. *Museums only* €3.50; €2 reductions. *Temporary exhibitions* €3.50; €2 reductions. Free under-12s, 1st Sun of mth. No credit cards. **Map** p75 C3 ❷

The Natural History Museum now comprises the zoology and geology museums in the Parc de la Ciutadella. Both suffer from old-school presentation: dusty glass cases are filled with moth-eaten stuffed animals and serried rows of rocks. However the zoology museum is redeemed by its location in the Castell dels Tres Dragons, which was built under the aegis of Domènech i Montaner as the café-restaurant for the 1888 Exhibition. The geology part of the musuem is for aficionados only, with a dry display of minerals, painstakingly classified, alongside explanations of geological phenomena found in Catalonia. More interesting is the selection from the museum's collection of 300,000 fossils, many found locally. A combined ticket also grants entrance to the Jardí Botànic (p113) on Montjuïc.

Event highlights The Myth of Origins; Belief and Science (until 25 Oct 2007).

Museu de la Xocolata

C/Comerç 36, Sant Pere (93 268 78 78/ www.museudelaxocolata.com). Metro Arc de Triomf or Jaume I. **Open** 10am-7pm Mon, Wed-Sat; 10am-3pm Sun. **Admission** €3.80; €3.20 reductions; free under-7s. **Map** p75 C3 ❸

The best-smelling museum in town draws chocaholics of all ages to its collection of *mones* (chocolate sculptures) made by Barcelona's master *pastissers* for the annual Easter competition. The *mones* range from multicoloured models of Gaudí's Casa Batlló to extravagant scenes of Don Quixote tilting at windmills. Inevitably, this is not a collection that ages well: photos have replaced most of the older sculptures, and those that are not in glass cases bear the ravages of hands-on appreciation from the museum's smaller visitors.

Museu Picasso

C/Montcada 15-23, Born (93 256 30 00/www.museupicasso.bcn.cat). Metro Jaume I. **Open** (last ticket 30mins before closing) 10am-8pm Tue-Sun. **Admission** *Permanent collection only* €6; €4 reductions. *With temporary exhibition* €8.50; €5.50 reductions; free under-16s. Free (museum only) 1st Sun of mth. **Map** p75 B4 ❹

The Picasso Museum takes up a row of medieval mansions, with the main entrance now at the Palau Meca, and the exit at the Palau Aguilar. By no means an overview of the artist's work, it is a record of the vital formative years that the young Picasso spent nearby at La Llotja art school (where his father taught), and later hanging out with Catalonia's fin-de-siècle avant-garde.

The presentation of Picasso's development from 1890 to 1904, from deft pre-adolescent portraits to sketchy landscapes to the intense innovations of his Blue Period, is seamless and unbeatable; the collection then leaps to a gallery of mature Cubist paintings from 1917. The pièce de résistance, however, is the complete series of 57 canvases based on Velázquez's famous *Las Meninas*, donated by Picasso himself, and now stretching through three

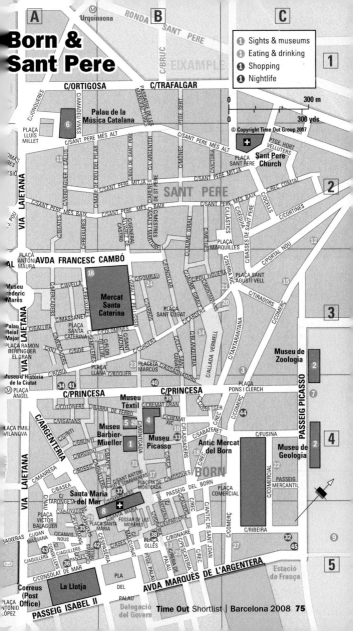

Santa Maria del Mar

tomb, through to Karl Lagerfeld. Among curiosities such as the world's largest collection of kid-skin gloves or an 18th-century bridal gown in black figured silk, the real highlight is the fashion collection – from baroque to 20th-century – one of the finest of its type anywhere. Recent important donations include more than 100 pieces by Spanish designer Cristóbal Balenciaga, who is famous for the 1958 baby-doll dress and pillbox hat. The museum shop is a great place to pick up presents, and there's a wonderful café outside in the courtyard.

Palau de la Música Catalana

C/Sant Francesc de Paula 2, Sant Pere (93 295 72 00/www.palaumusica.org). Metro Urquinaona. **Open** *Box office* 10am-9pm Mon-Sat. *Guided tours* 9.30am-3pm daily. **Admission** €8; €7 reductions. No credit cards (under €20). **Map** p75 A2 ⑥

Possibly the most extreme expression of Modernista architecture ever built, the façade of Domènech i Montaner's concert hall, with its bare brick, busts and mosaic friezes representing Catalan musical traditions and composers, is impressive enough, but is surpassed by the building's staggering interior. Making up for its famously poor acoustics, decoration erupts everywhere: the ceiling centrepiece is of multicoloured stained glass; 18 half-mosaic, half-relief figures representing the musical muses appear out of the back of the stage; and on one side, massive Wagnerian valkyries ride out to accompany a bust of Beethoven. By the 1980s, the Palau was bursting under the pressure of the musical activity going on inside it, and a 20-year renovation project involved the demolition of the ugly church next door to make way for the extension of the façade, a subterranean concert hall and a new entrance.

There are guided tours every 30 minutes or so, in either English, Catalan or Spanish. If you do have the chance, though, it's preferable to see the hall by catching a concert.

rooms. The display later ends with a wonderful collection of ceramics that were donated by Picasso's widow. Temporary exhibitions are held under the magnificent coffered ceiling of the Palau Finestres.

Event highlights Picasso's private collection of artworks (Dec 2007); Velázquez' influence on Picasso (Mar-May 2008); How Picasso, Juan Gris, Joan Miró and others transformed life into death and death into life (Nov 2008).

Museu Tèxtil

C/Montcada 12, Born (93 319 76 03/ www.museutextil.bcn.cat). Metro Jaume I. **Open** 10am-6pm Tue-Sat; 10am-3pm Sun. **Admission** *Combined admission with Museu de les Arts Decoratives & Museu de Ceràmica* €3.50; €2 reductions; free under-16s. Free 1st Sun of mth. No credit cards. **Map** p75 B4 ⑤

Housed in two adjoining mansions, the extensive Textile Museum is divided into three main sections: textiles, liturgical vestments, tapestry and rugs; clothing and accessories; and the city's lace and embroidery collection. The permanent exhibition provides a chronological tour of clothing and fashion, from its oldest piece, a man's Coptic tunic from a seventh-century

Parc de la Ciutadella

Passeig Picasso, Born (no phone).
Metro Arc de Triomf. **Open** 10am-
sunset daily. **Map** p75 C4 **❼**
Named after the hated Bourbon citadel
– the largest in Europe – that occupied
this site from 1716 to 1869, this elegant
park contains a host of attractions,
including the city zoo, the Natural
History Museum, a boating lake and
more than 30 pieces of imaginative
statuary. The giant mammoth statue
at the far side of the boating lake is a
huge hit with kids, as is the trio of
prancing deer by the zoo dedicated to
Walt Disney. In the north-east corner
is the *Cascade*, an ornamental fountain
topped with Aurora's chariot, on which
a young Gaudí worked as assistant to
Josep Fontseré, the architect of the
park. Not to be missed are Fontseré's
slatted wooden Umbracle (literally,
'shade house'), which provides a pocket of tropical forest within the city, and
the elegant Hivernacle ('winter garden')
designed by Josep Amargós in 1884, an
excellent example of the iron and glass
architecture of the Eiffel Tower period.
Outside, on the Passeig Picasso, is
Antoni Tàpies's *A Picasso*, which is a
giant Cubist monument to the artist.

Santa Maria del Mar

Plaça de Santa Maria, Born (93 310
23 90). Metro Jaume I. **Open** 9am-
1.30pm, 4.30-8pm Mon-Sat; 10am-
1.30pm, 4.30-8pm Sun. **Admission**
free. **Map** p75 B5 **❽**
Possibly the most perfect surviving
example of the Catalan Gothic style, this
graceful basilica stands out for its char-
acteristic horizontal lines, large bare sur-
faces, square buttresses and flat-topped
octagonal towers. Its superb unity of
style is down to the fact that it was built
relatively quickly, with construction
taking just 55 years (1329-1384). Named
after Mary in her role as patroness of
sailors, it was built on the site of a small
church known as Santa Maria del
Arenys (sand), for its position close to
the sea. In the broad, single-nave interi-
or, two rows of perfectly proportioned
columns soar up to fan vaults, creating

an atmosphere of space around the
light-flooded altar. There's also superb
stained glass, especially the great 15th-
century rose window above the main
door. The original window, built only
slightly earlier, fell down during an
earthquake, killing 25 people and injur-
ing dozens more.
Event highlights Handel's *Messiah*
(Christmas 2007 & 2008); Mozart's
Requiem (Easter 2008).

Zoo de Barcelona

Parc de la Ciutadella, Born (93 225
67 80/www.zoobarcelona.com). Metro
Barceloneta or Ciutadella-Vila Olímpica.
Open *Nov-Feb* 10am-5pm daily. *Mar,*
Oct 10am-6pm daily. *Apr-Sept* 10am-
7pm daily. **Admission** €14.50; €8.75
3-12s; free under-3s. **Map** p75 C5 **❾**
The live dolphin shows (hourly at
weekends) are the big draw, but other
favourites include the hippos, sea lions,
elephants and wide-open monkey
houses, although there's barely enough
room to move in some of the enclo-
sures. Child-friendly features include a
farmyard zoo, pony rides, plenty of pic-
nic areas and a brand-new adventure
playground. If all that walking is too
much, there's a mini-train, or you can
rent electric cars from the C/Wellington
entrance. Bear in mind that on hot days
many of the animals are sleeping and
out of sight.

Eating & drinking

La Báscula

C/Flassaders 30, Born (93 319 98 66).
Metro Jaume I. **Open** 7pm-midnight
Wed-Fri; 1pm-midnight Sat. No credit
cards. **€**. **Vegetarian**. **Map** p75 B4 **❿**
Under threat from the demolition
demons at City Hall (sign the petition
near the till), this former chocolate factory is a real find, with excellent vegetarian food and a deceptively large
dining room situated out back. An
impressively encyclopaedic list of
drinks runs from chai to *Glühwein*, taking in cocktails, milkshakes, smoothies
and iced tea, and the pasta and cakes
are as good as you'll find anywhere.

Dive time

It's been a difficult few years for committed barflies, with the Ajuntament cracking down on late-night drinking dens. But where there's a will there's a surreptitiously raised shutter and a crusty old bar willing to chance it. Despite the closure or gussying-up of some of Barna's classics, the humble dive bar is still alive and well in the city's back streets.

Papillon (C/Neu de Sant Cugat 7, no phone) lurks behind a metal door (ring the bell) in the seedier part of the Born. It opens around 2am and occasionally you have to do some sucking up to 'security' on the door. Generally though, anything goes and this beloved boozer offers cold beers, a pool table and turns a blind eye to the various nefarious activities within.

Not far away, **Brigadoon** (C/Brosolí 6, no phone) is small, grubby and smoky – and packed to the rafters every night. The transformation from local bar to dive diva occurs when it batons down the shutters around 2am, and you have to rattle on the door to get in. As indeed you do at **Flor del Norte** (Passeig Colom 10, 93 315 26 59), a good bet for dive-bar virgins looking for a gentler introduction. Not much more than a hole in the wall, it's a shade more upmarket than most with a door policy to match. Hunt in pairs; big gangs get turned away.

Situated between the Ronda Sant Antoni and Paral·lel, **Los Juanele** (C/Aldana 4, no phone) is a law unto itself hours-wise but is good for a taste of an authentic Andalucian *peña*, the sultry song of the Spanish guitar filling the air most Thursday, Friday and Saturday nights. A thin, barely discernible piece of string hanging to the left of the door is your ticket in, and if you're lucky you'll find a crowd of flamenco-loving revellers going until the wee hours. If you're very lucky, fried egg sandwiches are passed around at about 4am.

So raise your glasses please: *Vive le dive!*

El Bitxo

*C/Verdaguer i Callis 9, Sant Pere
(93 268 17 08). Metro Urquinaona.*
Open 1-4pm, 7pm-midnight Mon-Thur,
Sun; 1-4pm, 7pm-1am Sat. **No credit
cards. €. Tapas.** Map p75 A2 ⓫

A small, lively tapas bar, specialising
in excellent cheese and charcuterie
from the small Catalan village of Oix.
Kick off the evening with a 'Power
Vermut' (which is made of red vermouth, Picon, gin and Angostura
Bitters) and end it with a bottle of the
gutsy house red.

Bocamel

NEW *C/Comerç 8, Sant Pere (93 268
72 44/www.bocamel.com). Metro Arc
de Triomf.* **Open** *Sept-July* 8.30am-
8.30pm Mon-Fri; 8.30am-3pm, 5-8.30pm
Sat; 8.30am-3pm Sun. *Aug* 8.30am-4pm
Mon-Wed; 8.30am-8pm Thur, Fri;
8.30am-3pm Sat, Sun. **Café.**
Map p75 C3 ⓬

It's the mouthwatering, home-made
chocolate bonbons, Sachertorte, petits
fours and brownies that bring most customers through the door, but Bocamel
is also worth knowing about for its
breakfast pastries and a short but sweet
lunch menu. Needless to say, it's a good
idea to hold out for pudding.

Cal Pep

*Plaça de les Olles 8, Born (93 310
79 61/www.calpep.com). Metro
Barceloneta.* **Open** 8-11.45pm Mon;
1.30-4pm, 8-11.45pm Tue-Sat. Closed
Aug. **€€€. Seafood tapas.**
Map p75 B5 ⓭

Cal Pep is always packed: get here
early for the coveted seats at the front.
There is a cosy dining room at the
back, but it's a shame to miss the show
behind the bar. Neophytes are steered
towards the *trifásico* – a mélange of
fried whitebait, squid rings and
shrimp. Other favourites are the
exquisite little *tallarines* (wedge clams),
and *botifarra* sausage with beans.

Casa Paco

*C/Allada Vermell 10, Sant Pere
(no phone). Metro Arc de Triomf or
Jaume I.* **Open** *Apr-Sept* 9am-2am
Mon-Thur, Sun; 9am-3am Fri, Sat.
Oct-Mar 6pm-2am Tue-Thur, Sun;
6pm-3am Fri, Sat. **No credit cards.**
Bar. Map p75 B3 ⓮

Sounds like an old man's bar, looks like
an old man's bar, but this scruffy yet
amiable hole-in-the-wall has been *the*
underground hit of recent years,
thanks largely to occasional visits
from Barcelona's DJ-in-chief, Christian

El Bitxo

Vogel. Other contributing and crucial factors include a sprawling terrace and the biggest V&Ts in the known world.

Comerç 24

C/Comerç 24, Sant Pere (93 319 21 02/www.comerc24.com). Metro Arc de Triomf. **Open** *1.30-3.30pm, 8.30pm-midnight Mon-Sat.* **€€€€. Modern tapas.** Map p75 C3 ⓯

An urbane and sexy restaurant, where celeb chef Carles Abellan defines the new-wave tapas movement. Most of the selection of playful creations change seasonally, but signature dishes include a 'Kinder egg' (lined with truffle); tuna sashimi and seaweed on a wafer-thin pizza crust; a densely flavoured fish *suquet*; or a fun, truffled-edged take on the *bikini* (a cheese and ham toastie).

Cuines Santa Caterina

Mercat Santa Caterina, Avda Francesc Cambó, Sant Pere (93 268 99 18). Metro Jaume I. **Open** *1-4pm, 8-11.15pm Mon-Wed, Sun; 1-4pm, 8pm-12.15am Thur-Sat.* **€€€. Global.** Map p75 A3 ⓰

It's not quite as dazzling as it was when it opened in 2005, with higher prices and a slightly more lax attitude to quality control, but CSC still has its charms. The menu is nothing if not varied, with dishes from langoustine tempura to a baked spud with cheese and sausage. The rice, flour, crates of veg and so on arrayed along the vast windows, coupled with the well-made olive wood furniture, give a pleasantly honest, Mediterranean feel.

Euskal Etxea

Placeta Montcada 1-3, Born (93 310 21 85). Metro Jaume I. **Open** *Bar 6.30-11.30pm Mon; 11.30am-4pm, 6.30-11.30pm Tue-Sat. Restaurant 8.30-11.30pm Mon; 1.30-4pm, 8.30-11.30pm Tue-Sat.* **€. Tapas.** Map p75 B4 ⓱

A Basque cultural centre and *pintxo* bar, where you can help yourself to chicken tempura with saffron mayonnaise, dainty *jamón serrano* croissants, melted provolone with mango and crispy ham, or a mini-brochette of pork. Make sure you hang on to the toothpicks spearing each one: they'll be counted and charged for at the end.

Gimlet

C/Rec 24, Born (93 310 10 27). Metro Jaume I. **Open** *10pm-3am daily. No credit cards.* **Cocktails.** Map p75 B4 ⓲

On a quiet night, this subdued little wood-panelled cocktail bar has something of an Edward Hopper feel. The long mahogany counter has been burnished by the same well-clad elbows and patrolled by the same laconic barman for many years, and Gimlet is considered something of a classic, but the measures can be a little too lady-like for modern tastes.

Itztli

C/Mirallers 7, Born (93 319 68 75/ www.itztli.es). Metro Jaume I. **Open** *noon-11pm Tue-Sun.* **€. Mexican.** Map p75 B4 ⓳

Fortify yourself in the interminable queue for the Picasso Museum with a takeaway chicken burrito from this

La Paradeta

handily proximate Mexican snack bar. Keenly priced around the €3.50 mark, burritos also come with beef, chilli con carne or veg, as do tacos. Also on offer are quesadillas, wraps, nachos and salads, and there's a good range of Mexican beers, tinned goods and fiery chilli sauces for sale.

Mosquito

C/Carders 46, Sant Pere (93 268 75 69/www.mosquitotapas.com). Metro Arc de Triomf or Jaume I. **Open** 1pm-1am Tue-Thur, Sun; 1pm-3am Fri, Sat. **€€. Asian tapas. Map** p75 C3 ⓴
Don't be put off. The announced 'exotic tapas' are not another lame attempt to sex up fried calamares by way of tower presentation and yucca chips, but tiny versions of good to excellent dishes from the subcontinent and elsewhere in Asia. Food ranges from chicken tikka to Thai omelettes and masala dosas, with sushi at lunchtime.

Mundial Bar

Plaça Sant Agusti Vell 1, Sant Pere (93 319 90 56). Metro Arc de Triomf or Jaume I. **Open** 1-4pm, 8.30-11.30pm Tue-Sat; noon-3.30pm Sun. Closed Aug. **€€€. Seafood. Map** p75 C3 ㉑
Recently given a rosy-pink lick of paint, the Mundial's cave-like interior is nothing if not cosy. It has become increasingly pricey of late but, while the mainstay is still no-frills platters of seafood, steaming piles of razor clams, shrimp, oysters, spider crabs and the like, there are now fancy desserts and a more extensive wine list.

La Paradeta

C/Comercial 7, Born (93 268 19 39). Metro Arc de Triomf or Jaume I. **Open** 8-11.30pm Tue-Fri; 1-4pm, 8pm-midnight Sat; 1-4pm Sun. **€€.** No credit cards. **Seafood. Map** p75 C4 ㉒
Superb seafood, served refectory style. Choose from glistening mounds of clams, mussels, squid, spider crabs and whatever else the boats have brought in, let them know how you'd like it cooked (grilled, steamed or a la marinera), pick a sauce (Marie Rose, spicy local *romesco, all i oli* or onion

Rococó

with tuna), buy a drink and wait for your number to be called. A great – and cheap – experience for anyone not too grand to clear their own plate.

Re-Pla

C/Montcada 2, Sant Pere (93 268 30 03). Metro Jaume I. **Open** 1.30-4pm, 8.30pm-midnight daily. **€€€.**
Global. Map p75 B3 ㉓
A casually hip but nonetheless welcoming restaurant serving Asian-Mediterranean fusion. The wildly varied menu might include anything from a sushi platter to ostrich with green asparagus, honey and grilled mango slices. Veggie options are clearly marked, and desserts are rich and creative. For once, the lighting is wonderfully romantic and the sleek artwork easy on the eye, though some may feel uncomfortable with the sort of waiters who pull up a chair while recounting the day's specials.

Rococó

NEW *C/Gombau 5-7, Sant Pere (93 269 16 58). Metro Jaume I.* **Open** 9am-midnight Mon-Thur; 9am-1am Fri, Sat. **€€. Café. Map** p75 B3 ㉔
On the ground floor of a new and not especially characterful apartment

block, Rococó manages to live up to its name thanks to an array of red velvet seating, along with flock wallpaper and gilt-edged paintings. The Vietnamese rolls and chocolate brownies are fun, but the real stars are the *bocadillos* on home-made ciabatta.

La Strada

C/Pescateria 6, Born (93 268 27 11). Metro Barceloneta. **Open** 1.30-3.30pm Mon; 1.30-3.30pm, 9-11.30pm Tue-Fri; 9-11.30pm Sat. **€€€**. **Italian**. Map p75 B5

A peaceful little spot decorated in pale autumnal shades, hidden down an easily missed side street off the Avda Marquès de l'Argentera. Its lunch menu comprises simple Italian food made with high-quality ingredients: bruschetta pomodori; farfalle alla pesto; salmon trout with garlic, chives and toasted almonds, and lemon zabaglione. The set dinner is more of a tasting menu – as well as home-made gnocchi, pasta and risotto there are less predictable offerings such as carpaccio of venison with redcurrants.

Tèxtil Cafè

C/Montcada 12, Born (93 268 25 98). Metro Jaume I. **Open** 10am-midnight Tue-Thur, Sun; 10am-2am Fri, Sat. **€€**. **Café**. Map p75 B4

Perfectly placed for visitors to the various C/Montcada museums, and with a graceful 14th-century courtyard, Tèxtil Cafè is an elegant place in which to enjoy a coffee in the shade or under gas heaters in winter. There are decent breakfast and lunch menus to boot. For music lovers, a DJ plays on Wednesday and Sunday evenings followed, on Sunday, by live jazz (this attracts a €5 supplement, however).

Thai Cafè/Come Vida

C/Comerç 27, Born (93 268 39 59). Metro Jaume I. **Open** 12.30-4pm, 8pm-midnight Mon-Thur; 8pm-1am Fri, Sat. **€€€**. **Thai**. Map p75 C5

Thai Cafè's hot pink and lime-green candy stripes along the walls, its aromatic tom kha gai soup, chicken with holy basil and pad thai have

inexplicably been failing to pull in the lunchtime punters of late, so new measures have been called for. These include an incongruous salad bar and a new daytime incarnation as 'Come Vida' – which serves a scaled-down list of Thai favourites, pasta dishes and grilled meats.

Va de Vi

C/Banys Vells 16, Born (93 319 29 00). Metro Jaume I. **Open** 6pm-1am Mon-Wed, Sun; 6pm-2am Thur; 6pm-3am Fri, Sat. **Wine bar**. Map p75 B4

Owned by a former sommelier, artist and sculptor, this Gothic-style wine bar lists over 1,000 wines, many by the *cata* (tasting measure). The usual Spanish selections are accompanied by wines from the New World and elsewhere.

La Vinya del Senyor

Plaça Santa Maria 5, Born (93 310 33 79). Metro Barceloneta or Jaume I. **Open** noon-1am Mon-Thur; noon-2am Fri, Sat; noon-midnight Sun. **Wine bar/tapas**. Map p75 A5

La Strada

Another classic wine bar, this one with an unmatchable position right in front of the basilica of Santa Maria del Mar. With high-quality tapas and so many excellent wines on its list (the selection changes every two weeks), however, it's a crime to do as most tourists do and take up those terrace tables just to take in the view.

Wushu

NEW *C/Colomines 2, Sant Pere (310 73 13/www.wushu-restaurant.com). Metro Jaume I.* **Open** noon-midnight Tue-Sat. **€€€. Pan-Asian. Map** p75 A3 ⑳
Within a month of Wushu's opening, its six tables were some of the Born's most sought after. The formula is hard to beat: superb Asian wok cooking (pad thai, *lo mein* and the only *laksa* to be found in Barcelona) courtesy of Australian chef Bradley Ainsworth; with charming service; scrumptious desserts, and reasonable prices – particularly for the superb €9.90 set lunch. In fact, it's only thanks to the all-day opening that you can count on getting a seat at all.

El Xampanyet

C/Montcada 22, Born (93 319 70 03). Metro Jaume I. **Open** noon-4pm, 7-11.30pm Tue-Sat; noon-4pm Sun. Closed Aug. **Bar. Map** p75 B4 ㉛
The eponymous poor man's champagne is actually a fruity and drinkable sparkling white, served here in old-fashioned saucer glasses and best accompanied by the house *tapa*, a little plateful of delicious fresh anchovies from Cantábria. Run by the same family since the 1930s, El Xampanyet is lined with coloured tiles, barrels and antique curios, and has a handful of marble tables.

Shopping

Adolfo Domínguez

C/Ribera 16, Born (93 319 21 59/ www.adolfodominguez.com). Metro Barceloneta. **Open** 11am-9pm Mon-Sat. **Map** p75 C5 ㉜
Men's tailoring remains Domínguez's forte, with his elegantly cut suits and shirts. The women's line reciprocates with tame but immaculately refined outfits that are also squarely aimed at the 30- to 45-year-old market. The more casual U de Adolfo Domínguez line courts the younger traditionalist, but doesn't quite attain the panache of its grown-up precursor. This under-visited two-storey flagship store is supplemented by several other locations around the city.

Almacen Marabi

NEW *C/Flassaders 30, Born (no phone/ www.almacenmarabi.com). Metro Jaume I.* **Open** noon-2.30pm, 5-8.30pm Tue-Fri; 5-8.30pm Sat. **No credit cards. Map** p75 B4 ㉝
Mariela Marabi has created a felt funland with just a sewing machine and her imagination. Although she says she makes toys for adults, children will love her finger puppets and stuffed animals, and they'll be intrigued by her anatomically correct fabric dolls.

Arlequí Mascares

C/Princesa 7, Born (93 268 27 52/ www.arlequimask.com). Metro Jaume I. **Open** 10.30am-8.30pm Mon-Sat; 10.30am-4.30pm Sun. **Map** p75 A4 ㉞
The walls at Arlequí Mascares drip with masks crafted from papier mâché and leather. Whether gilt-laden or done in feathered commedia dell'arte style, simple Greek tragicomedy versions or traditional Japanese or Catalan varieties, they make striking fancy dress or decorative staples. Other trinkets and toys include finger puppets, mirrors and ornamental boxes.

Bubó

C/Caputxes 10, Born (93 268 72 24/ www.bubo.ws). Metro Jaume I. **Open** 3-10pm Mon; 10am-10pm Tue, Wed, Sun; 10am-11pm Thur; 10am-1am Fri, Sat. **Map** p75 A5 ㉟
The place for cakes. Be a hit at any dinner party with a box of Bubó's exquisitely sculpted petits fours, or make afternoon tea fashionable again with a tray of its colourful fruit sablés, raspberry and almond brandy snaps, or dreamily rich sachertorte.

Casa Antich SCP

*C/Consolat del Mar 27-31, Born
(93 310 43 91/www.casaantich.com).
Metro Jaume I.* **Open** *9am-8.30pm
Mon-Fri; 9.30am-8.30pm Sat.*
Map p75 A5

Under the arches at the southern edge
of the Born you'll find a luggage shop
that in levels of service and size of
stock recalls the golden age of travel.
Here you can still purchase trunks for
a steam across the Atlantic and ladies'
vanity cases perfect for a sojourn on
the Orient Express. But you'll also find
cutting-edge laptop cases and slouchy
shoulder bags from the likes of
Samsonite and Mandarina Duck.

Casa Gispert

*C/Sombrerers 23, Born (93 319 75
35/www.casagispert.com). Metro
Jaume I.* **Open** *Jan-Sept 9.30am-2pm,
4-7.30pm Tue-Fri; 10am-2pm, 5-8pm
Sat. Oct-Dec 9.30am-2pm, 4-7.30pm
Mon-Fri; 10am-2pm, 5-8pm Sat.*
Map p75 B4

Casa Gispert radiates a warmth that
emanates from something more than
its wood-fired nut and coffee roaster.
The shop's Dickensian wooden cabinets and shelves groan with the finest

and most fragrant nuts, spices, pre-
serves, sauces, oils and, most impor-
tantly, its huge hand-made chocolate
truffles. The pre-packaged kits for
making various local specialities such
as *panellets* (Hallowe'en bonbons)
make great gifts.

Custo Barcelona

*Plaça de les Olles 7, Born (93 268 78
93/www.custo-barcelona.com). Metro
Jaume I.* **Open** *10am-10pm Mon-Sat.*
Map p75 B5

The Catalan Dalmau brothers had to
make it in LA before bringing their
bright and brash, cut-and-paste style
T-shirts back home, but now the
Custo look is synonymous with
Barcelona style, and has spawned a
thousand imitations. Custo's signature prints can be found on everything
from coats to jeans to swimwear, but
a T-shirt is still the most highly prized
(and highly priced) souvenir for any
visiting fashionista.

Demasié

NEW *C/Princesa 28, Born (93 310 42
25). Metro Jaume I.* **Open** *noon-8pm
Mon, Sun; 10.30am-9pm Tue-Sat.*
Map p75 B4

Bubó p83

Cookies large and small – iced and plain; sweet and savoury; crumbly and dunkable. An impressive and distinctive range of flavours takes in pesto or mustard through to the more usual dark chocolate with ginger – all of them packaged in Barcelona's trademark lower-case, minimalist style.

On Land

C/Princesa 25, Born (93 310 02 11/ www.on-land.com). Metro Jaume I. **Open** *Sept-July* 5-8.30pm Mon; 11am-2pm, 5-8.30pm Tue-Fri; 11am-8.30pm Sat. *Aug* 11am-2pm, 5-8.30pm Tue-Sat. **Map** p75 B4 ⓵

On Land shows a refreshing lack of pretension, with simple decor and a hint of playfulness echoed in the fashions it stocks: local boy Josep Font's girly frocks are made for fun rather than flouncing, Petit Bateau's cute T-shirts are perfect for playing sailor girl, and Divinas Palabras' cartoony T-shirts put a smile on your face.

El Rei de la Màgia

C/Princesa 11, Born (93 319 39 20/ www.elreidelamagia.com). Metro Jaume I. **Open** *Sept-July* 10am-2pm, 5-8pm Mon-Fri; 11am-2pm Sat. *Aug* 11am-2pm, 5-8pm Mon-Fri. **Map** p75 A4 ⓵

Harry Potter syndrome has no doubt lured many a young visitor to the 'King of Magic'. Although it's a serious set-up that prepares stage-ready illusions for pros, it also welcomes the amateur magician, curious fan and prank-obsessed schoolboy, who may levitate with joy on seeing its fine range of fake turds, itching powder and the like.

U-Casas

C/Espaseria 4, Born (93 310 00 46/ www.casasclub.com). Metro Jaume I. **Open** 10.30am-9pm Mon-Thur; 10.30am-9.30pm Fri, Sat. **Map** p75 A5 ⓵

The pared-down, post-industrial decor so beloved of this neighbourhood provides the perfect backdrop for bright and quirky shoes. Strange heels and toes are out in force this season, and after all those snub-nosed winkle-pickers and rubber wedgies

from the likes of Helmut Lang, Fly, Fornarina and Irregular Choice, you can rest your weary pins on the giant, shoe-shaped chaise longue.

Vila Viniteca

C/Agullers 7, Born (93 268 32 27/ www.vilaviniteca.es). Metro Jaume I. **Open** *Sept-June* 8.30am-2.30pm, 4.30-8.30pm Mon-Sat. *July-Aug* 8.30am-2.30pm, 4.30-8.30pm Mon-Fri; 8.30am-2.30pm Sat. **Map** p75 A5 ⓵

This family-run business has built up a stock of over 6,000 wines and spirits since 1932. With everything from a 1953 Damoiseau rum, which costs as much as €500, through to €6 bottles of table wine, the selection is mostly Spanish and Catalan, but it also takes in some international favourites. The new food shop, situated just next door at no.9, stocks fine cheeses, cured meats and oils.

Nightlife

Club Mix

NEW *C/Comerç 21, Born (93 319 46 96/www.clubmixbcn.com). Metro Jaume I.* **Open** 8pm-3am daily. **Admission** free. **Map** p75 C4 ⓵

Opened in January 2007, Mix is an urbane and classy DJ bar, serving cocktails and 'international tapas' to a grown-up crowd. As well as occasional live acts (most regularly, jazz on Wednesdays), DJs spin rare groove, neo soul and the like from a deeply cool booth set high up in a copper-panelled wall.

Diobar

NEW *C/Marquès de L'Argentera 27, Born (93 221 19 39). Metro Barceloneta.* **Open** 11pm-3am Thur-Sat. **Admission** free. **Map** p75 C5 ⓵

The latest underground hit has popped up in the most unlikely place – in the basement of a Greek restaurant. Thursday through Saturday nights, this cosy, stone-walled space transforms into a temple of funk and soul as the sofas and dancefloor host lounging urbanites and DJ Fred Spider hits the decks.

Raval

Upper Raval

From La Rambla, signposts for the MACBA carefully guide visitors along the gentrified 'tourist corridors' of C/Tallers and C/Bonsuccès to a bourgeois bohemian's playground of cafés, galleries and boutiques. The centre of the Upper Raval is the Plaça dels Àngels, where the 16th-century **Convent dels Àngels** houses both the **FAD** design institute and a gigantic almshouse, the **Casa de la Caritat**, converted into a cultural complex housing the **MACBA** and the **CCCB**. When the clean, high-culture MACBA opened in 1995, it seemed to embody everything the Raval was not, but it profoundly influenced what the Raval was to become.

Below here C/Hospital and C/Carme meet at the Plaça Pedró, where the tiny Romanesque chapel (and ex-lepers' hospital) of **Sant Llàtzer** sits. From La Rambla, the area is accessed along either street or through the **Boqueria** market, itself the site of the Sant Josep monastery until the sale of church lands led to its destruction in the 1830s. Behind the Boqueria is the **Antic Hospital de la Santa Creu**, which took in the city's sick from the 15th century until 1926 (it now houses Catalonia's main library and the headquarters of the Institute of Catalan Studies); and **La Capella**, an attractive exhibition space. C/Carme is capped at the Rambla end by the 18th-century **Església de Betlem** (Bethlehem) with its serpentine pillars and geometrically patterned façade.

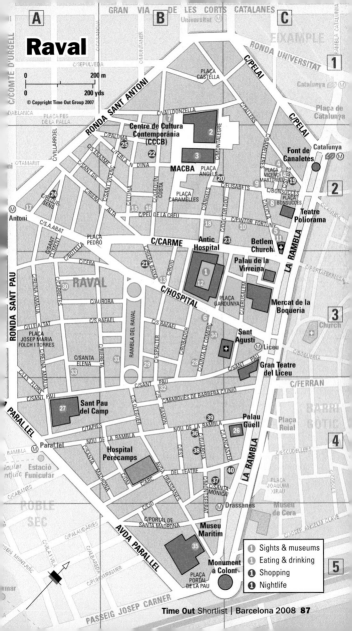

Raval

GRAN VIA DE LES CORTS CATALANES

EIXAMPLE

RONDA UNIVERSITAT

C/PELAI

Plaça de Catalunya

Font de Canaletes

Catalunya

PLAÇA CASTELLA

Centre de Cultura Contemporània (CCCB)

MACBA

PLAÇA ÀNGELS

PLAÇA CARAMELLES

Teatre Poliorama

PLAÇA VICENÇ MARTORELL

PLAÇA BONSUCCES

Antic Hospital

Betlem Church

Palau de la Virreina

RAVAL

C/HOSPITAL

PLAÇA GARDUNYA

Mercat de la Boqueria

Church

Sant Agustí

Liceu

Gran Teatre del Liceu

C/FERRAN

BARRI GÒTIC

Sant Pau del Camp

Palau Güell

Plaça Reial

PARAL·LEL

Paral·lel

Hospital Perecamps

Estació Funicular

POBLE SEC

PLAÇA JOAQUIM XIRAU

Museu de Cera

Museu Marítim

AVDA PARALLEL

Monument a Colom

PLAÇA PORTAL DE LA PAU

PASSEIG JOSEP CARNER

① Sights & museums
① Eating & drinking
① Shopping
① Nightlife

© Copyright Time Out Group 2007

Its name features on many shop signs nearby; older residents still refer to this part of the Raval as Betlem.

Sights & museums

Antic Hospital de la Santa Creu & La Capella

C/Carme 47-C/Hospital 56 (no phone/ La Capella 93 442 71 71). Metro Liceu. **Open** 9am-8pm Mon-Fri; 9am-2pm Sat. *La Capella* noon-2pm, 4-8pm Tue-Sat; 11am-2pm Sun. **Admission** free. **Map** p87 B3 ❶

There was a hospital on this site as early as 1024, but in the 15th century it expanded to centralise all the city's hospitals and sanatoriums. By the 1920s it was hopelessly overstretched and its medical facilities moved uptown to the Hospital Sant Pau. One of the last patients was Gaudí, who died here in 1926; it was also here that Picasso painted one of his first important pictures, *Dead Woman* (1903).

The buildings combine a 15th-century Gothic core with baroque and classical additions. They're now given over to cultural institutions, among them Catalonia's main library. Highlights include a neo-classical lecture theatre complete with revolving marble dissection table, and the entrance hall of the Casa de Convalescència, tiled with lovely baroque ceramic murals telling the story of Sant Pau (St Paul); one features an artery-squirting decapitation scene. La Capella, the hospital chapel, was rescued from a sad fate as a warehouse and sensitively converted to an exhibition space for contemporary art. The beautifully shady colonnaded courtyard is a popular spot for reading or eating lunch.

CCCB (Centre de Cultura Contemporània de Barcelona)

C/Montalegre 5 (93 306 41 00/ www.cccb.org). Metro Catalunya. **Open** *Mid June-mid Sept* 11am-8pm Tue-Sat; 11am-3pm Sun. *Mid Sept-mid June* 11am-2pm, 4-8pm Tue,

Thur, Fri; 11am-8pm Wed, Sat; 11am-7pm Sun. **Admission** *1 exhibition* €4.40; €3.30 reductions & Wed. *2 exhibitions* €6; €5.50 reductions & Wed. Free under-16s. **Map** p87 B2 ❷

Spain's largest cultural centre was opened in 1994 at the huge Casa de la Caritat, built in 1802 on the site of a medieval monastery to serve as the city's main workhouse. The massive façade and part of the courtyard remain from the original building; the rest was rebuilt in dramatic contrast, all tilting glass and steel. As a centre for contemporary culture, the CCCB tends to pick up whatever falls through the cracks elsewhere: a slew of film cycles and multimedia presentations, and various flamenco, literary, music and dance festivals.

Event highlights 'Apartheid' looks at the origins of racism through photos and paintings (26 Sept 2007-13 Jan 2008); 'World Press Photo, the best of the world's photojournalists' (9 Oct 2007-25 Nov 2007); 'In Transition', studying the complex transition from dictatorship to democracy (20 Nov 2007-Feb 2008).

MACBA (Museu d'Art Contemporani de Barcelona)

Plaça dels Àngels 1 (93 412 08 10/ www.macba.es). Metro Catalunya. **Open** *June-Sept* 11am-8pm Mon, Wed-Fri; 10am-8pm Sat; 10am-3pm Sun. *Oct-May* 11am-7.30pm Mon, Wed-Fri; 10am-8pm Sat; 10am-3pm Sun. **Admission** *Museum* €7.50; €6 reductions. *Temporary exhibitions* €4; €3 reductions. **Map** p87 B2 ❸

No work of art inside the MACBA can quite live up to the wow factor of Richard Meier's cool iceberg of a museum set in the vast skateboarder plains of the Plaça dels Àngels. Even some of the best sculptures are on the outside: *La Ola* (The Wave), a curving bronze behemoth by Jorge Oteiza, and the monochrome mural *Barcelona*, by Eduardo Chillida. Since it opened in 1995, the place has fattened up its holdings considerably, but the shows are often heavily political in concept and occasionally radical to the point of inaccessibility. If you can't or won't see the socio-political implications of, say, a roomful of beach balls, the MACBA may leave you cold.

The exhibits cover the last 50 years or so. The earlier pieces are strong on artists such as Antonio Saura and Tàpies (of whom director Manuel Borja Villel is an ardent fan), who were members of the Dau-al-Set, a group of radical writers and painters, much influenced by Miró, who kickstarted the Catalan art movement after the post-Civil War years of cultural apathy. Jean Dubuffet, and Basque sculptors Jorge Oteiza and Eduardo Chillida also feature. Works from the last 40 years are more global, with the likes of Joseph Beuys, Jean-Michel Basquiat, AR Penck and photographer Jeff Wall; the contemporary Spanish collection includes Catalan painting (Ferran García Sevilla, Miquel Barceló) and sculpture (Sergi Aguilar, Susana Solano).

Event highlights Joan Jonas, multimedia artist (20 Sept 2007-7 Jan 2008); 'Under the bomb: the transatlantic war of images', the Cold War artistic rivalry between New York and Paris.

Eating & drinking

Bar Kasparo

Plaça Vicenç Martorell 4 (93 302 20 72). Metro Catalunya. **Open** *May-Aug* 9am-midnight daily. *Sept-Apr* 9am-10pm daily. Closed mid Dec-mid Jan. No credit cards. €€. **Café**. **Map** p87 C2 ④

The favourite bar of Barcelona's beleaguered parents, Australian-run Bar Kasparo has outdoor seating (only) overlooking a playground on a quiet, traffic-free square. As well as sandwiches and tapas, there is a daily-changing selection of dishes from around the globe, soups and salads, and the kitchen stays open all day.

Bar Lobo

NEW *C/Pintor Fortuny 3 (93 481 53 46).* **Open** noon-midnight Mon-Wed, Sun; noon-2am Thur-Sat. €€€. **Bar/Global**. **Map** p87 C2 ⑤

A starkly monochrome space, with high ceilings and punky artwork from celebrated graffiti artists. The watchword is moody (not least among the waiting staff) but the bar comes alive with DJs and studied lounging on the mezzanine at night, and by day its terrace is a peaceful, sunny space for coffee or a light lunch.

BARCELONA BY AREA

Antic Hospital

CCCB p88

staff will make up an appropriate medicinal tea from the shop's stock of more than 100 herbs.

Buenas Migas

Plaça Bonsuccés 6 (93 318 37 08). Metro Liceu. **Open** *June-Sept* 10am-midnight Mon-Thur, Sun; 10am-1am Fri, Sat. *Oct-May* 10am-11pm Mon-Thur, Sun; 10am-midnight Fri, Sat. **€€. Vegetarian. Map** p87 C2 ❽
'Good Crumbs' (from a phrase meaning 'to get on with someone'), is a ferociously wholesome kind of place, all gingham and pine and chewy spinach tart. The speciality is tasty focaccia with various toppings, along with the usual high-fibre, low-fat cakes you expect to find in a vegetarian café. This branch has several tables outside.

Elisabets

C/Elisabets 2-4 (93 317 58 26). Metro Catalunya. **Open** 7am-11pm Mon-Sat. Closed 3wks Aug. **€€.** No credit cards. **Bar/Catalan. Map** p87 C2 ❾
Elisabets maintains a sociable local feel, despite the recent gentrification of its street. Dinner (Fridays only) is actually a selection of tapas, and otherwise only the set lunch or myriad *bocadillos* are served. The lunch deal is terrific value, however, with osso buco, vegetable and chickpea stew, baked cod with garlic and parsley, and roast pork knuckle all making an appearance on the menu with gratifying regularity.

Flamingo's

[NEW] *C/Pintor Fortuny 15 (93 301 23 22). Metro Catalunya.* **Open** 5pm-2am Mon-Thur; 5pm-3am Fri, Sat. **Café. Map** p87 C2 ❿
Flamingo's is like a Club Tropicana party held in the Tardis. Each night sees a crowd of cool-cat cocktail sippers squeezed into this hot, hip and refreshingly unpretentious bar. Tapas are served on Friday nights and DJs wedge in at weekends.

Granja M Viader

C/Xuclà 4-6 (93 318 34 86). Metro Liceu. **Open** 5-8.45pm Mon; 9am-1.45pm, 5-8.45pm Tue-Sat. Closed 3wks Aug. **€€. Tearoom. Map** p87 C2 ⓫

Bar Mendizábal

C/Junta de Comerç 2 (no phone). Metro Liceu. **Open** *June-Oct* 10am-1am daily. *Nov-May* 10am-midnight daily. No credit cards. **Bar. Map** p87 B3 ❻
An emblematic Raval bar, its multi-coloured tiles featuring in many thousands of holiday snaps, Mendizábal has been around for decades but is really little more than a pavement stall. On offer are myriad fruit juices, *bocadillos* and, in winter, soup, served to tables across the road in the tiny square opposite.

Baraka

[NEW] *C/Valldonzella 25 (93 304 10 61). Metro Universitat.* **Open** 11am-10.30pm Mon-Fri; 4-10.30pm Sat. **Café. Map** p87 B1 ❼
At the back of a beautiful old building converted into a health-food shop is this cosy little bar where everything, from the wine and beer to the milk used in the fair-trade coffee, is organic and cheap – not a common combination. And should anything ail you,

The chocolate milk drink Cacaolat was invented in this old *granja* in 1931, and is still on offer, along with strawberry and banana milkshakes, *orxata* (tiger nut milk) and hot chocolate. It's an evocative, charming place with century-old fittings and enamel adverts, but the waiters refuse to be hurried. Popular with Catalan families on the way back from picking up the children, and couples meeting after work.

El Jardi

NEW *C/Hospital 56 (93 329 15 50). Metro Liceu.* **Open** 10am-11pm Mon-Sat. €€. **Café**. **Map** p87 B3 ⑫

A small terrace café in the dusty tree-lined grounds of the Antic Hospital (p88), providing a spot of tranquillity just off La Rambla. Breakfast pastries and all the usual tapas are present and correct, along with pasta dishes, quiches and salads.

Juicy Jones

C/Hospital 76 (93 443 90 82). Metro Liceu. **Open** noon-11pm daily. €€. No credit cards. **Vegetarian**. **Map** p87 B3 ⑬

A new branch of this riotously colourful, backpacker-oriented vegan restaurant, with an endless and inventive list of juices, salads and filled baguettes. Staffed, it would seem, by slightly clueless language exchange students, its heart is in the right place, but this is not somewhere you can expect a speedy lunch. Bring a book.

Lili Deliss

NEW *Plaça Vicenç Martorell 2 (mobile 639 743 221). Metro Catalunya.* **Open** 9.30am-7.30pm Mon-Sat. €€. No credit cards. **Café**. **Map** p87 C2 ⑭

A respectable alternative when Bar Kasparo (p89) is full, this tiny French-run café also has tables in the shade overlooking the cheerful Plaça Vicenç Martorell. A short list of eating options includes filled baguettes, quiche, crêpes and home-made cakes. No alcohol.

Mam i Teca

C/Lluna 4 (93 441 33 35). Metro Sant Antoni. **Open** 1-4pm, 8.30pm-midnight Mon, Wed-Fri, Sun; 8.30pm-midnight

Mam i Teca

Sat. Closed 2wks Aug. €€. **Tapas**. **Map** p87 B2 ⑮

A bright little tapas restaurant with only three tables, so it pays to reserve. All the usual tapas, from anchovies to cured meats, are rigorously sourced, and complemented by superb daily specials such as organic *botifarra*, pork confit and asparagus with shrimp. The bar (which is also open afternoons) is worth mentioning for its superior vodka and tonic.

Ravalo

Plaça Emili Vendrell 1 (93 442 01 00). Metro Sant Antoni. **Open** 8pm-midnight Tue-Sun. €€. **Pizzeria**. **Map** p87 B2 ⑯

Perfect for fans of thin and crispy, Ravalo's table-dwarfing pizzas take some beating, thanks to flour, and a chef, imported from Naples. Most pizzas, like the Sienna, are furnished with the cornerstone toppings you'd expect – in this case mozzarella di bufala, speck, cherry tomatoes and rocket – but less familiar offerings include the pizza soufflé, which is filled with ham, mushrooms and an eggy

Giménez y Zuazo

mousse (better than it sounds, really). The terrace overlooking a quiet square is open year-round.

Sésamo
C/Sant Antoni Abat 52 (93 441 64 11). Metro Sant Antoni. **Open** 1-3.30pm Mon; 1-3.30pm, 8.30-11.30pm Wed-Sat; 8.30-11.30pm Sun. €€. **Vegetarian.** Map p87 A2 ⑰
Another veggie restaurant that doesn't take itself too seriously (yoga ads, but no whale song), Sésamo offers a creative bunch of dishes in a cosy, buzzing back room. Salad with risotto and a drink is a bargain at €6.50, or try cucumber rolls stuffed with smoked tofu and mashed pine nuts, crunchy polenta with baked pumpkin, gorgonzola and radicchio, or the delicious spicy curry served in popadom baskets with dahl and wild rice.

Silenus
C/Àngels 8 (93 302 26 80). Metro Liceu. **Open** 1.30-4pm, 8.30pm-11.30am Mon-Thur; 1.30-4pm, 8.30pm-midnight Fri, Sat. €€€. **Mediterranean.** Map p87 B2 ⑱

Run by arty types for arty types, Silenus works hard on its air of scuffed elegance, with carefully chipped and stained walls on which the ghost of a clock is projected and the faded leaves of a book float up on high. The food, too, is artistically presented, and never more so than with the lunchtime tasting menu. This offers a tiny portion of everything on the menu, from French onion soup to a flavoursome haricot bean stew and entrecôte with mash.

Shopping

Discos Castelló
C/Tallers 3, 7, 9 & 79 (93 302 59 46/www.discoscastello.es). Metro Catalunya. **Open** 10am-8.30pm Mon-Sat. Map p87 C2 ⑲
Discos Castelló is a homegrown cluster of small shops, each with a different speciality: no.3 is devoted to classical; the largest, no.7, covers pretty much everything; no.9 does hip hop, rock and alternative pop plus T-shirts and accessories; and no.79 is best for jazz and 1970s pop. The latter is good for ethnic music and electronica.

Giménez y Zuazo
C/Elisabets 20 (93 412 33 81/ www.boba.es). Metro Catalunya. **Open** 10.30am-3pm, 5-8.30pm Mon-Sat. Map p87 B2 ⑳
This effortlessly cool designer duo has always been quirky. Previously, they've let themselves go when it comes to colour and print, although they have remained quite restrained with the silhouette of their women's clothing line. However, recently they seem to have thrown the A-line shape rule book out of the window and have started playing with layers and asymmetric cuts.

Le Swing
C/Riera Baixa 13 (93 324 84 02). Metro Liceu. **Open** 10.30am-2.30pm, 4.30-8.30pm Mon-Sat. No credit cards. Map p87 B3 ㉑
Today's second-hand is known as 'vintage', and thrift is not on the agenda. Fervent worshippers of Pierre Cardin,

YSL, Dior, Kenzo and other fashion deities scour all corners of the sartorial stratosphere and deliver their booty back to this little powder puff of a boutique. The odd Zara number and other mere mortal brands creep in as well.

Nightlife

Benidorm

C/Joaquín Costa 39 (no phone). Metro Universitat. **Open** *Apr-mid Oct* 8pm-2.30am Mon-Thur, Sun; 8pm-3am Fri, Sat. *Mid Oct-Mar* 7pm-2.30am Mon-Thur, Sun; 7pm-3am Fri, Sat. Closed Aug. No credit cards. **Map** p87 B2 ㉒

This lively, smoky little place is a kitsch paradise of brothel-red walls, crystal lanterns and 1980s disco paraphernalia, boasting the world's smallest toilet, dancefloor and chill-out room. The sounds being absorbed by the mass of humanity packed in here on weekends (watch your wallet) range from hip hop to 1970s, although in the main they are variations on the same electronica theme.

Dos Trece

NEW *C/Carme 40 (93 301 73 06/ www.dostrece.net).* Metro Liceu. **Open** 10pm-3am Thur-Sun. Live music from 10pm Wed. **Map** p87 C2 ㉓

The downstairs lounge at Dos Trece restaurant has made a welcome return, after being closed for a few years. The remodelled basement lounge has a Moroccan feel to it, but it's the programming of live music and DJs that has been most anticipated. Funk, soul and afrobeat sessions predominate, with live jazz, bossa nova and bolero on Wednesdays.

Jazz Sí Club

C/Requesens 2 (93 329 00 20/www.tallerdemusics.com). Metro Sant Antoni. **Open** 5pm-2.30am Mon-Thur, Sun; 5pm-3am Fri, Sat. No credit cards. **Map** p87 A2 ㉔

This tiny music school auditorium and bar is a space where students, teachers and music lovers can meet, perform and listen. Every night is dedicated to a different musical genre: there's trad

jazz on Monday; pop, rock and blues jams on Tuesday; jazz sessions on Wednesday; Cuban music on Thursday; flamenco on Friday; and rock on Saturday and Sunday.

La Paloma

C/Tigre 27 (93 301 68 97/www.la paloma-bcn.com). Metro Universitat. **Open** 6-9.30pm, 11.30pm-5am Thur; 6-9.30pm, 11.30pm-2am, 2.30am-5am Fri, Sat; 5.45-9.45pm Sun. **Admission** (incl 1 drink) €3-€8. No credit cards. **Map** p87 B2 ㉕

If the Addams family ran a club, it'd be something like La Paloma: refined, steeped in history and a little bit nuts. The chandeliers, velvet curtains and dancers create a burlesque vibe oddly complemented by the varied range of nights. There's Swasthya Yoga on Tuesdays; Thursday's Bongo Lounge continues to pump out Latin tunes and funk, while the weekend's So Rebel Club!, depending on who's on the decks (from Justice to Jon Carter), can be anything from techno to pop and rock. The second Wednesday of every month is the eclectic mini-festival of sorts, Rawal Launch, which brings together international dance, food and DJs.

Lower Raval

The lower half of the Raval, from C/Hospital downwards, is generally referred to as the **Barrio Chino** ('Barri Xino' in Catalan). The nickname was coined in the 1920s by a journalist comparing it to San Francisco's Chinatown, and referred to its underworld feel rather than to any Chinese population. The authorities have long been working on cleaning up the area. Whole blocks with associations to prostitution or drugs have been demolished, a sports centre, a new police station and office blocks have been constructed, and some streets have been pedestrianised. But the most dramatic plan was to create a 'Raval obert al cel' ('Raval open to the sky'), the most tangible result of which is the sweeping, palm-lined Rambla del Raval, completed in 2000. Current efforts to fill the rather empty new *rambla* include licences for new clubs and bars, Botero's deliciously bulging *Gat* ('Cat') sculpture and an ethnic weekend market.

C/Nou de la Rambla, the area's main street, is home to Gaudí's first major project, the **Palau Güell**. Nearby, in C/Sant Pau, is a Modernista landmark, Domènech i Montaner's **Hotel España**, and at the end of the street sits the Romanesque tenth-century church of **Sant Pau del Camp**. Iberian remains dating to 200 BC have been found next to the edifice, marking it as one of the oldest parts of the city. At the lower end of the area were the **Drassanes** (shipyards), now home to the **Museu Marítim**. Along the Paral·lel side of this Gothic building is the only remaining large section of Barcelona's 14th-century city wall.

Sights & museums

Palau Güell

C/Nou de la Rambla 3 (93 317 39 74). Metro Drassanes or Liceu. **Admission** tbc. **Map** p87 C4 ㉖

The Palau Güell is due to reopen in early 2008, after major structural renovation. A fortress-like edifice shoehorned into a narrow six-storey sliver, it was Gaudí's first major commission, begun in 1886 for textile baron Eusebi Güell. The tour starts in the subterranean stables, with an exotic canopy of stone palm fronds on the ceiling. On the next floor, the vestibule has ornate mudéjar carved ceilings from which the Güells could snoop on their arriving guests through the jalousie trelliswork; at the heart of the house lies the spectacular six-storey hall complete with musicians' galleries and topped by a dome covered in cobalt honeycomb

tiles. The antidote to this dark and gloomy palace lies on its roof terrace, decorated with a rainbow forest of 20 mosaic-covered chimneys.

Sant Pau del Camp

C/Sant Pau 101 (93 441 00 01). Metro Paral·lel. **Open** *Visits* noon-1pm; 7.30-8.30pm Mon-Fri. *Mass* 8pm Sat; noon Sun. **Admission** €1. **Map** p87 A4 ㉗

The name, St Paul in the Field, reflects a time when this was still countryside. This little Romanesque church goes back 1,000 years; indeed, the date carved on its most prestigious headstone – that of Count Guifré II Borell, son of Wilfred the Hairy and inheritor of all Barcelona and Girona – is AD 912.

The church's impressive façade includes sculptures of fantastical flora and fauna along with human grotesques. The tiny cloister features extraordinary Visigoth capitals and some triple-lobed arches. Restored after stints serving as a school in 1842, as an army barracks from 1855 to 1890 and as a bomb site during the Civil War, Sant Pau is now a national monument.

Eating & drinking

Biblioteca

C/Junta de Comerç 28 (93 412 62 21). Metro Liceu. **Open** 1-4pm, 8.30-11.30pm Tue-Sat. Closed 2wks Aug. €€€.
Mediterranean. **Map** p87 B3 ㉘

A very Zen space with beige minimalist decor, Biblioteca is all about food. Food and books about food, that is. From Bocuse to Bourdain, they are all for sale, and their various influences collide in some occasionally sublime cooking. Beetroot gazpacho with live clams and quail's egg is a dense riot of flavour, and the endive salad with poached egg and *romesco* wafers is superb. Mains aren't quite as head-spinning, but are accomplished nevertheless.

Cafè de les Delícies

Rambla del Raval 47 (93 441 57 14). Metro Liceu. **Open** 6pm-2am Mon, Tue, Thur, Sun; 6pm-3am Fri, Sat. Closed 3wks Aug. €. No credit cards.
Café. **Map** p87 B3 ㉙

The trash pack

The Spanish have always been a resourceful lot, as evinced by the age-old tradition of leaving unwanted furniture on the streets on Thursday nights for collection by those that need it. Despite the authorities' disapproval and occasional efforts to crack down on this environmentally friendly and eminently sensible system, a Thursday night stroll remains the favourite way to furnish the city's student digs. With recycling deeply ingrained in local culture, it is hardly surprising that there are now people who have made an art out of it.

Local eco-design crew **Demano** (93 300 48 07, www.demano.net) turns obsolete PVC street flags into colourful bags, hats and wellies, which can be bought on their website or in design stores such as **Anna Povo** (C/Vidrieria 11, Barri Gòtic, 93 319 35 61) or **Vinçon** (p137). **Vaho** (C/Cotoners 8, Born, 93 268 05 30, www.vaho.ws) offers a cheerful Boldo bag range, this time made of canopy material. For sophisticated, heavy-duty furniture, **Homâ** (C/Rec 20, Born, 93 315 27 55) is an atmospheric grotto that contains lamps, twisted bed-frames and ingenious bicycles made from recycled iron.

The association **Drap-Art** centres on the small shop and exhibition space **La Carboneria** (C/Groch 1, Barri Gòtic, 93 268 48 89, www.drapart.org) and offers a kaleidoscope of curiosities. Run by Tanja Grass, Drap-Art provides a city foothold for eco-artists such as the Barcelona design duo Bel y Bel (www.belybel.com), who transform scrapped SEATs and Vespas into savvy swivel chairs and retro lamps; or artisans (Zenzele or Fantastik), bringing tin can and wire animal sculpture from Africa and India. Accessories abound, from chunky jewellery fashioned from buttons, typing keys, seeds and feathers or slithers of mirror, to recycled leather purses and condom-holders.

Once a year, the CCCB (see p88) hosts Drap-Art's **International Festival of Artistic Recycling** (14-16 December 2007), which incorporates a market, performances and recycling workshops. In the summer months, a fashion show in La Carboneria features prêt-à-porter recycled printed T-shirts, or Tetra Brik bras and bottle dresses, for those with more individual tastes.

David Soul! Boney M! Olivia Newton-John! The functioning 1970s jukebox is reason enough to visit this cosy little bar, even without the excellent G&Ts, the chess, the variety of teas, the terrace and the shelves of books for browsing. A coveted alcove with a sofa, low armchairs and magazines is opened at busy times, or there is a quiet dining room at the back.

Las Fernández

C/Carretes 11 (93 443 2043). Metro Paral·lel. **Open** *9pm-2am Tue-Sun.* **€€. Spanish. Map** p87 A3 ③⓪
An inviting entrance, coloured pillar-box red, is a beacon of cheer on one of Barcelona's more insalubrious streets. Inside, the three Fernández sisters have created a bright and unpretentious bar-restaurant that specialises in wine and food from their native León. Alongside regional specialities *cecina* (dried venison), gammon and sausages are lighter, Mediterranean dishes and generous salads; smoked salmon with mustard and dill, pasta filled with wild mushrooms, and sardines with a citrus escabeche.

Madame Jasmine

NEW *Rambla del Raval 22 (no phone). Metro Liceu.* **Open** *10am-2.30am Tue-Fri, Sun; 10am-3am Fri, Sat.* **€.** *No credit cards.* **Café. Map** p87 B3 ③①
Kitted out like a slightly bizarre and crumbling old theatre set, Madame Jasmine sports silver spray-painted geckos, oriental lamps and feather boas amid its beams and retro '70s tiling. Its generous salads and heaped *bocadillos* are named after historical Raval characters and local street names.

Marsella

C/Sant Pau 65 (93 442 72 63). Metro Liceu. **Open** *10pm-2.30am Mon-Thur; 10pm-3am Fri, Sat.* *No credit cards.* **Bar. Map** p87 B4 ③②
Marsella was opened in 1820 by a native of Marseilles, who may have changed the course of Barcelona's artistic endeavour by introducing absinthe, still a mainstay of the bar's delights. Untapped 100-year-old bottles of the stuff sit in glass cabinets alongside old

mirrors and William Morris curtains, probably covered in the same dust kicked up by Picasso and Gaudí.

Mesón David

C/Carretes 63 (93 441 59 34). Metro Paral·lel. **Open** *1-4.30pm, 8-11.45pm Mon, Tue, Thur-Sun. Closed Aug.* **€. Spanish. Map** p87 A3 ③③
Rough and ready, noisy, chaotic and a lot of fun, Mesón David is also one of the cheapest restaurants in Barcelona. Be prepared to share a table. Mainly Galician dishes include *caldo gallego* (cabbage broth) or fish soup to start, followed by *lechazo* (a vast hunk of roast pork) or grilled calamares. Of the desserts, the almond *tarta de Santiago* battles for supremacy with fresh baby pineapple doused in Cointreau.

Organic

C/Junta de Comerç 1 (93 301 0902). Metro Liceu. **Open** *12.30pm-midnight daily.* **€€. Vegetarian. Map** p87 B3 ③④

Sant Pau del Camp p94

The last word in refectory chic, Organic is better designed and lighter in spirit (its motto: 'Don't panic, it's organic!') than the majority of the city's vegetarian restaurants. Options include an all-you-can-eat salad bar, a combined salad bar and main course, or the full whammy – salad, soup, main course and dessert. Beware the extras (such as drinks), which hitch up the prices.

Spiritual Café

Museu Marítim, Avda Drassanes (mobile 677 634 031/reservations 93 317 52 56). Metro Drassanes. **Open** *May-mid Oct 9pm-3am Wed-Sun.* **€€€**. **Café**. **Map** p87 B5 ㉟

Deliciously different, this late-night alfresco lounge bar fills the patio of the Maritime Museum in summer with chilled sounds and zephyrs of incense. Low, round tables scrawled with Arabic script and lit with candles float on a sea of rugs and cushions, while a team of student waiters offers massages, acrobatics, juggling, Tibetan chants and poetry.

Shopping

Torres

NEW *C/Nou de la Rambla 25 (93 317 32 34/www.vinosencasa.com). Metro Drassanes or Liceu.* **Open** *9am-2pm, 4-9pm Mon-Sat.* **Map** p87 B4 ㊱

After moving from its old and dusty grocery store across the road, Torres' shiny new shop is a bit out of place in the scruffy Lower Raval. It stocks an excellent range of Spanish wines (with a particularly good cava section), including black Mallorcan absinthe.

Nightlife

Bar Pastis

C/Santa Mònica 4 (93 318 79 80). Metro Drassanes. **Open** *7.30pm-2.30am Tue-Thur, Sun; 7.30pm-3.30am Fri, Sat.* **Map** p87 B4 ㊲

This quintessentially Gallic bar once served pastis to visiting sailors and the denizens of the Barrio Chino underworld. It still has a louche Marseilles feel, floor-to-ceiling indecipherable oil paintings (by the original owner when drunk, apparently), Edith Piaf on the stereo, and latter-day troubadours on Tuesdays, Wednesdays and Sundays.

La Concha

C/Guàrdia 14 (93 302 41 18). Metro Drassanes. **Open** *5pm-2.30am Mon-Thur, Sun; 5pm-3am Fri, Sat. No credit cards.* **Map** p87 B4 ㊳

Though it's not as gay as it used to be under its new management, the homo-to-hetero ratio of the crowd that packs La Concha every night to sip cocktails and dance to Moroccan pop, salsa and flamenco remains the highest for blocks. As does the camp factor, with Sara Montiel, queen of the Spanish silver screen, watching over her loyal subjects from hundreds of faded photographs.

Guru

NEW *C/Nou de la Rambla 22 (93 318 08 40/www.gurubarcelona.com). Metro Liceu.* **Open** *8pm-2.30am daily.* **Admission** €3. No credit cards. **Map** p87 B4 ㊴

Guru is set on becoming the sleekest new addition to the newly hip Raval but, palm trees and mood lighting aside, its white padded walls do make it look rather like an asylum. As it has not yet achieved the exclusive status it's aiming for, Cosmo-sipping, black-clad Parisiennes are still having to deal with gangs of tipsy Scousers hopping about to live salsa. For the moment.

Moog

C/Arc del Teatre 3 (93 301 72 82/www.masimas.com). Metro Drassanes. **Open** *midnight-5am daily.* **Admission** €9. **Map** p87 C4 ㊵

A night in Moog is a bit like partying on an aeroplane: it's long, narrow and enclosed, with full-blast air-conditioning and service with a smile. Some fine techno and house keep everything ticking along just right; Angel Molina, Laurent Garnier and Jeff Mills, among countless others, have all played here, with Wednesday nights being especially popular. Upstairs there's a tiny concession to those not feeling the bleeps – an even smaller dancefloor that plays R&B and 1970s tunes.

Wounded Star

Barceloneta & the Ports

Barceloneta

Once a working-class neighbourhood dependent on fishing and heavy industry, this triangular spit of land is now a prime slice of seafront real estate where many of the famously tiny apartments are being converted into short-stay holiday flats. But Barceloneta has not completely lost its charm; the interior of this cramped and chaotic neighbourhood (hidden behind the restaurant-lined boulevard of Passeig Joan de Borbó) is a real slice of old Barcelona.

Since the beach clean-up, Barceloneta has enjoyed a higher profile, and current redevelopment includes university housing and Enric Miralles's towering Gas Natural headquarters, which is covered in mirrored glass. In the heart of the neighbourhood is the new **market** designed by Josep Mias (see box p105). The area has also been the beneficiary of a staggering amount of sculpture (the Wounded Star, for example) particularly around the Port Vell.

Eating & drinking

Agua

Passeig Marítim 30 (93 225 12 72/ www.aguadeltragaluz.com). Metro Barceloneta, then bus 45, 57, 59, 157. **Open** 1.30-3.45pm, 8.30-11.30pm Mon-Thur, Sun; 1.30-4.30pm, 8pm-12.30am Fri, Sat. **€€€. Mediterranean.** **Map** p101 E4 ❶

One of the freshest, most relaxed places to eat in the city, with a large terrace smack on the beach and an animated sunny interior. The menu rarely changes, but regulars never seem to tire of the competently executed monkfish tail with tomato and onion, the risotto with partridge, and fresh pasta with juicy little prawns. Scrummy puddings include marron glacé mousse and a sour apple sorbet.

Bestial

C/Ramón Trias Fargas 2-4 (93 224 04 07). Metro Barceloneta. **Open** 1-4pm, 8-11.30pm Mon-Thur; 1.30-5pm, 8.30pm-12.30am Fri, Sat. **€€€**. **Italian**. **Map** p101 E4 ❷

Its tiered wooden decking and ancient olive trees make Bestial a peerless spot for alfresco seaside dining. At weekends, coloured lights play over the tables as a DJ takes to the decks. The food is modern Italian: dainty little pizzas, rocket salads with parma ham and a lightly poached egg, tuna with black olive risotto and all the puddings you'd expect to find – panna cotta, tiramisu and limoncello sorbet.

Can Ramonet

C/Maquinista 17 (93 319 30 64). Metro Barceloneta. **Open** 10.30am-4pm, 8pm-midnight Mon-Sat; 10.30am-4pm Sun. Closed 2wks Jan, 2wks Aug. **€€€**. **Seafood**. **Map** p101 D3 ❸

A classic among Barceloneta's seafood restaurants, this quaint, rose-coloured space with two quiet terraces is mostly overlooked by tourists, being deep in the heart of the neighbourhood. Consequently, it suffers none of the drop in standards of those paella joints on nearby Passeig Joan de Borbó. Spectacular displays of fresh seafood show what's on offer that day, but it's also worth sampling the velvety fish soup and the generous paellas.

Can Solé

C/Sant Carles 4 (93 221 50 12). Metro Barceloneta. **Open** 1.30-4pm, 8-11pm Tue-Thur; 1.30-4pm, 8.30-11pm Fri, Sat; 1.30-4pm Sun. Closed 2wks Aug. **€€€**. **Seafood**. **Map** p100 C4 ❹

One of Barceloneta's most traditional seafood restaurants, where for over a century portly, jovial waiters have been charming moneyed regulars. Over the years many of these have added to the framed photos, sketches and paintings that line the walls. What continues to lure them is the freshest shellfish (share a plate of chipirones in onion and garlic, Cantabrian anchovies or red shrimp to start) and fillets of wild turbot, lobster stews and sticky paellas. Beware the steeply priced extras (coffee, cover).

La Cova Fumada

C/Baluard 56 (93 221 40 61). Metro Barceloneta. **Open** 8.30am-3.30pm Mon-Wed; 8.30am-3.30pm, 6-8.30pm Thur, Fri; 8.30am-1.30pm Sat. Closed Aug. **€**. No credit cards. **Tapas**. **Map** p100 C4 ❺

This cramped little *bodega* is the birthplace of the potato *bomba*, served with a fiery chilli sauce. Especially tasty are the chickpeas with morcilla sausage, roast artichokes and the marinated sardines. Its huge following of lunching workers means it's hard to get a table after 1pm.

Daguiri

C/Grau i Torras 59 (93 221 51 09). Metro Barceloneta. **Open** *June-Oct* 11am-2am Mon-Fri, Sun; 10am-1am Sat. *Nov-May* 11am-2am Mon, Thur-Sun. **€€**. **Café**. **Map** p100 C4 ❻

Daguiri works hard not to become a one-trick seaside summer terrace, with a raft of measures aimed squarely at foreign residents. Wi-fi, a language exchange, Murphy's, Guinness and a stack of newspapers from around the world feature among them. Throughout the day, there's cheesy garlic bread, delectable filled ciabatta, tapas, dolmades and dips, and home-made chocolate or carrot cake.

La Miranda del Museu

Museu d'Història de Catalunya, Plaça Pau Vila 3 (93 225 50 07). Metro Barceloneta. **Open** 10am-7pm Tue, Wed; 10am-7pm, 9-11pm Thur-Sat; 10am-4pm Sun. **€€**. **Café**. **Map** p100 C3 ❼

BARCELONA BY AREA

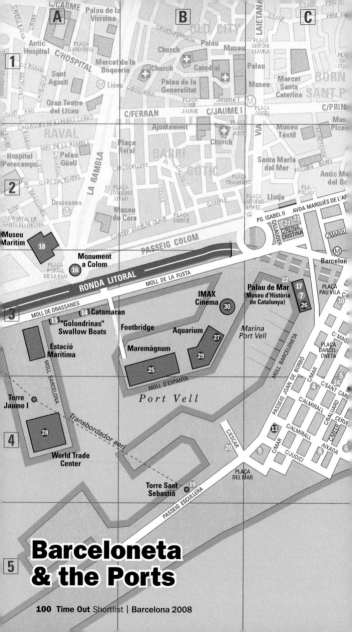

Barceloneta
& the Ports

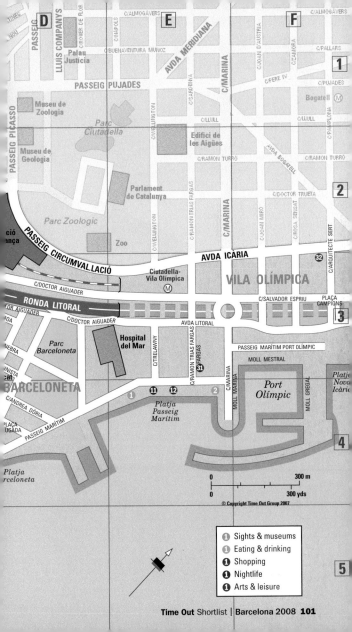

Don't go spreading this about, but there's a secret café with terrific views, cheap and reasonable food and a vast terrace, sitting right at the edge of the marina, perched high above the humdrum tourist traps. Stroll into the Catalan History Museum and take the lift to the top floor. You don't need a ticket.

La Piadina

C/Meer 48 (mobile 660 806 172). Metro Barceloneta. **Open** 1-10pm Tue-Sun. **€.** No credit cards. **Italian. Map** p100 C4 ⑧
A *piadina* is a warmed Italian wrap, made using something akin to a large pitta. Fillings here come in 30 different permutations on the basic tomato, mozzarella, ham, rocket and mushroom theme. To find the place, turn inland at Rebecca Horn's tower of rusting cubes on the beach.

El Suquet de l'Almirall

Passeig Joan de Borbó 65 (93 221 62 33). Metro Barceloneta. **Open** 1-4pm, 9-11pm Tue-Sat; 1-4pm Sun. Closed 2wks Aug. **€€€. Seafood. Map** p100 C4 ⑨
El Suquet remains a friendly family concern despite the smart decor and mid-scale business lunchers. Fishy favourites range from *xató* salad to *arròs negre* and

a variety of set menus, including the 'blind' selection of tapas, a gargantuan taster menu and, most popular, the *picapica*, which includes roast red peppers with anchovies, steamed cockles and clams, and a heap of *fideuà* with lobster.

El Vaso de Oro

C/Balboa 6 (93 319 30 98). Metro Barceloneta. **Open** 9am-midnight daily. Closed Sept. No credit cards. **€€. Tapas. Map** p100 C3 ⑩
The enormous popularity of this long, narrow bar, styled like a cruise ship, tells you everything you need to know about the tapas. It also means that he who hesitates is lost when it comes to ordering. Elbow out a space and demand, loudly, *choricitos*, *patatas bravas*, cubed steak (*solomillo*) or spicy tuna (*atún*).

Nightlife

CDLC

Passeig Marítim 32 (93 224 04 70/www. cdlcbarcelona.com). Metro Ciutadella-Vila Olímpica. **Open** 10pm-2.30am Mon-Wed; noon-3am Thur-Sun. **Admission** free. **Map** p101 E4 ⑪
The Carpe Diem Lounge Club remains at the very forefront of Barcelona's

La Cova Fumada p99

Suite Royale

NEW *Passeig Joan de Borbó 54 (93 268 00 12). Metro Barceloneta.* **Open** 10pm-3am daily. **Admission** free. **Map** p100 C4 ⓭

Barcelona night owls suffered last year when hotspot Café Royale closed, but the same crew have revamped the club in a new portside hotel. Jazz-funk DJ Fred Guzzo still has his swing, while the softly lit, retro bachelor pad decor has been successfully reproduced in a cosy subterranean setting.

Port Vell

Barcelona's first wharves were not built until the Middle Ages, when the city was on its way to being the dominant power in the western Mediterranean. The immense Drassanes Reials (Royal Shipyards) are among the world's finest surviving pieces of civilian Gothic architecture; they now house the **Museu Marítim** and bear witness to the sovereignty of the Catalan navy as the city became a military centre and the hub of trading routes between Africa and the rest of Europe. The city's power was dealt a blow when Christopher Columbus sailed west and found what he thought was the East; soon the Atlantic became the important trade route and Barcelona went into recession.

Despite putting the city out of business, Columbus was commemorated in 1888 with the **Monument a Colom**, a statue inspired by Nelson's Column, complete with eight majestic lions. Nearby is the **World Trade Center**, a ship-shaped construction built on a jetty and housing offices, a five-star hotel and a tower for the **Transbordador Aeri** cable car. The **Moll d'Espanya** wharf is an artificial island housing the **Maremàgnum** shopping mall, an

splash-the-cash, see-and-be-seen celeb circuit – the white beds flanking the dancefloor, guarded by a clipboarded hostess, are perfect for showing everyone who's the daddy. Or, for those not celebrating six-figure record deals, funky house and a busy terrace provide an opportunity for mere mortals (and models) to mingle and discuss who's going to finance their next drink and how to get chatting to whichever member of the Barça team has just walked in.

Shôko

Passeig Marítim 36 (93 225 92 03/ www.shoko.biz). Metro Ciutadella-Vila Olímpica. **Open** 11.30pm-3am daily. **Admission** free. **Map** p101 E4 ⓬

Another semi-exclusive restaurant-club concept in the Port Olímpic. The tried and tested formula continues to go down a treat with Sarrià's pseudo-fashionistas – all Britney hats, spray-on jeans and little wiggles – as they strut their stuff on the dancefloor, gutted they couldn't get into the more exclusive CDLC. Meanwhile, outside on the terrace, civilised sets of chino-clad tourists recline on the comfy beds sipping cocktails.

IMAX cinema and **L'Aquàrium**. It's linked to land by the undulating **Rambla de Mar** footbridge.

Sights & museums

Catamaran Orsom

Portal de la Pau, Port de Barcelona (93 441 05 37/www.barcelona-orsom.com). Metro Drassanes. **Sailings** (approx 1hr 20mins) *Mar-Oct* noon-8pm 3-4 sailings daily. All sailings subject to weather conditions. **Tickets** €12-€14.50; €6-€9 reductions. No credit cards. **Map** p100 A3 ⑭

This 23-metre (75ft) catamaran – departing from the jetty by the Monument a Colom – chugs round the Nova Bocana harbour development, before unfurling its sails and peacefully gliding across the bay. There are 8pm jazz cruises from June to September or the catamaran can be chartered for private trips along the Costa Brava.

Las Golondrinas

Moll de Drassanes (93 442 31 06/www. lasgolondrinas.com). Metro Drassanes. **Tickets** €9.20-€4; €6.80-€2 reductions; free under-4s. **Map** p100 A3 ⑮

For over 115 years the 'swallow boats' have chugged all around the harbour, giving passengers a bosun's-eye view of Barcelona's now rapidly changing seascape. The fleet is made up of three double-decker pleasure boats and two glass-bottomed catamarans, moored next to the Orsom catamaran. Boats leave around every 35 minutes for the shorter trip, and approximately every hour for the longer one.

Monument a Colom

Plaça Portal de la Pau (93 302 52 24). Metro Drassanes. **Open** 9am-8.30pm daily. **Admission** €2.30; €1.50 reductions; free under-4s. No credit cards. **Map** p100 A3 ⑯

Where La Rambla meets the port is the Columbus monument, designed for the 1888 Universal Exhibition. It's hard to believe from ground level, but Colom himself is actually 7m (23ft) high; his famous white barnet comes courtesy of the city pigeons. A tiny lift takes you up inside the column to a circular viewing bay for a panoramic view of city and port. The claustrophobic and acrophobic should stay away; the slight sway is particularly unnerving.

Museu d'Història de Catalunya

Plaça Pau Vila 3 (93 225 47 00/www. mhcat.net). Metro Barceloneta. **Open** 10am-7pm Tue, Thur-Sat; 10am-8pm Wed; 10am-2.30pm Sun. **Admission** €3; €2.10 reductions; free under-7s. Free to all 1st Sun of mth. No credit cards. **Map** p100 C3 ⑰

Located in a lavishly converted 19th-century port warehouse, the Museum of Catalan History's compass runs from the Paleolithic era right up to Jordi Pujol's proclamation as President of the Generalitat in 1980. With very little in the way of original artefacts, it is more a virtual chronology of the region's past revealed through two floors of text, photos, film, animated models and reproductions of everything from a medieval shoemaker's shop to a 1960s bar. Hands-on activities such as trying to lift a knight's armour or irrigating lettuces with a Moorish water wheel add a little pzazz to the rather dry displays. Every section has a decent introduction in English, but the reception desk will also lend copies of the more detailed museum guide. Upstairs is a café with terrace and an unbeatable view.

Museu Marítim

Avda de les Drassanes (93 342 99 29/ www.museumaritimbarcelona.com). Metro Drassanes. **Open** 10am-8pm daily. **Admission** €6.40; €3 reductions; free under-7s. *Temporary exhibitions varies. Combined ticket with Las Golondrinas (35 mins)* €8.30; €6.10-€4.40 reductions; free under-4s. **Map** p100 A2 ⑱

A full-scale replica of Don Juan de Austria's royal galley, from which he led the ships of the Holy League to victory against the invading Ottomans at Lepanto, is the mainstay of the collection at the Museu Marítim, complete with a ghostly crew of oarsmen projected on to

Market values

There's nothing like an iconic piece of architecture to signal the gentrification of a neighbourhood. Set on prime beachfront real estate, the old maritime district of Barceloneta has had it coming for a while: its brand new market, which finally opened in March 2007, comes hot on the heels of a rash of high-profile building work, including the mirror-coated Gas Natural skyscraper, resculpted beaches and swanky new hotels.

The seven-million-euro project is designed by Josep Miàs, disciple and erstwhile right-hand man of the late Enric Miralles (the man behind the mosaic-roofed Santa Caterina market). Miàs has largely preserved the original iron structure of Antoni Rovira i Trias's 1884 design, and blinged it all up with some wavy pergolas and a lot of sheet glass. The roof may look like it is covered in duct tape but those grey strips are actually 180 solar panels which generate 40

per cent of the market's energy requirements. Further green credentials include advanced recycling and rubbish separation.

Following the mall-type trend of the other revamped municipal markets, the number of stalls has almost halved from 60 to 34, opening hours have extended (the market is open until 8.30pm, Tue-Fri) and much floor space has been turned over to a Caprabo supermarket, a mezzanine hall for cultural activities and two restaurants. One is a gleaming white minimalist effort from the hotel and restaurant chain Husa, serving modern versions of Barceloneta paellas and seafood; the other serves gourmet tapas and exclusive tasting menus. Neither establishment bears much relation to the bank accounts of the many low-rent grannies and working class families who live hereabouts, but perhaps that is not the point.

Wave goodbye

As city beaches go, Barceloneta (pictured) has never been a great beauty. Artificial, overcrowded and distinctly urban, its main selling point is convenience. Whenever city life got too much, you could just go and gaze at the horizon. All that has changed. Faced with the annual task of replacing the vast quantities of sand that were washed away whenever a storm rolled in, and with local elections imminent, the city council finally decided to throw in the towel. Citing emergency legislation in order to avoid a full inquiry, they rushed through plans for a wall to keep out the waves.

The result will be an eyesore that ruins the view – and the surf, much to the disgust of the local surfing community. The Med occasionally throws up the odd day of surfable waves, especially between October and April. Hawaii it ain't, but it's certainly better than nothing for anyone with a surfboard in the hall.

Swimmers are perhaps the people who will suffer most, however. It's true that Barceloneta beach was never likely to win any clean beach awards, with its summer broth of plastic bags, sanitary towels and suntan oil, and the nearby sewage plant that overflows whenever it rains for more than 20 minutes. But with a dirty great wall impeding water circulation, not only will there be even more detritus floating around, but higher temperatures will make it the perfect breeding ground for all sorts of unpleasant bacteria.

As for Barcelona's other beaches beyond the Port Olímpic, they too are threatened by breakwaters. Following vociferous protests by the surfing community, these will be a couple of metres below the surface, softening the main force of the waves while still leaving them surfable, and allowing some water flow to sluice out the primordial ooze. Better still, the view won't be disturbed, so gazing continues to be on the horizon.

the rowing banks. The original ship was built in these very same shipyards, one of the finest examples of civil Gothic architecture in Spain and a monument to Barcelona's importance in Mediterranean naval history. With the aid of an audio guide, the maps, nautical instruments, multimedia displays and models show how shipbuilding and navigation techniques have developed and evolved over the years. Admission also covers the *Santa Eulàlia* schooner docked in the Moll de la Fusta.

Transbordador Aeri

Torre de Sant Sebastià, Barceloneta (93 441 48 20). Metro Barceloneta. Also Torre de Jaume I, Port Vell, to Ctra Miramar, Montjuïc. Metro Drassanes. **Open** *Mid June-mid Sept* 10.45am-7.15pm daily. *Mid Sept-mid June* 10.30am-5.45pm daily. **Tickets** €9 single; €12.50 return; free under-3s. No credit cards. **Map** p100 B4 ⑲
Designed as part of the 1929 Expo, these rather battered old cable cars run between the Sant Sebastià tower at the very far end of Passeig Joan de Borbó to the Jaume I tower in front of the World Trade Center; the final leg ends at the Miramar lookout point on Montjuïc. The towers are accessed by lifts.

Eating & drinking

Bar Colombo

C/Escar 4 (93 225 02 00). Metro Barceloneta. **Open** noon-3am daily. Closed 2wks Jan-Feb. No credit cards. **Bar**. **Map** p100 B4 ⑳
Deckshod yachties and chic moneyed locals stroll by all day, oblivious to this unassuming little bar and its sunny terrace overlooking the port. In fact, nobody seems to notice it, odd given its fantastic location and generous portions of *patatas bravas*. The only drawback is the nerve-jangling techno that occasionally fetches up on the sound system.

Can Paixano

C/Reina Cristina 7 (93 310 08 39/www.canpaixano.com). Metro Barceloneta.

Open 9am-10.30pm Mon-Sat. Closed 3wks Aug-Sept. No credit cards. **Bar**. **Map** p100 C2 ㉑
It's impossible to talk, get your order heard or move your elbows, yet the 'Champagne Bar', as it's invariably known, has a global following. Its smoky confines are always mobbed with Catalans and adventurous tourists making the most of dirt-cheap house Cava and sausage *bocadillos* (you can't buy a bottle without a couple). A must.

Luz de Gas – Port Vell

Opposite the Palau de Mar, Moll del Dipòsit (93 484 23 26). Metro Barceloneta or Jaume I. **Open** *Apr-Oct* noon-3am daily. Closed mid Nov-mid Mar. **Bar**. **Map** p100 C3 ㉒
It's cheesy, but this boat/bar also has its romantic moments. By day, bask in the sun with a beer on the upper deck, or rest in the shade below. With nightfall, candles are brought out, wine is uncorked and, if you can blot out the Lionel Richie, it's everything a holiday bar should be.

Set Portes

Passeig Isabel II 14 (93 319 30 33/www.7portes.com). Metro Barceloneta. **Open** 1pm-1am daily. €€€. **Seafood**. **Map** p100 C2 ㉓
The eponymous seven doors open on to as many dining salons, all kitted out in elegant 19th-century decor. Regional dishes are served in enormous portions and include a stewy fish *zarzuela* with half a lobster, and a different paella daily (shellfish, for example, or with rabbit and snails). Reservations are only available for certain tables (two to three days in advance is recommended); without one, get there early or expect a long wait outside.

Somorrostro

C/Sant Carles 11, Barceloneta (93 225 00 10). Metro Barceloneta. **Open** 7-11.30pm Mon, Thur-Sun. €€€. **Global**. **Map** p100 C4 ㉔
Named after the shanty town of Andalucian immigrants that once stood nearby on the beach, Somorrostro is a refreshingly non-fishy, non-traditional

restaurant for these parts. Its bare-bricked walls and red and black decor attract a young, buzzy crowd, attended to by permanently confused waiters. The food ranges from cucumber, tomato and yoghurt soup to an unexpectedly successful tandoori duck magret.

Shopping

Maremàgnum

Moll d'Espanya (93 225 81 00/www. maremagnum.es). Metro Drassanes. **Open** 10am-10pm daily. **Map** p100 B3 **25**
After years of declining popularity, the Maremàgnum shopping centre has been spruced up, ditched most of the bars and discos and taken a step upmarket with shops such as Xocoa (for mouthwatering chocolate), Calvin Klein and Parisian accessories from boudoirish Lollipops. The high-street staples are all present and correct – Mango, H&M, Women's Secret and so on – and the ground floor still focuses on the family market with sweets, clothes for children and a Barça shop. There's also a Starbucks and a handful of tapas bars and restaurants.

Nightlife

Le Kasbah

Plaça Pau Vilà (Palau del Mar) (93 238 07 22/www.ottozutz.com). Metro Barceloneta. **Open** 11pm-3am daily. **Admission** free. **Map** p100 C3 **26**
A white awning heralds the entrance to this louche bar behind the Palau de Mar. Inside, a North African harem look seduces a young and up-for-it mix of tourists and students on to its plush cushions for a cocktail or two before going out. As the night progresses so does the music, from chill-out early on to full-on boogie after midnight.

Mondo

NEW *Edifici IMAX, Moll d'Espanya (93 221 39 11/www.mondobcn.com). Metro Barceloneta or Drassanes.* **Open** 11.30pm-3am Wed-Sat. **Map** p100 B3 **27**
Arrive by yacht or by Jaguar – anything less might not get you past the door.

Upscale dining alongside amazing views of the port precede late-night caviar and champagne house parties with DJs from Hed Kandi and Hotel Costes. Multiple intimate VIP rooms provide privacy, pleasure and prestige.

Sugar Club

World Trade Center, Moll de Barcelona (93 508 83 25/www.sugarclub-barcelona. com). Metro Drassanes. **Open** 8pm-4am Wed-Sat. **Admission** free. **Map** p100 A4 **28**
Grupo Salsitas continues its cool quest, with this latest addition to the stable of Danzatoria, Danzarama et al. Beautiful people and a twinkling view across the marina provide the decoration in this otherwise minimal couple of spaces, one small and intimate with a splash of smooth and soulful vocal house, the other a large dancefloor with sofas. DJs blend tribal, electro and tech house beats with the odd remixed 1980s classic.

Arts & leisure

L'Aquàrium

Moll d'Espanya (93 221 74 74/www. aquariumbcn.com). Metro Barceloneta or Drassanes. **Open** Oct-May 9.30am-9pm Mon-Fri; 9.30am-9.30pm Sat, Sun. *June, Sept* 9.30am-9.30pm daily. *July, Aug* 9.30am-11pm daily. **Admission** €15; €10 reductions; free under-4s. **Map** p100 B3 **29**
The aquarium houses more than 450 species of Mediterranean marine life. Miniaquària is devoted to the smaller animals such as sea cucumbers and sea-horses, but the main draw here is the Oceanari, a giant shark-infested tank traversed via a glass tunnel. The upstairs section is devoted to children, with knobs-and-whistles style activities for pre-schoolers or Planet Aqua – an extraordinary, split-level circular space with Humboldt penguins and a walk-through model of a sperm whale.

IMAX Port Vell

Moll d'Espanya (93 225 11 11/www. imaxportvell.com). Metro Barceloneta or Drassanes. **Tickets** €7-€10. **Map** p100 B3 **30**

Monument a Colom p103

theme pubs. Wide empty boulevards lend themselves well to large-scale sculpture; landmark pieces include a jagged **pergola** on Avda Icària by Enric Miralles and Carme Pinós, in memory of the ripped-up industrial railway tracks, and Antoni Llena's abstract **David i Goliat** in the Parc de les Cascades.

Nightlife

Around the Port Olímpic, you'll find endless dance bars interspersed with seafood restaurants, fast-food outlets and mock-Irish pubs.

Club Catwalk

C/Ramon Trias Fargas s/n (93 221 61 61/www.clubcatwalk.net). Metro Ciutadella-Vila Olímpica. **Open** midnight-5.30am Wed-Sun. **Admission** €15-€18. **Map** p101 E3 ❸
Maybe it's the name or maybe it's the location (slap bang under celeb-tastic Hotel Arts), but most of the Catwalk queue seems to think they're headed for the VIP room – that's crisp white collars and gold for the boys and short, short skirts for the girls. Inside it's suitably snazzy; upstairs there's R&B and hip hop, but the main house room is where most of the action is, with regular appearances from the likes of Erick Morillo and Roger Sánchez keeping the club's prestige firmly intact.

Arts & leisure

Yelmo Icària Cineplex

C/Salvador Espriú 61, Vila Olímpica (information 93 221 75 85/tickets 902 22 09 22/www.yelmocineplex.es). Metro Ciutadella-Vila Olímpica. **Tickets** *Mon* €5. *Tue-Sun* €6.50; €5 before 3pm & reductions. No credit cards. **Map** p101 F3 ❷
The Icària has all the atmosphere of the empty shopping mall that surrounds it, but what it lacks in charm, it makes up for in choice, with 15 screens offering a commercial roster of mainstream films. Queues tend to be slow-moving; it's worth booking your seat online.

A squat white hulk in the middle of the marina, the IMAX has yet to persuade many that it's anything more than a gimmick. Predictable programming covers fish, birds, ghosts and adventure sports.

Vila Olímpica

The land further up the coast was once an area of thriving industry, but by the 1980s it had fallen into disuse and presented the perfect blank slate for a team of 30 prize-winning architects to design the model neighbourhood of the Olympic Village, with accommodation for 15,000 athletes, parks, a metro stop, four beaches and a leisure marina. The result is a spacious district but the lack of cafés and shops leaves it devoid of bustle, unless you count the weekend skaters and cyclists.

Most social activity takes place in the seafront Port Olímpic, home to docked sailboats, restaurants, beaches, a large casino, and a waterfront strip of cheesy clubs and

BARCELONA BY AREA

Pavelló Mies van der Rohe p116

Montjuïc & Poble Sec

In a city with as few parks as Barcelona, the pretty gardens, spectacular views, museums and galleries of Montjuïc hill offer a precious escape. Yet, despite the attractions, difficult access means that Montjuïc's green spaces are greatly underused by local citizens; plans to convert it into the 'Central Park' of Barcelona involve opening up access from the neighbourhood of Poble Sec with broad boulevards and escalators leading up to Avda Miramar; as a temporary boost, the Ajuntament has already launched a new Montjuïc bus service (p113).

The mists of time obscure the etymology of Montjuïc, but an educated guess is that 'juïc' comes from the old Catalan word meaning Jewish. It was here that the medieval Jewish community buried their dead; some of the excavated headstones are now kept in the Museu Militar, inside the 17th-century Castell de Montjuïc. This was rebuilt in its current form after Philip V's troops broke the siege of Barcelona in 1714. From its vantage point overlooking the city, the central government was able to impose its will on the unruly populace until the death of Franco.

The most popular access to the park is still the long way from Plaça d'Espanya, with the climb eased by a sequence of open-air escalators. Where Avda Paral·lel meets Plaça d'Espanya is Las Arenas, the old bullring. The last bull met its fate

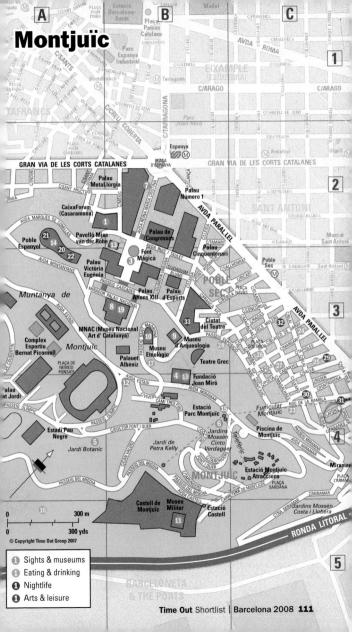

here in the 1970s and until 2003 the bullring lay derelict. The ubiquitous Lord Rogers is currently overseeing a mammoth transformation project, to be completed in 2008, which will turn the ring into a circular leisure complex while restoring the original neo-Mudéjar façade. The vision encompasses a 'piazza in the sky', a giant roof terrace that will allow for alfresco events and offer panoramic views over Barcelona.

Sights & museums

CaixaForum

Casaramona, Avda Marquès de Comillas 6-8 (93 476 86 00/www.fundacio. lacaixa.es). Metro Espanya. **Open** 10am-8pm Tue-Sun. **Admission** free. **Map** p111 A/B2 ❶

One of the masterpieces of industrial modernism, this former red-brick yarns and textiles factory was designed by Puig i Cadafalch in 1911. It spent most of the last century in a sorry state, acting briefly as a police barracks and then falling into dereliction. Fundació La Caixa, the charitable arm of Catalonia's largest savings bank, bought it and gave it a huge rebuild. The brick factory was supported while the ground below was excavated to house an entrance plaza by Arata Isozaki (who designed the Palau Sant Jordi on the other side of the hill), a Sol LeWitt mural, a 350-seat auditorium, bookshop and library. In addition to the smaller permanent contemporary art collection, upstairs there are three impressive spaces for temporary exhibitions – often among the most interesting in the city.

Cementiri del Sud-oest

C/Mare de Déu de Port 54-58 (93 484 17 00). Bus 38. **Open** 8am-6pm daily. **Admission** free. **Map** p111 A4 ❷

This enormous necropolis, perched at the side of the motorway out of town, serves as a daily reminder to commuters of their own mortality. It has housed the city's dead since 1883, originally placing them in four sections:

one for Catholics, one for Protestants, one for non-Christians and a fourth for unborn babies. It now stretches over the entire south-west corner of the mountain, with family tombs stacked up to six storeys high. Many, notably those belonging to the city's gypsy community, are a riot of colour.

Font Màgica de Montjuïc

Plaça d'Espanya (93 316 10 00/www. bcn.es/fonts). Metro Espanya. **Fountain** *May-Sept* 8pm-11.30pm Thur-Sun; music every 30mins 9.30pm-midnight. *Oct-Apr* 7-9pm Fri, Sat; music every 30mins 7-9pm. **Map** p111 B3 ❸

Still using its original art deco waterworks, the 'magic fountain' works its wonders with the help of 3,600 pieces of tubing and 4,500 light bulbs. Summer evenings after nightfall see the multiple founts swell and dance to various hits ranging from Sting to the *1812 Overture*, showing off its kaleidoscope of pastel colours, while searchlights play in a giant fan pattern over the palace dome. Tacky but unmissable.

Fundació Joan Miró

Fundació Joan Miró

Parc de Montjuïc (93 329 19 08/ www.bcn.fjmiro.es). Metro Paral·lel then Funicular de Montjuïc/bus 61. **Open** *July-Sept* 10am-8pm Tue, Wed, Fri, Sat; 10am-9.30pm Thur; 10am-2.30pm Sun. *Oct-June* 10am-7pm Tue, Wed, Fri, Sat; 10am-9.30pm Thur; 10am-2.30pm Sun. *Guided tours* 11.30pm Sat, Sun. **Admission** *All exhibitions* €7.50; €5 reductions. *Temporary exhibitions* €4; €3 reductions. Free under-14s. **Map** p111 B4 ❹

Josep Lluís Sert, who spent the years of the dictatorship as Dean of Architecture at Harvard University, designed one of the world's great museum buildings on his return. Approachable, light and airy, these white walls and arches house a collection of more than 225 paintings, 150 sculptures and all of Miró's graphic work, plus some 5,000 drawings. The permanent collection, highlighting Miró's trademark use of primary colours and simplified organic forms symbolising stars, the moon, birds and women, occupies the second half of the space. On the way to the sculpture gallery is Alexander Calder's lovely reconstructed *Mercury Fountain*, which was originally seen at the Spanish Republic's Pavilion at the 1937 Paris Fair. In other works, Miró is shown as a Cubist (*Street in Pedralbes*, 1917), Naïve (*Portrait of a Young Girl*, 1919) or Surrealist (*Man and Woman in Front of a Pile of Excrement*, 1935). The works downstairs were donated to the museum by 20th-century artists. In the upper galleries large, black-outlined paintings from the final period precede a room of works with political themes.

Temporary shows vary wildly in content and quality, but at best can match the appeal of the permanent exhibition. The Espai 13 in the basement features young contemporary artists. Outside is a pleasant sculpture garden with fine work by some contemporary Catalan artists.

Event highlights Sean Scully (until 30 Sept 2007); 'A body without limits', the human body in contemporary art (25 Oct 2007-27 Jan 2008).

Jardí Botànic

C/Doctor Font i Quer (93 426 49 35). Metro Espanya. **Open** *Apr-June, Sept* 10am-5pm Mon-Fri; 10am-8pm Sat, Sun. *July, Aug* 10am-8pm daily. *Oct-Mar* 10am-5pm daily. **Admission** €3; €1.50 reductions; free under-16s. Free last Sun of mth. No credit cards. **Map** p111 A4 ❺

The botanic garden was opened in 1999, with the idea of collecting plants from the seven global regions that share a western Mediterranean climate. The result is highly impressive. Everything about the futuristic design, from the angular concrete pathways to the raw sheet-steel banking, is the antithesis of the more naturalistic, Jekyll-inspired gardens of England. It is meticulously kept, with the added advantage of wonderful views across the city. There is a small space housing occasional temporary exhibitions and free audio guides to lead visitors through the gardens.

Event highlights 'The Hidden Colours of Nature' (until 31 Dec 2007).

Jardins Mossèn Costa i Llobera

Ctra de Miramar 1. Metro Drassanes or Paral·lel. **Open** 10am-sunset daily. **Admission** free. **Map** p111 B4 ❻

The port side of Montjuïc is protected from the cold northerly wind, which creates a microclimate that is some two degrees warmer than the rest of the city. This has made it perfect for 800 species of the world's cacti. It is said to be the most complete collection of its type in Europe. Along with the botanical curiosities, there is a vast bronze of a young girl making lace.

Montjuïc Tourist Bus

NEW *Plaça d'Espanya (93 415 60 20). Metro Espanya.* **Open** *Mid Sept-June* 10am-9.20pm Sat, Sun. *July-mid Sept* 10am-9.20pm daily. **Tickets** Day pass €3; €2 reductions. No credit cards. **Map** p111 B2 ❼

A new, open-top tourist bus. There are actually two routes: the blue line starts and ends here at Plaça Espanya, the red one at Portal de la Pau (p100 A3), near

Curtain call for the can-can

In the 1890s Avda Paral·lel was known as the Montmartre of Barcelona, crammed with music halls and cafés entertaining the local factory workers. The most notorious was El Molino, a music hall with a famously daring programme starring Europe's sauciest vedettes.

It started life in 1899 as a cabaret café called La Pajarera Catalana, but in 1913 was rebuilt as a Parisian-style music hall fronted by a revolving windmill. It was rechristened Le Petit Moulin Rouge, but with the arrival of the Franco dictatorship in 1939, its name was switched to Spanish, El Molino (quietly dropping the *rouge*, now the colour of the political left).

The post-war decline in the popularity of music hall forced the closure of even the much-loved El Molino in the 1990s. Its derelict state was symbolic of the general shabbiness of the Paral·lel, lined with abandoned theatres and once decadent cafés converted into cheap kebab joints.

Suggestions for El Molino's future included a dance school, a university residence and a mini opera house, but the final plan obeyed local wishes to keep it as a musical theatre. The new Molino will specialise in cabaret, flamenco, magic and comedy.

Renovation started in March 2007 and the neon red sails are due to turn again in late 2008. The old Modernista façade will front a 27-metre-high (89-foot) curving glass tower, a metaphor for the wind that blows the sails below. Work will cost an estimated €6.5 million and new amenities will include state-of-the art technical facilities and a terrace cocktail bar with views over the remodelled Plaça del Molino.

This project is the figurehead for the Ajuntament's plan to recover the spirit of the area and create a Barcelona Broadway; next up for renovation is the neighbouring, 100-year-old Teatre Arnau, which is to be converted into a cultural centre for performance arts.

the Monument a Colom; they coincide at the Olympic stadium and the castle. Tickets are valid for both routes.

MNAC (Museu Nacional d'Art de Catalunya)

Palau Nacional, Parc de Montjuïc (93 622 03 76/www.mnac.es). Metro Espanya. **Open** 10am-7pm Tue-Sat; 10am-2.30pm Sun. **Admission** *Permanent exhibitions* €8.50; €6 reductions. *Temporary exhibitions* €3-€5. Free under-7s and 1st Thur of mth. **Map** p111 B3 ❽

The National Museum of Catalan Art gives a dizzying overview of Catalan art from the 12th to the 20th centuries. Newly renovated, the museum has a whole extra floor to absorb holdings of the Thyssen-Bornemisza collection previously kept in the convent in Pedralbes, along with Modernista work from the former Museum of Modern Art in Ciutadella park.

The highlight of the museum, however, is still the Romanesque collection, with 21 murals rescued from Pyrenean churches, including the tremendous *Crist de Taüll* from the 12th-century church of Sant Climent de Taüll.

The Gothic collection is also excellent and starts with some late 13th-century frescoes. There are carvings and paintings from local churches, including works of the Catalan masters of the Golden Age, Bernat Martorell and Jaume Huguet. The highlight of the Thyssen collection is Fra Angelico's *Madonna of Humility* (c1430s), while the Cambó bequest contains some stunning Old Masters – Titian, Rubens and El Greco. Also unmissable is the Modernista collection, which includes the original mural of *Ramon Casas and Pere Romeu on a Tandem* (1897), which decorated Els Quatre Gats. The rich collection of decorative arts includes furniture from Modernista houses such as the Casa Amatller and Gaudí's Casa Batlló.

Event highlights 'Drawings by Santiago Rusiñol' (until Apr 2008); 'Napper and Frith, a photographic journey through the Iberian peninsula of the 19th century' (Oct 2007-Jan 2008); 'Yves Tanguy, the surrealist universe' (22 Oct 2007-13 Jan 2008).

Museu d'Arqueologia de Catalunya

Passeig de Santa Madrona 39-41 (93 423 21 49/93 423 56 01/www.mac.es). Metro Poble Sec. **Open** 9.30am-7pm Tue-Sat; 10am-2.30pm Sun. **Admission** €2.40; €1.70 reductions; free under-16s. No credit cards. **Map** p111 B3 ❾

The time frame for this archaeological collection starts with the Palaeolithic period, and there are relics of Greek, Punic, Roman and Visigoth colonisers, up to the early Middle Ages. A massive Roman sarcophagus is carved with scenes of the rape of Persephone, and an immense statue of Asklepios, the god of medicine, towers over one room. The display ends with the marvellous, jewel-studded headpiece of a Visigoth king. One of the best-loved pieces is an alarmingly erect Priapus, found during building work in Sants in 1848 but kept under wraps 'for moral reasons' until 1986.

Museu Etnològic

Passeig de Santa Madrona s/n (93 424 68 07/www.museuetnologic.bcn.es). Metro Poble Sec. **Open** *Late June-late Sept* noon-8pm Tue-Sat; 11am-3pm Sun. *Late Sept-late June* 10am-7pm Tue, Thur; 10am-2pm Wed, Fri-Sun. **Admission** €3; €1.50 reductions; free under-16s, over-65s & 1st Sun of mth. No credit cards. **Map** p111 B3 ❿

Recently spruced up and expanded, the Ethnology Museum houses a vast collection of items, from Australian Aboriginal boomerangs to rugs and jewellery from Afghanistan, although by far the most comprehensive collections are from Catalonia. Of the displays upstairs, most outstanding are the Moroccan, Japanese and Philippine exhibits, though there are also some interesting pre-Columbian finds. Of the attempts to arrange the pieces in thematically interesting ways, 'Taboo' turns out to be a rather limp look at nudity in different cultures; more successful is 'Sacred', a run through the world of religious rituals.

BARCELONA BY AREA

Museu Militar

Castell de Montjuïc, Ctra de Montjuïc 66 (93 329 86 13). Metro Paral·lel, then funicular & cable car. **Open** *Apr-Oct* 9.30am-8pm Tue-Sun. *Nov-Mar* 9.30am-5pm Tue-Fri; 9.30am-8pm Sat, Sun. **Admission** €2.50; €1-€1.25 reductions; free under-7s. No credit cards. **Map** p111 B5 ⑪

Appropriately housed in one wing of the old hilltop castle, the Military Museum is a grim slice of local history. The fortress was used to bombard rather than protect Barcelona in past conflicts, and as a prison and place of execution, the castle has strong repressive associations. The exhibits here include armour, swords, lances, muskets, rifles and pistols. Other highlights include 23,000 lead soldiers representing a Spanish division of the 1920s. Oddly, a display of Jewish tombstones from the mountain's desecrated medieval cemetery is the only direct reminder of death within its thick walls. If the Spanish government cedes the castle to the city of Barcelona, there are plans to turn part of the building into a centre for peace studies.

Museu Olímpic i de l'Esport

NEW *Avda Estadi 60 (93 292 53 79). Bus 50, 55, 61.* **Open** *Apr-Sept* 10am-6pm Mon, Wed-Sun. *Oct-Mar* 10am-1pm, 4-6pm Mon, Wed-Sun. **Admission** €8; €6 reductions; free under-5s. **Map** p111 B4 ⑫

Opened in 2007 in a new building across from the stadium, the Olympic and Sports Museum gives an overview of the Games (and indeed, all games) from Ancient Greece onwards. As well as photos and videos of great sporting moments and heroes, there are objects such as Ronaldinho's boots or Mika Häkkinen's Mercedes, along with a collection of opening ceremony costumes and Olympic torches. Perhaps more entertaining are the interactive displays, such as one that compares your effort at the long jump with that of the pros.

Pavelló Mies van der Rohe

Avda Marquès de Comillas (93 423 40 16/www.miesbcn.com). Metro Espanya.

Open 10am-8pm daily. **Admission** €3.50; €2 reductions; free under-18s. No credit cards. **Map** p111 B2 ⑬

Mies van der Rohe built the Pavelló Alemany (German Pavilion) for the 1929 Exhibition not as a gallery, but as a simple reception space, sparsely furnished by his trademark 'Barcelona Chair'. The pavilion was a founding monument of modern rationalist architecture, with its flowing floor plan and revolutionary use of materials. Though the original was demolished after the Exhibition, a fine replica was built on the same site in 1986, the simplicity of its design setting off the warm tones of the marble and expressive Georg Kolbe sculpture in the pond.

Poble Espanyol

Avda Marquès de Comillas (93 325 78 66/www.poble-espanyol.com). Metro Espanya. **Open** 9am-8pm Mon; 9am-2am Tue-Thur; 9am-4am Fri, Sat; 9am-midnight Sun. **Admission** €7.50; €5.50 reductions; €15 family ticket; free under-7s. **Map** p111 A2 ⑭

Built for the 1929 Universal Exhibition, this mock Spanish village is a minimally cheesy architectural theme park with reproductions of traditional buildings from every region in Spain. The cylindrical towers at the entrance are copied from the walled city of Ávila and lead on to a typical Castilian main square from which visitors can explore a tiny whitewashed street from Arcos de la Frontera in Andalusia, then on to the 16th-century House of Chains from Toledo, and so on. There are numerous bars and restaurants, a flamenco *tablao* and more than 60 shops selling Spanish crafts. The Poble is unmistakably aimed at tourists, but it has been working to raise its cultural profile, with the Fundació Fran Daurel collection of contemporary art, hosting music festivals such as B-estival and the recent opening of a quality gallery of Iberian arts and crafts.

Telefèric de Montjuïc

Estació Funicular, Avda Miramar (93 443 08 59/www.tmb.net). Metro Paral·lel, then funicular. **Map** p111 B4 ⑮

The cable cars, running from the funicular to the castle, were due to reopen in summer 2007 after renovation and the introduction of new eight-person cars.

Eating & drinking

La Caseta del Migdia

Mirador de Migdia, Passeig del Migdia s/n, Montjuïc (mobile 617 956 572). Bus 55 or bus Parc de Montjuïc/funicular de Montjuïc, then 10min walk. Follow signs to Mirador de Montjuïc. **Open** *June-Sept* 8pm-2.30am Thur, Fri; 11am-2.30am Sat; 11am-1am Sun. *Oct-May* 10am-6pm Sat, Sun. No credit cards. **Bar**. **Map** p111 A5 ⑯

Follow the Camí del Mar footpath around Montjuïc castle to find one of the few places in the city from which to watch the sun set. Entirely alfresco, high up in a clearing among the pines, this is a magical space, scattered with deckchairs, hammocks and candlelit tables. DJs spinning funk, rare groove and lounge alternate in surreal fashion with a faltering string quartet.

La Font del Gat

Passeig Santa Madrona 28 (93 289 04 04). Funicular Parc Montjuïc/bus 55. **Open** 1-4pm Tue-Sun. Closed 3 wks Aug. €€. **Catalan**. **Map** p111 B3 ⑰

A welcome watering hole perched high on Montjuïc between the Miró and Ethnological Museum. Most come for the set lunch: start with scrambled egg with Catalan sausage and peppers or a salad, follow with baked cod or chicken with pine nuts and basil, and finish with fruit or dessert. Tables outside attract a surcharge, but enjoy fantastic views.

Fundació Joan Miró

Parc de Montjuïc (93 329 07 68). Metro Paral·lel, then Funicular de Montjuic. **Open** *July-Sept* 10am-7.30pm Tue-Sat; 10am-2.30pm Sun. *Oct-June* 10am-6.30pm Tue-Sat; 10am-2.30pm Sun. €€. **Café**. **Map** p111 B4 ⑱

Inside the Miró museum is this pleasant restaurant and café; the former overlooks the sculpture garden, while the latter has tables outside in a grassy courtyard dotted with Miró's pieces.

Poble Espanyol

The sandwiches made of 'Arab bread' are expensive but huge; there are also pasta dishes and daily specials.

Oleum

MNAC, Palau Nacional, Montjuic (93 289 06 79). Metro Espanya. **Open** 1-4pm Tue-Sun. **€€€€**. **Modern Mediterranean**. Map p111 B3 ⓲

That the MNAC's restaurant is to be considered a serious contender is indicated by two Antoni Tàpies canvases flanking the wonderful view across the city. Dishes run from scallops on squid ink noodles with lime foam to suckling pig with an onion tarte tatin, or St Peter's fish poached in a fennel broth. The place has only been open a year or two, and despite some teething troubles (distracted service and a couple of deliquescent foams), your average museum caff this is not.

Nightlife

Discothèque

Poble Espanyol, Avda Marquès de Comillas (93 511 57 64). Metro

Quimet i Quimet p120

Espanya. **Open** midnight-6am Fri, Sat.
Admission (incl 1 drink) €12 with
flyer, €15 without. **Map** p111 A2 ⓴
New promoters have taken on the ardu-
ous task of keeping Discothèque at the
forefront of the A-list clubs. A snaking
queue of the young and the beautiful
use looks and attitude to blag their way
in. Nights with names like 'Ken loves
you' or 'Fuck me, I'm famous' mix up
house and techno in the main room,
while hip hop and R&B fill the smaller
room. Projections, drag queens, podium
dancers and a VIP bar create the Ibiza-
when-it-was-still-hot vibe.

La Terrrazza

*Poble Espanyol, Avda Marquès de
Comillas (93 272 49 80/www.laterrrazza.
com). Metro Espanya.* **Open** *May-
mid Oct* midnight-6am Thur-Sat.
Admission (incl 1 drink) €15 with
flyer, €18 without. **Map** p111 A2 ㉑
Driven by resident DJ Sergio Patricio,
the city's best-loved club packs them in
on its huge outdoor space that moves
to a tech house beat. Compilation
albums, international guest DJs and
partner club Fellini on La Rambla (p69)
make it one energetic enterprise. If you
only go to one nightclub in Barcelona,
or indeed Spain, make it this one. A
long cold drink on a balmy night
checking the eye-candy is hard to beat.

Arts & leisure

El Tablao de Carmen

*Poble Espanyol, Avda Marquès de
Comillas, Montjuïc (93 325 68 95/www.
tablaodecarmen.com). Metro Espanya.*
Open 7pm-2am Tue-Sun. *Shows*
7.45pm, 10pm Tue-Sun. Closed 2wks
Jan. **Admission** *Show & 1 drink* €31.
Show & dinner €59. **Map** p111 A3 ㉒
This rather sanitised version of the traditional flamenco *tablao* sits in faux-
Andalucian surroundings in the Poble
Espanyol. You'll find both established
stars and new young talent, displaying
the various styles of flamenco singing,
dancing and music. The emphasis is on
panache rather than passion, so you
might prefer your flamenco with a bit
more spit and a little less polish. You

must reserve in advance, which will
allow you to enter the Poble Espanyol
free after 7pm.

Poble Sec & Paral·lel

Poble Sec, the name of the
neighbourhood between Montjuïc
and the Avda Paral·lel, means
'dry village', which is explained
by the fact that it was 1894 before
the thousands of poor workers
who lived on the flanks of the hill
celebrated the installation of the
area's first water fountain (which
is still standing in C/Margarit).

The name Avda Paral·lel derives
from the fact that it coincides exactly
with 41° 44' latitude north, one of
Ildefons Cerdà's more eccentric
conceits. The avenue was the
prime centre of Barcelona nightlife
in the first half of the 20th century,
and was full of theatres, nightclubs
and music halls.

Today, Poble Sec is a friendly,
working-class area of quiet streets
and leafy squares. On the stretch of
the Paral·lel opposite the city walls,
three tall chimneys stand amid
modern office blocks. They are all
that remains of the Anglo-Canadian-
owned power station known locally
as **La Canadença** ('The Canadian').
This was the centre of the city's
largest general strike, in 1919.
Beside the chimneys an open space
has been created and dubbed the
Parc de les Tres Xemeneies
(Park of the Three Chimneys).

Towards the Paral·lel are
some distinguished Modernista
buildings, which local legend has
maintained were built for *artistas*
from the nude cabarets by their
rich sugar daddies. At C/Tapioles
12 is a beautiful, narrow wooden
Modernista door with particularly
lovely writhing ironwork, while
at C/Elkano 4 is La Casa de les
Rajoles, which is known for its
peculiar mosaic façade.

Sights & museums

Refugi 307

*C/Nou de la Rambla 169 (93 319 02 22).
Metro Paral·lel.* **Open** *Guided tour* 11am
1st Sat of mth (by appointment only).
Call to book 10am-2pm Mon-Fri; 4-6pm
Tue, Thur. *Meeting place* Biblioteca
Francesc Boix, C/Blai 34. **Admission**
€3.20; free under-7s. No credit cards.
Map p111 C4 ㉓

About 1,500 Barcelona civilians were
killed during the vicious air bombings
of the Civil War, a fact that the government long silenced. As Poble Sec
particularly suffered the effects of
bombing, a large air-raid shelter was
built partially into the mountain at the
top of C/Nou de la Rambla; one of some
1,200 in the entire city. Now converted
into a museum, it is worth a visit. The
guided tour takes 90 minutes.

Eating & drinking

La Bella Napoli

*C/Margarit 14 (93 442 50 56). Metro
Paral·lel.* **Open** 8.30pm-midnight Mon,
Tue; 1.30-4pm, 8.30pm-midnight Wed-
Sun. €€. **Pizzeria. Map** p111 C3 ㉔

The once-legendary queues at La
Bella Napoli are happily a thing of the
past, thanks to a major renovation and
the addition of a new and spacious
bare-brick dining room. Welcoming
Neapolitan waiters, in nifty red T-
shirts to match the red gingham tablecloths, are able to talk you through the
long, long list of antipasti and pasta
dishes, but you can't go wrong with
the crispy baked pizzas, such as the
Sofia Loren, with provolone, basil,
bresaola, cherry tomatoes, rocket and
parmesan. Beer is Moretti and the
wine list is all-Italian.

Quimet i Quimet

*C/Poeta Cabanyes 25 (93 442 31 42).
Metro Paral·lel.* **Open** noon-4pm, 7-
10.30pm Mon-Fri; noon-4pm Sat. Closed
Aug. €€. **Tapas. Map** p111 C3 ㉕

Packed to the rafters with dusty bottles of wine, this miniscule bar makes
up for in tapas what it lacks in space.
The speciality is preserved clams,

cockles, mussels and so on, which are
not to all tastes, but the *montaditos*,
sculpted tapas served on bread, are
spectacular. Try salmon sashimi with
cream cheese, honey and soy, or cod,
passata and black olive pâté.

La Soleá

*Plaça del Sortidor 14 (93 441 01 24).
Metro Poble Sec.* **Open** noon-midnight
Tue-Sat; noon-4pm Sun. €€. No credit
cards. **Global. Map** p111 C3 ㉖

From the name to the sprawling terrace
and the cheerful waiters to the orange
and yellow decor, everything about La
Soleá radiates sunshine. There's barely
a continent that hasn't been visited on
the menu, which holds houmous,
tabouleh and goat's cheese salad
alongside juicy burgers served with
roquefort or mushrooms, smoky tandoori chicken, Mexican tacos, vegetable
samosas and slabs of Argentine beef.

Tapioles 53

*C/Tapioles 53 (93 329 22 38/www.
tapioles53.com). Metro Paral·lel or
Poble Sec.* **Open** 9-11.30pm Tue-Sat.
€€€. **Global. Map** p111 C3 ㉗

Eating at Tapioles 53 would be just like
eating at a friend's house; if, that is, you
happened to have friends who could
cook this well and had as canny an eye
for seductive lighting. It's the brain-
child of Australian chef Sarah Stothart,
who wanted to create a cosy atmosphere in which to serve accomplished
but unpretentious food – such dishes
as fabulous home-made bread with
wild mushroom soup; fresh pasta with
baby broad beans and artichokes;
boeuf bourguignon; rosewater rice pudding with pomegranate, or ginger and
mascarpone cheesecake.

Xemei

NEW *Passeig de la Exposició 85 (93 553
51 40). Metro Poble Sec.* **Open** 1-3pm,
9.30pm-midnight Mon, Wed-Sun. €€€.
Italian. Map p111 B3 ㉘

Heartwarming Venetian country cooking, from home-made pasta to peppered
ribbons of liver and onions with fried
polenta. The *cicchetti* is a great way to
start: a plate of antipasti involving

fresh anchovies, figs with pecorino and *sarda in saor* (sardines marinated in vinegar and onions), while peach crostata makes for an indulgent finish. When the weather allows, book a pavement table; the dining room can get a little cramped and noisy.

Nightlife

Barcelona Rouge

C/Poeta Cabanyes 21 (93 442 49 85). *Metro Paral·lel.* **Open** 11pm-4am Tue-Sat. **Admission** free. No credit cards. **Bar**. Map p111 C3 ㉙
A hidey-hole of a place, small enough to get packed even though it's little known, hard to get into and hard on the wallet. Once inside there's ambient music, good cocktails and battered sofas draped with foreign and local thirtysomethings – those with a bit of money and a bit of class who want to avoid the more obvious nightspots. Ring the buzzer to get in.

Maumau

C/Fontrodona 33 (93 441 80 15/ *www.maumaunderground.com). Metro* *Paral·lel.* **Open** 11pm-2.30am Thur; 11pm-3am Fri, Sat; 7pm-midnight Sun. **Admission** *Membership* €5. No credit cards. **Map** p111 C4 ㉚
Behind the anonymous grey door (ring the bell), first-timers to this likeable little chill-out club pay €5 to become members, though in practice it rarely charges out-of-towners. Inside, a large warehouse space is humanised with colourful projections, IKEA sofas and scatter cushions, and a friendly, laid-back crowd. DJ Wakanda schools us in the finer points of deep house, jazz, funk or whatever takes his fancy.

Sala Apolo

C/Nou de la Rambla 113 (93 441 *40 01/www.sala-apolo.com). Metro* *Paral·lel.* **Open** midnight-5am Wed, Thur; midnight-7am Fri, Sat; 10.30pm-3am Sun. **Admission** varies. No credit cards. **Map** p111 C4 ㉛
Who'd have thought one of the most popular clubs in this most stylish city would be a poorly lit 1940s dancehall. A

new, more intimate space downstairs hosts relaxed gigs from up-and-coming talent, while upstairs features bigger and international acts. Afterwards, Wednesdays and Thursdays are an upbeat affair, with an international crowd of music buffs, from hipster geeks to hip hop gals, trekking across the Raval for funk and Latin grooves. And, ten years on, there are still epic queues for the weekend's bleepity-bleep techno extravaganza, Nitsa.

Tinta Roja

C/Creu dels Molers 17 (93 443 32 43/ *www.tintaroja.net). Metro Poble Sec.* **Open** *Bar* 8pm-2am Wed, Thur; 8pm-3am Fri, Sat; 7pm-1am Sun. *Shows* 10pm-midnight Wed-Sat. Closed 2wks Aug. **Admission** *Bar* free. *Shows* (incl 1 drink) €8-€10. No credit cards. **Map** p111 C3 ㉜
Push through the depths of the bar and you'll find yourself transported to a Buenos Aires bordello/theatre/circus/cabaret by the array of plush red velvet sofas, smoochy niches and an ancient ticket booth. It's an atmospheric place for a late-ish drink, and a distinctly different entertainment experience from Friday to Sunday when you'll get to take in live tango, jazz and flamenco in a small theatre at the back. Tango classes are also offered.

Arts & leisure

Mercat de les Flors

Plaça Margarida Xirgú, C/Lleida *59 (93 426 18 75/www.mercat* *flors.com). Metro Poble Sec.* **Box** **office** 1hr before show. Advance tickets also available from Palau de la Virreina. **Tickets** varies. No credit cards. **Map** p111 B3 ㉝
A huge converted flower market housing three performance spaces, the Mercat is one of the most innovative venues in town. Performances here experiment with unusual formats and mix new technologies, pop culture and the performing arts. Film nights and DJ sessions also feature; events include June's Marató de l'Espectacle and the Festival Asia in autumn.

BARCELONA BY AREA

Casa Batlló

Eixample

In contrast to the narrow alleys and winding streets that characterise much of Barcelona, the vast, grid-patterned Eixample ('enlargement') seems rather out of character. It was a late 19th-century extension to Barcelona that has now become home to some of the city's most elegant buildings, its swankiest shops and some of its most well-heeled residents. Its showpiece is the plush bisecting avenue of **Passeig de Gràcia**.

The period of construction coincided with Barcelona's golden age of architecture: the city's bourgeoisie employed Gaudí, Puig i Cadafalch, Domènech i Montaner and the like to build them a series of increasingly daring townhouses in an orgy of avant-garde one-upmanship.

The result is extraordinary but can be tricky to negotiate on foot; the lack of open spaces and similarity of many streets can leave you somewhat confused. The city council, meanwhile, is attempting to make the area more liveable: in 1985 the ProEixample was set up to reclaim some of the courtyards proposed in the plans of the original design of the Eixample, drawn up by Ildefons Cerdà, so that everybody living in the area should be able to find an open space within 200 metres (650 feet) of their home. Two of the better examples are the palm-fringed mini-beach around the **Torre de les Aigües** water tower (C/Roger de Llúria 56) and the patio at **Passatge Permanyer** (C/Pau Claris 120).

Sights & museums

Casa Àsia

Avda Diagonal 373 (93 238 73 37/
www.casaasia.es). Metro Diagonal.
Open 10am-8pm Mon-Sat; 10am-2pm
Sun **Admission** free. **Map** p125 D2 ❶
This much-needed Asian contribution
to Barcelona's cultural scene is located
in another of Modernista architect Puig
i Cadafalch's creations, the Palau Baró
de Quadras. The Casa Àsia cultural
centre acts as both an exhibition space
and ambassador for all things in Asia
and the Asian Pacific. Recent exhibitions include rare documentary films,
photos on the anniversary of Hiroshima
and Tarun Chopras's pictures of life in
urban India. It also features an oriental
café on the ground floor and an excellent multimedia library. Forthcoming
events for 2007 include a series of crit-
ical readings on Krishnamurti, and
courses ranging from Japanese culture
to Chinese astrology.

Casa Batlló

Passeig de Gràcia 43 (93 216 03 06/
www.casabatllo.es). Metro Passeig
de Gràcia. **Open** 9am-8pm daily.
Admission €16.50; €13.20 reductions;
free under-7s. **Map** p124 C3 ❷
For many people the Casa Batlló is the
most telling example of Gaudí's pre-
eminence over his Modernista contem-
poraries; the comparison is easy, since
it sits in the same block as masterworks by his two closest rivals, Puig i
Cadafalch and Domènech i Montaner.
Opinions differ on what the building's
remarkable façade represents, with its
polychrome shimmering walls, the sinister skeletal balconies and the hump-
backed, scaly roof. Some maintain it
shows the spirit of carnival, others
insist it is a cove on the Costa Brava.
The most popular theory, however,
which takes into account the architect's
patriotic feelings, is that it depicts Sant
Jordi and the dragon. The idea is that
the cross on top of the building is the
knight's lance, the roof is the back of
the beast, and the balconies below are
the skulls and bones of its victims.

Exploring the interior (at a cost)
offers the best opportunity of under-
standing how Gaudí, who is sometimes
considered the lord of the bombastic
and overblown, was really the master
of tiny details. Witness the ingenious
ventilation in the doors and the amazing natural light reflecting off the azure
walls of the inner courtyard, or the way
in which the brass window handles are
curved to fit precisely the shape of a
hand. An apartment within Casa Batlló
is now open to the public, along with
the the roof terrace and attic: the whitewashed arched rooms of the top floor,
which were originally used for wash-
ing and hanging clothes, are among the
master's most atmospheric spaces.

Fundació Antoni Tàpies

C/Aragó 255 (93 487 03 15/www.
fundaciotapies.org). Metro Passeig
de Gràcia. **Open** 10am-8pm Tue-Sun.
Admission €4.20; €2.10 reductions;
free under-16s. **Map** p124 C3 ❸
Antoni Tàpies is Barcelona's most celebrated living artist. In 1984 he set up
the Tàpies Foundation in the former
publishing house of Muntaner i Simon,
dedicating it to the study and appreciation of contemporary art. He promptly
crowned the building with a glorious
tangle of aluminium piping and ragged
metal netting (*Núvol i Cadira*, meaning
'cloud and chair'). This was a typically
contentious act by an artist whose
work, a selection of which remains on
permanent display on the top floor of
the gallery, has been causing controversy ever since he burst on to the art
scene in the 1960s. 'Give the organic its
rights', he proclaimed, and devoted his
time to making the seemingly insignif-
icant significant, using such everyday
materials as mud, string, rags and
cardboard to build his rarely pretty but
always striking works.

Fundacion Francisco Godia

C/València 284 pral (93 272 31 80/
www.fundacionfgodia.org). Metro
Passeig de Gràcia. **Open** 10am-8pm
Mon, Wed-Sun. Closed Aug. **Admission**
€4.50; €2.10 reductions; free under-5s.
No credit cards. **Map** p125 D3 ❹

Eixample

Godia's first love was motor-racing: he was a Formula 1 driver for Maserati in the 1950s. His second, though, was art, which is how this private museum has come to house an interesting selection of medieval religious art, historic Spanish ceramics and modern painting. Highlights include Alejo de Vahía's medieval *Pietà* and a baroque masterpiece by Luca Giordano, along with some outstanding Romanesque sculptures, and 19th-century oil paintings by Joaquín Sorolla and Ramon Casas. The modern collection has works by Miró, Julio González, Tàpies and Manolo Hugué.

Hospital de la Santa Creu i Sant Pau

C/Sant Antoni Maria Claret 167 (93 291 90 00/www.santpau.es/www.ruta delmodernisme.com). Metro Hospital de Sant Pau. **Map** p125 F2 ⑤

Hospital de la Santa Creu i Sant Pau

Domènech i Montaner's 'garden city' of a hospital is a collection of pavilions abundantly adorned with the medieval flourishes that characterise the architect's style. The hospital, now a UNESCO World Heritage Site, is composed of 18 pavilions and connected by an underground tunnel system. It is a short walk from the madding crowds at the Sagrada Familia. Domènech i Montaner built the hospital very much with its patients in mind, convinced that pleasant surroundings and aesthetic harmony were good for the health. Unfortunately, the old buildings don't entirely suit the exigencies of modern medicine; patient care is being phased out and moved to a blocky white monstrosity of a building on the north side of the hospital grounds. The public has free access to the grounds; guided tours (€5, call 93 317 76 52) are offered every morning.

Museu de Carrosses Fúnebres

C/Sancho de Avila 2 (93 484 17 10). Metro Marina. **Open** 10am-1pm, 4-6pm Mon-Fri; 10am-1pm Sat, Sun (weekends call to check). **Admission** free. **Map** p125 F5 ⑥

Finding this, the most obscure and macabre museum in Barcelona, hasn't got any easier. You'll need to ask at the reception desk of the Ajuntament's funeral service and, eventually, a security guard will take you down to a perfectly silent and splendidly shuddersome basement housing the world's biggest collection of funeral carriages and hearses, dating from the 18th century through to the 1950s. There are ornate baroque carriages and more functional Landaus and Berlins, and a rather wonderful silver Buick. The white carriages were designed for children and virgins, and there's a windowless black velour mourning carriage for the forlorn mistress. The vehicles are manned by ghoulish dummies dressed in period gear whose eyes follow you around the room, making you glad of that security guard.

Museu de la Música

NEW *L'Auditori, C/Padilla 155 (93 256 36 50/www.museumusica. bcn.cat). Metro Glòries.* **Open** 11am-9pm Mon, Wed-Fri; 10am-7pm Sat, Sun. **Admission** €4; €3 reductions. **Map** p125 F5 ⑦

As part of the efforts to turn the Plaça de les Glòries into a cultural hub, the contents of the old Music Museum, which were under wraps for six years, have finally been rehoused in the Auditori concert hall. The idea behind the vast and glittering displays of instruments and fun interactive exhibits is not to provide a historical overview of the art, but to take a look at some of its defining moments.

Museu del Perfum

Passeig de Gràcia 39 (93 216 01 21/ www.museodelperfume.com). Metro Passeig de Gràcia. **Open** 10.30am-1.30pm, 4.30-8pm Mon-Fri; 10.30am-2pm Sat. **Admission** €5; €3 reductions. **Map** p124 C4 ⑧
In the back room of the Regia perfumery sits this collection of nearly 5,000 scent bottles, cosmetic flasks and related objects. On display you'll find such familiar perfume brands as Dior and Guerlain in extremely rare bottles – among them a garish creation by Dalí made for Schiaparelli and a set of really disturbing golliwog flasks for Vigny. The Museu del Perfum's most recent acquisitions include a collection of 19th-century perfume powder bottles and boxes.

Museu Egipci de Barcelona

C/València 284 (93 488 01 88/ www.fundclos.com). Metro Passeig de Gràcia. **Open** 10am-8pm Mon-Sat; 10am-2pm Sun. **Admission** *Museum* €6; €5 reductions; free under-5s. **Map** p125 D3 ⑨
Two floors of this museum showcase a well-chosen collection that spans some 3,000 years of Nile-drenched culture. Exhibits run from religious statuary, such as the massive baboon heads used to decorate temples, to everyday objects such as copper mirrors and alabaster headrests. Outstanding pieces include the painstakingly matched fragments from the Sixth Dynasty Tomb of Iny, a bronze statuette of the goddess Isis in the midst of breastfeeding her son Horus, and mummified cats, baby crocodiles and falcons.

Parc de l'Estació del Nord

C/Nàpols (no phone). Metro Arc de Triomf. **Open** 10am-sunset daily. **Admission** free. **Map** p125 F5 ⑩
This slightly shabby space is perked up by three pieces of land art in glazed blue ceramic by New York sculptor Beverley Pepper. Along with a pair of incongruous white stone entrance walls, *Espiral Arbrat* (*Tree Spiral*) is a spiral bench set under the shade of lime-flower trees and *Cel Caigut* (*Fallen Sky*) is a 7m-high (23ft) ridge rising from the grass, while the tilework recalls Gaudí's *trencadís* smashed-tile technique.

Parc Joan Miró (Parc de l'Escorxador)

C/Tarragona (no phone). Metro Tarragona or Espanya. **Open** 10am-sunset daily. **Map** p124 A3 ⑪
The demolition of the old slaughterhouse provided some much-needed urban parkland, although there's precious little greenery here. The rows of stubby *palmera* trees and grim cement lakes are dominated by a library and Miró's towering phallic sculpture *Dona i Ocell* (*Woman and Bird*).

La Pedrera (Casa Milà)

Passeig de Gràcia 92-C/Provença 261-5 (93 484 59 00/www.caixacatalunya.es). Metro Diagonal. **Open** 10am-8pm daily. **Admission** €8; €4.50 reductions; free under-12s. **Guided tours** (in English) 4pm Mon-Fri. **Map** p125 D3 ⑫
The last secular building designed by Antoni Gaudí, the Casa Milà (usually referred to as La Pedrera, 'the stone quarry') is a stupendous and daring feat of architecture, the culmination of the architect's experimental attempts to recreate natural forms with bricks and mortar. Its marine feel is complemented by Jujol's tangled balconies, doors of twisted kelp ribbon, sea-foamy ceilings and interior patios as blue as a mermaid's cave. Ridiculed when it was completed in 1912, it has become one of Barcelona's best-loved buildings, and is adored by architects for its extraordinary structure: it is supported entirely by pillars, without a single

master wall, allowing the vast asymmetrical windows of the façade to invite in great swathes of natural light.

There are three exhibition spaces. The first-floor art gallery hosts free exhibitions of eminent artists, you can visit a reconstructed Modernista flat on the fourth floor, and the attic holds a museum dedicated to an insightful overview of Gaudí's career. Best of all is the chance to stroll on the roof of the building amid its *trencadís*-covered ventilation shafts: their heads are shaped like the helmets of medieval knights. Informative titbit-filled guided tours in English are run daily at 4pm.

Sagrada Família

C/Mallorca 401 (93 207 30 31/
www.sagradafamilia.org). Metro
Sagrada Família. **Open** *Mar-Sept*
9am-8pm daily. *Oct-Feb* 9am-6pm
daily. **Admission** €8; €5 reductions;
€3 7-10 years; free under-6s. *Lift to*
spires €2. No credit cards. **Map**
p125 F3 ⑬

The Temple Expiatori de la Sagrada
Família manages to be both Europe's
most fascinating building site and
Barcelona's most emblematic creation.
In the 1930s anarchists managed to
destroy Gaudí's intricate plans and
models for the building by setting fire
to them, which means that the ongoing
work is a matter of conjecture and con-
siderable controversy; the putative
finishing date of 2020 is looking
increasingly optimistic. The church's
first mass has been put back a year and
is now scheduled for Sant Josep's day
(19 March) in 2008, 126 years after the
foundation stone was laid.

Gaudí, buried beneath the nave of the
Sagrada Família, dedicated more than
40 years of his life to the project, the
last 14 exclusively, and the crypt, the
apse and the nativity façade, all of
which were completed in his lifetime,
are the most beautiful elements of the
church. The latter, facing C/Marina,
looks at first glance as though some
careless giant has poured candlewax
over a Gothic cathedral, but closer
inspection reveals that every protu-
berance is an intricate sculpture of
flora, fauna or a human figure,
combining to form an astonishingly
moving stone tapestry depicting
scenes from Christ's life. The other
completed façade, the Passion, which
faces C/Sardenya, is more austere,
with vast diagonal columns in the
shape of bones and haunting sculptures by Josep Maria Subirachs.
Japanese sculptor Etsuro Sotoo has
chosen to adhere more faithfully to
Gaudí's intentions, and has fashioned
six more modest musicians at the rear
of the temple, as well as the exuber-
antly coloured bowls of fruit to the left
of the nativity façade.

Eating & drinking

Alkimia

C/Indústria 79 (93 207 61 15). Metro
Joanic or Sagrada Família. **Open** 1.30-
3.30pm, 8.30-11pm Mon-Fri. Closed
2wks Aug. €€€€. **Catalan**.
Map p125 F2 ⑭

It came as no surprise to the regulars
at Alkimia when it was awarded a
Michelin star (as a consequence of
which, making a reservation is now all
but essential). A great way to explore
what the restaurant has to offer is to
sample the gourmet menu, which
offers four savoury courses, including
complex dishes that play around with
the Spanish classics – for instance,
liquid *pa amb tomàquet* with *fuet*
sausage, wild rice with crayfish, strips
of tuna on a bed of foamed mustard –
and a couple of desserts.

Bar Mut

C/Pau Claris 192 (93 217 43 38). Metro
Diagonal. **Open** 8.30am-midnight Mon-
Fri; 10.30am-midnight Sat; noon-5pm,
8.30pm-midnight Sun. €€€. **Tapas**.
Map p125 D2 ⑮

There's more than a soupçon of the
16ème arrondissement about this
smart and traditional bar; well-heeled
Catalans, BCBG to the core, chatter
loudly and dine on excellent, well-
sourced tapas – foie, wild sea bass and
espardenyes (sea cucumbers). The wine
selection is similarly upmarket and
displayed so seductively behind glass
that you may find yourself drinking
and spending rather more than you
bargained for.

La Bodegueta

Rambla de Catalunya 100 (93 215 48
94). Metro Diagonal. **Open** 8am-2am
Mon-Sat; 6.30pm-1am Sun. Closed
2wks Aug. €€. No credit cards.
Tapas. **Map** p124 C3 ⑯

Resisting the rise of the surrounding
area, this former wine *bodega* is un-
reconstructed, dusty and welcoming,
supplying students, businessmen and
everyone in between with reasonably
priced wine, vermouth on tap and
prime-quality tapas amid the delicate

Kitchen confidential

Chef Jordi Artal explains what's hot in Cinc Sentits.

Born in Toronto to a Catalan mother and Canadian father, Jordi Artal threw away a successful career in Silicon Valley to move to the land of his European forefathers and indulge his real passion – for cooking. Together with his sister, sommelier Amèlia Artal, he set up Cinc Sentits (p131); one of the hottest restaurants of the moment.

What's cooking?

Hmm, langoustine tails with *botifarra* sausage and shellfish consommé is a great new dish, or the Iberian pork belly with apple risotto and rosemary is an old favourite revisited.

What's next?

We're introducing some great types of lesser-known, local

fish – so many are overlooked because the public demand is for sea bass, cod and so on. We're also looking at in-house smoking with herbs and woodchips. The idea is to bring certain dishes (like a smoky bonito broth which is poured over sushi-grade tuna belly) to the dining room under a glass cloche, and release a puff of the smoke at the table.

Inspirations?

More than any individual, I would say our dishes are inspired by the produce itself, and the changing tastes of the seasons. Apricots are really good right now, so we thought we'd use them to balance veal cheeks, along with a camomile gelée. I get depressed when I see peaches in the market in January. A properly ripened peach should trickle down the chin, that's the fun. Don't be eating them out of season.

What's different?

We like to muck around with people's expectations. Our amuse-bouche is a shot containing maple syrup, cava sabayon and a pinch of Maldon sea salt. It shouldn't work, but it wakes up the palate for what is to come.

Molecular gastronomy. Discuss.

It makes for an interesting experience, but it's not the kind of soul-satisfying food you want to eat often. Also, not everyone can be Ferran Adrià, Heston Blumenthal or Grant Achatz – what people don't realise is that these guys all have a solid base in classic cooking. Ferran, for example, spent years cooking French haute cuisine at El Bulli before starting to experiment.

patterns of tiling that's a century old. In summer, there are tables are outside on the almost pedestrianised Rambla de Catalunya.

Café Berlin

C/Muntaner 240-242 (93 200 65 42). Metro Diagonal. **Open** *Sept-July* 10am-2am Mon-Wed; 10am-3am Thur-Sat. *Aug* 5.30pm-2am Mon-Wed; 5.30pm-3am Thur-Sat. **€€**. **Café**. **Map** p124 B2 ⑰

Downstairs, low sofas fill up with amorous couples while upstairs all is sleek and light, with brushed steel, dark leather and a Klimtesque mural. A rack of newspapers and plenty of sunlight make it popular for coffee or snacks all day; as well as tapas there are pasta dishes, *bocadillos* and cheese-cake, but beware the 20% surcharge for pavement tables.

Casa Calvet

C/Casp 48 (93 412 40 12). Metro Urquinaona. **Open** 1-3.30pm, 8.30-11pm Mon-Sat. **€€€€**. **Catalan**. **Map** p125 D4 ⑱

One of Gaudí's more understated buildings from the outside, Casa Calvet has an interior full of glorious detail in the carpentry, stained glass and tiles. The food is up to par, with surprising combinations almost always hitting the mark: squab with puréed pumpkin, risotto of duck confit and truffle with yoghurt ice-cream, and smoked foie gras with mango sauce. The puddings are supremely good, particularly the pine nut tart with foamed *crema catalana*.

Cervesería Catalana

C/Mallorca 236 (93 216 03 68). Metro Passeig de Gràcia. **Open** 8am-1.30am Mon-Fri; 9am-1.30am Sat, Sun. **€€**. **Tapas**. **Map** p124 C3 ⑲

The 'Catalan Beerhouse' lives up to its name with a winning selection of brews from around the world, but the real reason to come is the tapas. A vast array is yours for the pointing; only hot *montaditos*, such as bacon, cheese and dates, have to be ordered from the kitchen. Arrive early for a seat at the bar, even earlier for a pavement table.

Cinc Sentits

C/Aribau 58 (93 323 94 90/www.cinc sentits.com). Metro Passeig de Gràcia or Universitat. **Open** 1.30-3.30pm Mon; 1.30-3.30pm, 8.30-11.15pm Tue-Sat. **€€€€**. **Modern Spanish**. **Map** p124 B3 ⑳

Run by Catalan-Canadian siblings, the 'Five Senses' is the most reasonably priced of Barcelona's top-end restaurants, and should be on everyone's dining agenda. Talented chef Jordi Artal shows respect for the classics (melt-in-the-mouth suckling pig with apple compôte; Catalan flat *coca* bread with foie gras and crispy leeks), while adding a personal touch in dishes such as lamb cutlets with a crust of porcini dust. To finish, try the artisanal Catalan cheese pairings or the 'five textures of lemon'. Reservations are generally essential at night; visit at lunch for a more peaceful experience.

Cremeria Toscana

C/Muntaner 161 (93 539 38 25). Metro Hospital Clínic. **Open** 1pm-midnight Tue-Thur; 1pm-1am Fri, Sat; noon-10pm Sun. **€**. No credit cards. **Ice-cream**. **Map** p124 B2 ㉑

In this charming little ice-cream parlour, with its lovely, antique-strewn mezzanine, around 20 authentically Italian flavours are made daily, ranging from zingy mandarin to impossibly creamy coconut. '*I dopocena*' ('after dinner') are miniature gourmet sundaes, mixing parmesan and pear flavours; mascarpone and tiramisu; chocolate and pistachio; or liquorice and mint.

Dolso

C/València 227 (93 487 59 64). Metro Passeig de Gràcia. **Open** 9am-10.30pm Mon; 9am-11.30pm Tue-Thur; 9am-1am Fri; 11am-1am Sat. **€€**. **Desserts**. **Map** p124 C3 ㉒

Heaven on earth for the sweet of tooth, Dolso is a 'pudding café' where even the retro-baroque wallpaper is the colour of chocolate. Desserts run from light (a gin and tonic rendered in clear jelly, lemon sorbet, candied peel and juniper berries) to wickedly indulgent (chocolate fondant with passion fruit sorbet and a sherry reduction). A short range of sandwiches and topped ciabatta keeps the spoilsports happy.

Dry Martini

C/Aribau 162-166 (93 217 50 72). FGC Provença. **Open** 1pm-2.30am Mon-Thur; 1pm-3am Fri; 6.30pm-3am Sat; 6pm-2.30am Sun. **Cocktail bar**. Map p124 B2 ㉓

A shrine to the eponymous cocktail, honoured in martini-related artwork and served in at least a hundred forms. All the trappings of a traditional cocktail bar are in place – the bow-tied staff, the leather banquettes, the drinking antiques and the wooden cabinets displaying a century's worth of bottles – but the stuffiness is absent: music owes more to trip hop than middle-aged crowd-pleasers, and the barmen welcome all comers.

Gaig

Hotel Cram, C/Aragó 214 (93 429 10 17/www.restaurantgaig.com). Metro Passeig de Gràcia. **Open** 9-11pm Mon; 1.30-3.30pm, 9-11pm Tue-Sat. €€€€. **Modern Catalan**. Map p124 B3 ㉔

Sadly displaced from its 130-year home in Horta after structural problems, Gaig has lost none of its shine despite its anodyne new surroundings. Carles Gaig's cooking never fails to thrill, from the crayfish tempura amuse-gueule, served with a dip of creamed eel salted with a piece of pancetta, through to a shot-glass holding layers of tangy lemon syrup, *crema catalana* mousse, caramel ice-cream and topped with burnt sugar (to be eaten by plunging the spoon all the way down).

Hanoi II

NEW *Avda Sarrià 37 (93 444 10 99). Metro Hospital Clínic.* **Open** 12.30-4pm, 8.30pm-midnight Mon-Sat; 8.30pm-midnight Sun. €€€. **Vietnamese**. Map p124 A1 ㉕

Opened in 2006, this little sister of the frenetic original Hanoi on C/Enric Granados is a muted version, with low lighting, teak chairs and prints of Miró paintings. It's also considerably easier to get a table. The menu is the same,

however, with duck or prawn *nem* rolls, chicken *musi* (chopped with water chestnuts and pine nuts and rolled in lettuce leaves) and beef *chempy* (with orange peel and vegetables, fried with honey).

Inopia

NEW *C/Tamarit 104 (93 424 52 31). Metro Poble Sec or Sant Antoni.* **Open** 7pm-midnight Mon-Fri; 1-3.30pm, 7pm-midnight Sat. Closed Aug. €€€. **Tapas**. Map p124 A5 ㉖

Being brother (and pastry chef) to infamous chef Ferran Adrià has been both a curse and a blessing for Albert Adrià. On the one hand, his traditional tapas bar has been rammed since it opened; on the other, its glaringly bright, old-school look and approach has disappointed those expecting El Bulli-style culinary fireworks. If classic tapas – *patatas bravas*, Russian salad, croquettes and tripe – are to your liking, however, Inopia does them better than anywhere.

Lasarte

Hotel Condes de Barcelona, C/Mallorca 259 (93 445 32 42/www.restaurant lasarte.com). Metro Passeig de Gràcia. **Open** 1.30-3.30pm, 8.30-11.30pm Mon-Fri. Closed Aug. €€€€. **Modern Basque**. Map p124 C3 ㉗

Triple-Michelin-starred San Sebastián chef Martín Berasategui has now established a culinary outpost over here, overseeing a menu that incorporates many of his signature dishes. One of the most spectacular of these is the layered terrine of foie gras, smoked eel and caramelised apple; other dishes of note include a succulent pigeon breast with a foie gras prepared from its own liver, or roast sea bass with hot citrus vinaigrette and creamed 'marrowbone' of cauliflower. Puddings range from superbly refreshing – apple 'ravioli' in a mint and lime jus with coconut ice-cream and rum granita – to impossibly indulgent: a rich bread and butter pudding with coffee ice-cream and plum compôte.

Casa Batlló p123

Moo

C/Rosselló 265 (93 445 40 00/www.
hotelomm.es). Metro Diagonal. **Open**
1.30-4pm, 8.30-11pm Mon-Sat. €€€€.
Modern European. Map p124 C3 ㉘
Superbly inventive cooking is overseen
by renowned Catalan chef Joan Roca
and designed as 'half portions', the better to experience the full range, from
sea bass with lemongrass to exquisite
suckling pig with a sharp Granny
Smith purée. Wines from a list of 500
are suggested to go with every course,
and many dishes are even built around
them: you can finish, for example, with
'Sauternes', the wine's bouquet perfectly rendered in mango ice-cream,
saffron custard and grapefruit jelly.

Noti

C/Roger de Llúria 35 (93 342 66 73).
Metro Passeig de Gràcia or Urquinaona.
Open 1.30-4pm, 8.30pm-midnight Mon-
Fri; 8.30pm-midnight Sat. €€€€.
Mediterranean. Map p125 D4 ㉙
With a new chef at the helm, Noti has
lost the French influences in its menu
and now marks more familiar

Barcelona territory with Mediterranean
dishes revisited Asian style – the catch
of the day with peanut sauce; tuna with
a sauce of Chardonnay and wasabi;
duck magret with lotus root, and so
on. The DJ bar at the front is now a
thing of the past, but the look is still
supremely cool, with reflective glass,
gold panelling and splashes of hot pink.

Ot

C/Corsega 537 (93 435 80 48). Metro
Sagrada Família. **Open** 1.30-3.30pm,
8.30-11pm Tue-Sat. Closed 3wks Aug.
€€€€. **Modern Mediterranean.**
Map p125 F2 ㉚
It's the extras that make the Ot experience memorable: an olive-oil tasting to
start; a shot of cauliflower soup speck-
led with herring eggs as an amuse-
bouche, or the sweet and sour layers of
coconut and hibiscus flower foam with
the coffee. There is no à la carte menu,
just a couple of set-price deals, but
these are very safe hands in which to
leave yourself: when they say chocolate soufflé needs basil ice-cream, by
Jove, they're right.

La Paninoteca Cremoni

C/Rosselló 112 (93 451 03 79). Metro Hospital Clínic. **Open** 9.30am-5pm, 7.30pm-midnight Mon-Fri; 1-5pm, 8.30pm-midnight Sat. Closed 3wks Aug. **€€**. **Panini**. Map p124 B2 ③①

Named after the 19th-century inventor of the celebrated Italian sandwich, this is a sunny spot, with a white-painted rustic look that is enlivened by a huge photograph of Sienna. Neither the owners nor the ingredients can make much claim to Italian provenance, but panini such as the *siciliano* – consisting of olive bread, mozzarella, tomato, aubergine and basil – make a wonderful change nonetheless from endless *bocadillos de jamón*.

Saüc

Ptge Lluis Pellicer 12 (93 321 01 89). Metro Hospital Clínic. **Open** 1.30-3.30pm; 8.30-10.30pm Tue-Sat. **€€€€**. **Modern Catalan**. Map p124 B2 ③②

Book early for one of the coveted tables at Saüc ('Elderberry'), particularly for lunch. The classy set lunch runs from accomplished Catalan comfort food in the shape of spicy Mallorcan sausage with potatoes and poached egg to more sophisticated fare such as cod with apple aïoli, cherry tomatoes and spinach. Excellent bread, a shot glass of pepper and potato soup with pancetta as an *aperitivo* and home-made petits fours are also unexpected touches in a *menú del día*.

Semproniana

C/Rosselló 148 (93 453 18 20). Metro Hospital Clínic. **Open** 1.30-4pm, 9-11.30pm Mon-Thur; 1.30-4pm, 9pm-midnight Fri, Sat. **€€€**. **Mediterranean**. Map p124 B2 ③③

The Old Curiosity Shop meets Tate Modern in this former printing house, which is wall-papered with defunct leaflets and pages from old books. The combination of antique furniture with arty mobiles made out of tortured kitchen utensils is as offbeat as the food, which might include such dishes as an all-white 'monochrome of cod and chickpeas'; turbot with passion fruit

and *escopinyes* (cockles); or a green salad served with a mad scientist's test-tube rack of 14 aerosol dressings.

Tapa Ç24

NEW *C/Diputació 269 (93 488 09 77). Metro Passeig de Gràcia.* **Open** 8am-midnight Mon-Sat. **€€€**. **Tapas**. Map p125 D4 ③④

A new venture from Carles Abellan of Comerç 24 fame (p80), this is ostensibly an old-school tapas bar, but among the lentils with chorizo or ham croquettes you'll find playful snacks more familiar to his fans. The McFoie Burger is an exercise in fast-food heaven, as is the Bikini – a small version of his signature take on the ham and cheese toastie, this one with truffle.

Toc

NEW *C/Girona 59 (93 488 11 48/ www.tocbcn.com). Metro Girona.* **Open** 1.30-3.30pm, 8.30-11.30pm Mon-Fri; 8.30-11.30pm Sat. **€€€€**. **Modern Catalan**. Map p125 E4 ③⑤

Minimalist to the point of clinical, Toc nonetheless offers a menu that is all heart and colour. Old Catalan favourites such as *esqueixada* (salt cod salad) and *cap i pota* (calves' head stew) are revived with pzazz alongside squab and truffled pâté or chilled beetroot gazpacho. Look out for the green-tea fruitcake with pears in red wine to finish, and a well-thought-out wine list that contains some excellent local bottles at low mark-ups.

Tragaluz

Ptge de la Concepció 5 (93 487 01 96). Metro Diagonal. **Open** 1.30-4pm, 8.30pm-midnight Mon-Wed, Sun; 1.30-4pm, 8.30pm-12.30am Thur-Sat. **€€€€**. **Mediterranean**. Map p124 C3 ③⑥

Tragaluz is the stylish flagship for an extraordinarily successful group of restaurants (which includes Agua, Bestial and Omm). Prices have risen a bit recently and the wine mark-up is hard to swallow, but there's no faulting tuna tataki with a cardamom wafer and a dollop of ratatouille-like *pisto*; monkfish tail in a sweet tomato *sofrito*

Saüc

Windsor

C/Còrsega 286 (93 415 84 83).
Metro Diagonal. **Open** 1-4pm, 8.30-
11pm Mon-Fri; 8.30-11pm Sat. Closed
Aug. €€€€. **Modern Catalan**.
Map p124 C2 ③⑧
Let down by a smart but drab dining
room and a preponderance of foreign
businessmen, Windsor nevertheless
serves some of the most creative food
around. Start with an amuse-gueule of
a tomato reduction with pistachio;
warm up with wild mushroom cannelloni in truffle sauce or divine foie gras
on thin slices of fruit cake; and peak
with turbot and a citrus risotto or
squab with a sauce of fortified wine.

Xix Bar

NEW *C/Rocafort 19 (93 423 43 14/*
www.xixbar.com). Metro Poble Sec.
Open 9am-4.30pm, 6.30pm-1.30am
Mon-Thur; 9am-4.30pm, 6.30pm-3am
Fri, Sat. No credit cards. **Cocktail
bar**. **Map** p124 A5 ③⑨
Xix (pronounced 'chicks', and a play on
the address, among other things) is a
new, unconventional cocktail bar in the
candlelit surroundings of an old tiled
granja (milk bar). It's dead cosy but a
little bit scruffy, which makes the list
of 20 brands of gin all the more unexpected. Simple pasta dishes, salads and
bocadillos are served during the day.

Shopping

Altaïr

Gran Via de les Corts Catalanes 616
(93 342 71 71/www.altair.es). Metro
Universitat. **Open** 10am-2pm, 4.30-
8.30pm Mon-Fri; 10am-3pm, 4-8.30pm
Sat. **Map** p124 C4 ④⓪
The largest travel bookshop in Europe,
where you can pick up guides to free
eating in Barcelona, tomes on geolin-
guistics, handbooks on successful outdoor sex and CDs of tribal music. Of
course, all the less arcane publications
are here too: maps for hikers, travel
guidebooks, multilingual dictionaries,
travel diaries and notebooks and select
equipment such as money belts and
mosquito nets.

with black olive oil; or juicy braised
oxtail with cabbage. Finish the meal
with cherry consommé or a thin tart of
white and dark chocolate.

Ty-Bihan

Ptge Lluís Pellicer 13 (93 410 90 02).
Metro Hospital Clínic. **Open** 1.30-3.30pm
Mon; 1.30-3.30pm, 8.30-11.30pm Tue-Fri;
8.30-11.30pm Sat. €€. **Breton**. **Map**
p124 B2 ③⑦
Functioning both as crêperie and
Breton cultural centre, Ty-Bihan has
chosen a smart, spacious look over
wheat sheaves and pitchforks. A long
list of sweet and savoury galettes
(crêpes made with buckwheat flour)
are followed up with scrumptious little
blinis smothered in strawberry jam
and cream and crêpes suzettes served
in a pool of flaming Grand Marnier.
The Petite menu will take care of *les
enfants*, while a bowl of cider takes
care of the grown-ups.

Camper

C/Pelai 13-37 (93 302 41 24/www. camper.com). Metro Catalunya. **Open** 10am-10pm Mon-Sat. **Map** p125 D3 ④

Mallorca-based eco shoe company Camper has sexed up its ladies' line recently. Each year it seems to flirt more with high heels (albeit rubbery wedgy ones) and girly straps. Of course, it still has its round-toed and clod-heeled classics, along with the iconic bowling shoes, but take another look if you've previously dismissed this lot.

Casa del Llibre

C/Passeig de Gràcia 62 (93 272 34 80/ www.casadellibro.com). Metro Passeig de Gràcia. **Open** 9.30am-9.30pm Mon-Sat. **Map** p125 D3 ④

Part of a well-established Spanish chain, this general bookstore offers a diverse assortment of titles, including some English-language fiction. Glossy Barcelona-themed coffee-table tomes with good gift potential sit by the front right-hand entrance.

Chocolat Factory

NEW *C/Provença 223 (93 215 02 73/ www.chocolatfactory.com). FGC Provença.* **Open** 10am-9pm Mon-Sat. **Map** p124 C3 ④

Belgian Chocolatier Michel Laline describes his shop as a 'Benetton of chocolate', with the cocoa sourced from Java, Venuezuela, Grenada and Papua New Guinea, among other places. The result is packaged in impressively hip fashion, with the aluminium 'pocket tubes' (think upmarket Smarties) or mill of 'chocolate rain' making perfect gifts.

El Corte Inglés

Plaça Catalunya 14 (93 306 38 00/ www.elcorteingles.es). Metro Catalunya. **Open** 10am-10pm Mon-Sat. **Map** p125 D5 ④

El Corte Inglés' flagship store is a dominant landmark in Plaça Catalunya. It flies in the face of Barcelona's retail traditions: the goods are easy to return, and staff are helpful when you want assistance, unobtrusive when you don't. The Plaça Catalunya branch is the place for cosmetics, clothes and homewares. It also houses a well-stocked but pricey supermarket and gourmet food store, plus services ranging from key cutting to currency exchange. The Portal de l'Àngel branch stocks music, books, stationery and sports gear from trainers to training bikes.

Delishop

NEW *C/Mallorca 241 (93 215 15 46/ www.delishop.com). Metro Diagonal.* **Open** 10am-9pm Mon-Sat. **Map** p124 C3 ④

Opened in November 2006 by a pair of well-travelled foodies, Delishop brings together several hundred products from around the world. Most are selected for taste, while some add colour with wonderful packaging. Plenty of recipes are laid on if you're unsure what to do with hoisin sauce or vine leaves.

FNAC

El Triangle, Plaça Catalunya 4 (93 344 18 00/www.fnac.es). Metro Catalunya. **Open** 10am-10pm Mon-Sat. **Map** p124 C5 ④

This French multimedia superstore supplies info and entertainment in all possible formats. The ground floor has a great selection of magazines, along with a small café, a ticket desk and a travel agent. Above this there are two floors of CDs, DVDs, software, hardware and peripherals, hi-fis, cameras, MP3 players, home cinema systems and books in various languages.

Mango

Passeig de Gràcia 65 (93 215 75 30/ www.mango.es). Metro Passeig de Gràcia. **Open** 10am-9pm Mon-Sat. **Map** p124 C3 ④

A small step up from Zara in quality and price, Mango's womenswear is less chameleon-like but still victim to the catwalks. Strong points include tailored trouser suits and skirts, knitwear and stretchy tops. Unsold items end up at the Mango Outlet (C/Girona 37, 93 412 29 35), which is packed with frenzied girls on a mission.

Other locations Passeig de Gràcia 8-10 (93 412 15 99).

Purificación García

*Passeig de Gràcia 21 (93 487 72 92/
www.purificaciongarcia.es). Metro
Passeig de Gràcia.* **Open** 10am-8.30pm
Mon-Sat. **Map** p124 C4 ❹❽

Purificación's sleek and sophisticated
creations have appeared in many film
and theatre productions. Indeed, there
is something dramatic about her use of
flashes of colour and tactile fabrics in
otherwise conservative designs. She
creates clothes for those who want to
make an subtle statement in the office
or at a dinner party.

Vinçon

*Passeig de Gràcia 96 (93 215 60 50/
www.vincon.com). Metro Diagonal.*
Open 10am-8.30pm Mon-Sat.
Map p125 D2 ❹❾

Vinçon is one of the vital organs that
keeps Barcelona's reputation as a city
of cutting-edge design alive. The building itself is a monument to the history
of local design: its furniture showroom,
located upstairs, is surrounded by
Modernista glory (and you get a peek
at Gaudí's La Pedrera); downstairs in
the kitchen, bathroom, garden and
various other departments, everything
is super-stylish. As you'd expect, there
is no shortage of design classics, ranging from a Bonet armchair to the so-
called 'perfect' corkscrew.
Other locations Tinc Çon, C/Rosselló
246 (93 215 60 50).

Nightlife

Antilla BCN Latin Club

*C/Aragó 141 (93 451 45 64/
www.antillasalsa.com). Metro Urgell.*
Open 11pm-3.30am Mon-Wed, Sun;
11pm-4.30am Fri, Sat. Gigs around
1am. **Admission** (incl 1 drink) €10.
No credit cards. **Map** p124 A3 ❺⓪

The Antilla prides itself on being a
'Caribbean cultural centre', but its true
calling lies in being the self-proclaimed
best *salsateca* in town, offering dance
classes (including acrobatic salsa and
Afro-Cuban styles) and a solid programme of live music, which covers all
Latin flavours from *son* to merengue
and Latin jazz.

Arena

Classic & Madre *C/Diputació 233.*
Map p124 C4 ❺❶
VIP & Dandy *Gran Via de les Corts
Catalanes 593.* **Map** p124 C4 ❺❷
All *93 487 83 42/www.arenadisco.com.
Metro Universitat.* **Open** 12.30am-5am
Fri, Sat. **Admission** (incl 1 drink) €5
Fri; €10 Sat. No credit cards.

The four different Arena discos offer
variations on familiar, well-worn gay
themes; you can switch between them
freely after getting your hand stamped
at the entrance. Of the four, Classic is
the most light-hearted, playing classic
hits from the 1980s and '90s, with a
campy-kitsch atmosphere and a
healthy mix of the sexes. The cav-
ernous Madre is more full-on, with a
darkroom, pounding house music and
current chart hits. It attracts a younger
crowd, and is more of a cattle market.
VIP and Dandy are probably the tack-
iest and are also the most mixed; again,
they are youthful venues with lots of
space, but nonetheless heave at weekends. VIP does its bit for the Spanish
retro pop industry, while Dandy bangs
away with more house tunes.

Buda Restaurante

*C/Pau Claris 92 (93 318 42 52/
www.budarestaurante.com). Metro
Catalunya.* **Open** 9pm-3am daily.
Admission free. **Map** p125 D4 ❺❸

The glamorous Buda Restaurante has
lots of throne-style furniture and gilded wallpaper, topped off with a simply
colossal chandelier. The laid-back
nature of the staff (dancing on the
bar seems to be thoroughly acceptable)
and upbeat house music make this an
excellent place for drinks and an ogle.
Tuesday is 'model's night' (which
model isn't clear), Wednesday is ballroom dancing night, and every second
Thursday is Asian night, complete
with geishas.

City Hall

*Rambla Catalunya 2-4 (93 317
21 77/www.grupo-ottozutz.com).
Metro Catalunya.* **Open** midnight-
6am Tue-Sun. **Admission** (incl 1
drink) €12. **Map** p124 C4 ❺❹

Soul City on Thursdays at City Hall has made a name for itself among the local NY-capped, billowing trouser-wearing posses by bringing acts like Killa Kela and the Scratch Perverts to Barcelona. The rest of the week it's a little more mixed, with music from deep house to electro rock, and an older post-work (even pre-work?) crowd joining the young, tanned and skinny to show the dancefloors some love. Outside, the terrace is a veritable (and in summer, literal) melting pot of tourists and locals, who rub shoulders under the watchful (anti-pot-smoking) eye of the bouncer.

Danzarama

Gran Via de les Corts Catalanes 604 (93 301 97 43/reservations 93 342 5070/www.gruposalsitas.com). Metro Universitat. **Open** 7pm-3am Mon-Sat. **Admission** free. **Map** p124 C4 ⑮

Make your way past the flash restaurant upstairs – we're talking white sofas swinging from the ceiling – and down on to the brick-walled, loud dancefloor. With no entry charge and lots of tables, Danzarama has become a popular pre-party venue for Pacha (on Thursdays; p159) and Catwalk (on Sundays; p109), with a free shuttle bus and thumping tunes making up for the club-priced drinks.

Distrito Diagonal

Avda Diagonal 442 (mobile 607 113 602/www.distritodiagonal.com). Metro Diagonal. **Open** midnight-6am Fri, Sat. **Admission** free before 4am, €15 (incl 1 drink) after. No credit cards. **Map** p125 D2 ⑯

Housed in the stunning Casa Comalat, Distrito Diagonal attracts a slightly older crowd with its easygoing atmosphere and sounds ranging from nu jazz to deep house. The interior is bathed in red light, and there are plenty of chairs to sink into. It is a sought-after venue for small promoters and one-off parties, which means the music veers from Bollywood to hip hop. On a Thursday night, Cabaret Club educates listeners with the latest indietronica.

L'Auditori

La Fira

C/Provença 171 (mobile 650 855 384). Metro Hospital Clínic. **Open** 10pm-3am Tue-Thur; 10pm-4.30am Fri, Sat. **Admission** free before 1am; €10 (incl 1 drink) after 1am. No credit cards. **Map** p124 B3 ⑰

It's called a 'bar-museum', but don't worry, you don't get served a history lesson along with your pint of lager. The exhibits are old fairground rides: bumper cars, merry-go-rounds, crazy mirrors… which can all seem a little bit spooky when you're in the middle of a dark, warehouse-sized space and surrounded by beered-up students flirting to a soundtrack of tacky pop.

Luz de Gas

C/Muntaner 246 (93 209 77 11/www.luzdegas.com). FGC Muntaner. **Open** 11.30pm-5am daily. *Gigs* 12.30am daily. **Admission** (incl 1 drink) €15. **Map** p124 B1 ⑱

This lovingly converted old music hall, garnished with chandeliers and classical friezes, occasionally hosts classic MOR acts: maybe Phil Collins or Bill Wyman's Rhythm Kings. Between these visits from international 'names', you'll find nightly residencies: blues on

Mondays, Dixieland jazz on Tuesdays, cover bands on Wednesdays, Saturdays and Sundays, soul on Thursdays and rock on Fridays.

Metro

C/Sepúlveda 185 (93 323 52 27/www. metrodisco.bcn). Metro Universitat. **Open** 1-5am Tue-Sun. **Admission** (incl 1 drink) €13. **Map** p124 B4 ❺❾

Metro has been fully refurbished. It has a redesigned bar and even what were the dingier corners have achieved a better shine. With stiffer competition around, it remains to be seen whether this will be enough to sustain it as the pre-eminent gay club in town. Latin beats prevail on the smaller dancefloor, with house on the main one to keep the boys entertained (when they're not entertaining each other).

Raum

NEW *Gran Via 593 (mobile 600 422 318/www.raum.es). Metro Universitat.* **Open** midnight-5am Thur. **Admission** €10. No credit cards. **Map** p124 C4 ❻⓪

Raum's cold industrial decor lends itself well to this weekly electronic night, during which the tunes run the gamut from minimal to hard techno to the occasional chunk of deep electro-house. The Thursday slot ensures the crowd – a chatty bunch of expats and locals – come for the tunes rather than to pose among the steel pillars and lunar-style projections.

Salvation

Ronda Sant Pere 19-21 (93 318 06 86/www.matineegroup.com). Metro Urquinaona. **Open** midnight-5am Thur-Sat. **Admission** (incl 1 drink) €15. No credit cards. **Map** p125 D5 ❻❶

It's been said of Salvation – one of the city's enduringly popular gay clubs – that 'everyone you see naked on Gaydar… you can see them in here with their clothes on'. One room is full of said tanned, buff torsos lurching around to house; in the other room, sprightly young things bounce about to pop. The hot staff lean towards the God-complex side of approachable.

Santa Locura

C/Consell de Cent 294 (93 200 14 66). Metro Passeig de Gràcia. **Open** midnight-5.30am Thur-Sat. **Admission** (incl 1 drink) €10. No credit cards. **Map** p124 C4 ❻❷

Perhaps Barcelona's most extraordinary clubbing experience, Santa Locura has three floors filled with weird and wonderful nocturnal pleasures: get married at the bar; plead guilty at the confessional box; watch a Chippendale-style show; and hit the dancefloor to the music of Kylie and her ilk.

Space Barcelona

C/Tarragona 141-147 (93 426 84 44/ www.spacebarcelona.com). Metro Tarragona. **Open** midnight-6am Fri, Sat. **Admission** (incl 1 drink) €15; €12 with flyer. No credit cards. **Map** p124 A3 ❻❸

Like superclub rival Pacha, Space tries hard to cash in on Barcelona's Balearic party aspirations, with equally limited success. A young crowd of pseudo-fashionistas and wannabe diehard clubbers descends en masse to strike poses under the deep lights and pounding bass, or to lean against one of the four bars. Occasional appearances from the likes of Carl Cox keep the brand's reputation safe; Sunday night's Gay T Dance is great if you're into ripped abs.

Arts & leisure

L'Auditori

C/Lepant 150 (93 247 93 00/www. auditori.org). Metro Marina. **Open** *Information* 8am-10pm daily. *Box office* noon-9pm Mon-Sat; 1hr before performance Sun. Closed Aug. **Map** p125 F5 ❻❹

Serious music lovers in Barcelona prefer concerts at Rafael Moneo's sleek L'Auditori: what it lacks in architectural warmth it more than makes up for in acoustics and facilities. The 2,400-seat hall has provided the city with a world-class music venue and a home to its orchestra, the OBC. The Museu de la Música opened in 2007 (p126), as did a new 600-seat auditorium that will add more variety to an already-impressive programme covering not just classical music, but jazz, contemporary and world music. A late-night bus service connects the Auditori with Plaça Catalunya after evening performances.

Casablanca-Kaplan

Passeig de Gràcia 115, Eixample (93 218 43 45). Metro Diagonal. **Tickets** €4.50 Mon; €6 Tue-Sun. No credit cards. **Map** p125 D2 ⑥⑤
This centrally located cinema is the smallest in Barcelona, with two screens offering independent Spanish and European films.

Cine Ambigú

NEW *Casablanca-Gràcia, C/Girona 173-175, (93 459 34 56/www.retinas.org). Metro Verdaguer.* Closed July-Sept. **Tickets** €5. No credit cards. **Map** p125 E2 ⑥⑥
After nine years and more than 200 screenings in the Sala Apolo dancehall, the Cine Ambigú has moved home to C/Girona. The cinema screens a couple of accessible but alternative arthouse films from around Europe each week. The website provides details of all the forthcoming shows.

FilmoTeca

Cinema Aquitania, Avda Sarrià 31-33, Eixample (93 410 75 90/ http://cultura.gencat.net/filmo). Metro Hospital Clínic. Closed Aug. **Tickets** €2.70; €2 reductions; €18 for 10 films. No credit cards. **Map** p124 A2 ⑥⑦
Funded by the Catalan government, the Filmoteca is a little dry for some tastes, offering comprehensive seasons of cinema's more recondite auteurs, alongside better-known classics, plus screenings each spring of all films nominated in the Goya Awards. Overlapping cycles last two or three weeks, with each film screened at least twice at different times. Books of 20 and 100 tickets bring down the price per film to a negligible amount.

Méliès Cinemes

C/Villarroel 102 (93 451 00 51/ www.cinesmelies.net). Metro Urgell. **Tickets** €2.70 Mon; €4 Tue-Sun. No credit cards. **Map** p124 B4 ⑥⑧

A small, two-screen cinema that is the nearest Barcelona comes to an art-house, with the familiar idiosyncratic roster of accessible classics alongside more recent films that aren't quite commercial enough for general release. This is where you get to bone up on the masterworks of Antonioni, Billy Wilder, Hitchcock and others.

Plaza de Toros Monumental

Gran Via de les Corts Catalanes 749 (93 245 58 04/93 215 95 70). Metro Monumental. **Open** *Bullfights* Apr-Sept 5.30-7pm Sun. *Museum* Apr-Sept 11am-2pm, 4-8pm Mon-Sat; 10.30am-1.30pm Sun. **Admission** *Bullfights* €20-€97. *Museum* €4; €3 reductions. No credit cards. **Map** p125 F4 ⑥⑨
In 2004 council voted the city to be *anti-taurino* (against bullfighting), although this was largely a symbolic gesture: 100 bulls are still killed every year at the city's single remaining bullring, although its future is in the balance. The *corridas* mostly take place in front of tourists and homesick Andalucíans.

Renoir-Floridablanca

C/Floridablanca 135 (93 228 93 93/ www.cinesrenoir.com). Metro Sant Antoni. **Tickets** €4.50 Mon; €4-€6 Tue-Fri; €6.20 Sat, Sun. **Map** p124 B5 ⑦⓪
The closest first-run original-version cinema you'll find to the centre of town. Renoir-Floridablanca has four screens and shows up to eight independent, off-beat foreign and Spanish films per day.

Teatre Nacional de Catalunya (TNC)

Plaça de les Arts 1 (93 306 57 00/ www.tnc.es). Metro Glòries. **Box office** 3-9pm Tue-Sun. **Tickets** €15-€25; €10-€15 reductions. **Map** p125 F4 ⑦①
Funded by the Generalitat and designed by architect Ricard Bofill, the huge Parthenon-like TNC has three superb performance spaces. Its main stage promotes large-scale Spanish classical theatre, while more contemporary European theatre and works by new writers are normally staged in the more experimental Sala Tallers.

Gràcia

It's hard to imagine that little more than 100 years ago, Gràcia was still a town in its own right. The construction of the Eixample in 1850, however, soon encroached on to the open fields between the Old City and Gràcia and, by 1897, it was pretty much engulfed. Gràcia's nominal independence was rendered more or less irrelevant and, amid howls of protest, the town was annexed. Since then, dissent has been a recurring feature in Gràcia's history: streets boast names such as Llibertat, Revolució and Fraternitat.

The political activity came from the effects of rapid industrial expansion. This was a mere village in 1821, centred around the 17th-century convent of Santa Maria de Gràcia, with just 2,608 inhabitants. By the time of annexation, however, the population had risen to 61,935, making it the ninth largest town in Spain and a hotbed of Catalanism, republicanism and anarchism. Today, few vestiges of radicalism remain, though the *okupa* squatter movement inhabits a relatively high number of buildings in the area and it isn't uncommon to see the odd anarchist protest.

Nowadays, the *barri* is a favourite hangout of the city's bohemians. The numerous small, unpretentious bars are frequented by artists, designers and students. However, Gràcia really comes into its own for a few days in mid August, when its famous *festa major* grips the entire city. Residents spend months in advance preparing original home-made street decorations, and all of Barcelona converges on the tiny *barri* to party.

Gràcia

Parc Monterols

Sant Gervasi

Casa Vicens

Sant Marc

Gràcia

Eixample

Casa Torres Germans

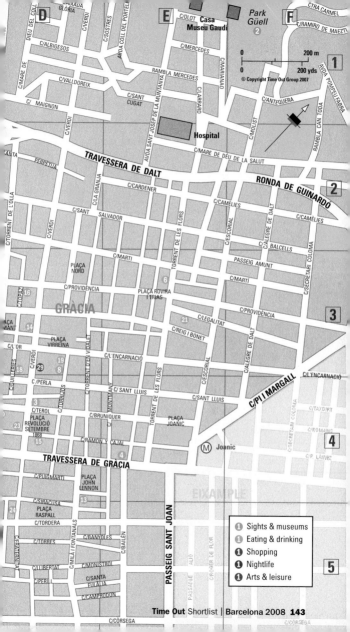

Sights & museums

Fundació Foto Colectània

C/Julián Romea 6, D2 (93 217 16 26/www.colectania.es). FGC Gràcia. **Open** 11am-2pm, 5-8.30pm Mon-Fri. Closed Aug. **Map** p142 B4 ❶

This private foundation is dedicated to the promotion of photography and collections of major Spanish and Portuguese photographers from the 1950s. It also has an extensive library of Spanish and Portuguese photography books, including out-of-print editions.

Park Güell

C/Olot (Casa-Museu Gaudí 93 219 38 11). Metro Lesseps/bus 24, 25. **Open** 10am-sunset daily. *Museum* Apr-Sept 10am-7.45pm daily. Oct-Mar 10am-5.45pm daily. **Admission** *Park* free. *Museum* €4; €3 reductions; free under-9s. No credit cards. **Map** p143 F1 ❷

Gaudí's brief for this spectacular project was to emulate the English garden cities so admired by his patron Eusebi Güell (hence the spelling of 'park'): to lay out a self-contained suburb for the wealthy, but also to design the public areas. The idea never took off and the Güell family donated the park to the city in 1922.

The fantastical exuberance of Gaudi's imagination is breathtaking. The visitor was previously welcomed by two life-sized mechanical gazelles – a religious reference to medieval Hebrew love poetry – although these were destroyed in the Civil War. The two gatehouses that do still remain were based on designs the architect made earlier for the opera *Hansel and Gretel*, one of them featuring a red and white mushroom for a roof. From here, walk up a splendid staircase flanked by multicoloured battlements, past the iconic mosaic lizard sculpture, to what would have been the marketplace. Here, 100 palm-shaped pillars hold up a roof, reminiscent of the hypostyle hall at Luxor. On top of this structure is the esplanade, surrounded by undulating benches in the form of a sea-serpent decorated with shattered tiles. The park's peak is marked by a large cross and offers an amazing panorama of Barcelona and the sea. Gaudi lived for a time in one of the two houses built on the site: it's since become the Casa-Museu Gaudi.

The best way to get to the park is by bus; if you go via Lesseps metro, be prepared for a steep uphill walk.

Eating & drinking

La Baignoire

C/Verdi 6 (mobile 606 330 460). Metro Fontana or Joanic. **Open** *June-Sept* 8pm-2am Mon-Thur, Sun; 8pm-3am Fri, Sat. *Oct-May* 6pm-2am Mon-Thur, Sun; 6pm-3am Fri, Sat. No credit cards. **Bar**. **Map** p143 D4 ❸

It means 'bathtub', which goes some way towards giving you an idea of the size, but the staff are unfailingly friendly, and slide projections and lounge music complement the mellow vibe. Fresh fruit juices are served in summer; cocktails and decent wine are available year round.

Bar Elèctric

Travessera de Gràcia 233 (no phone). Metro Joanic. **Open** 7pm-2am Tue-Thur, Sun; 7pm-3am Fri, Sat. Closed last wk July, 1st wk Aug. No credit cards. **Bar**. **Map** p143 E4 ❹

According to local legend, Elèctric was the first bar in Gràcia to be connected to the mains, yet this once bastion of modernity appears to have remained unchanged ever since. An innocuous entrance opens into a sprawling bohemian den that boasts an agenda as colourful as its clientele: theatre, puppetry and storytelling on weekdays, Brazilian jazz and cabaret at weekends.

Bo!

NEW *Plaça Rius i Taulet 11 (93 368 35 29). Metro Fontana.* **Open** 10am-1am Mon-Thur; 10am-2.30am Fri-Sun. **€€**. **Café**. **Map** p142 C4 ❺

Decent tapas, creative sandwiches and generous portions, plus plenty of terrace tables, make this a favourite spot in one of Gràcia's most emblematic, lively squares. If Bo!'s black chairs are all taken, you'll do nearly as well on one of neighbouring bar Amelie's white ones.

Bodega Manolo

C/Torrent de les Flors 101 (93 284 43 77). **Open** 9.30am-7pm Tue, Wed; 9.30am-1am Thur, Fri; 12.30-4.30pm, 8.30pm-1am Sat; 10.30am-3pm Sun. Closed Aug. No credit cards. **€€**.

Tapas. Map p143 E3 ⑥

Another old family *bodega* with faded, peeling charm, barrels on the wall and rows of dusty bottles, Manolo specialises not only in wine, but in classy food: we recommend the foie gras with port and apple. At the other end of the scale comes the 'Destroyer': egg, bacon, sausage and chips.

Botafumeiro

C/Gran de Gràcia 81 (93 218 42 30). Metro Fontana. **Open** 1pm-1am daily. **€€€€**. **Galician**. Map p142 C4

Love it or hate it (and the size, racket and overwhelmingly *arriviste* diners mean no one leaves undecided), there's no denying Botafumeiro's success, and its literally dozens of tables are rarely empty for very long. The speciality is excellent Galician seafood, served with military precision by the fleet of nautically clad waiters. Non-fishy dishes include a rich *caldo gallego* (cabbage and pork broth) and *lacón con grelos* (gammon with turnip tops).

Cantina Machito

C/Torrijos 47 (93 217 34 14). Metro Fontana or Joanic. **Open** 1-4pm, 7pm-12.30am daily. **€€**. **Mexican**. Map p143 D3 ⑧

One of life's perpetual mysteries is whether Mexican desserts are any good or not, given that no one has ever had room for one. Here, for example, 'your starter for ten' takes on a whole new meaning with the tasty but unfinishable *orden de tacos*, while mains largely comprise *enmoladas* or *enchiladas* the size of wine bottles, beached next to a sea of thick *mole* sauce. The tequila shots and Margaritas go without saying.

Casa Quimet

Rambla de Prat 9 (93 217 53 27). Metro Fontana. **Open** 6.30pm-2am Tue-Sun. Closed Aug. No credit cards. **Bar**. Map p142 C3 ⑨

Yellowing jazz posters cover every inch of wallspace, dozens of ancient guitars are suspended from the ceiling and a succession of ticking clocks compete to be heard over the voice of Billie Holiday. This other-worldly 'Guitar Bar' (as the place is invariably known to locals) occasionally springs to life with an impromptu jam session, but most of the time it remains a perfect study in melancholy.

Envalira

Plaça del Sol 13 (93 218 58 13). Metro Fontana. **Open** 1.30-4pm, 9pm-midnight Tue-Sat; 1.30-5pm Sun. Closed Aug. **€€**.

Spanish. Map p142 C4 ⑩

Old-school Spain lives on as penguin-suited waiters solemnly hand out brown PVC menus at plastic teak-effect tables under painfully austere lighting. But it's all worth it for the food: as traditionally brown as the drab decor, it runs the full gamut of hefty Iberian classics. Start with fish soups or lentils and go on to paellas, roast meats and seafood stews, followed by serious, own-made *crema catalana* or *tarta de Santiago*. Arrive early for the leather banquettes at the front.

Flash Flash

C/Granada del Penedès 25 (93 237 09 90). FGC Gràcia. **Open** 1.30pm-1.30am daily. **€€€**. **Tortillas/cocktails**. Map p142 B4 ⑪

Opened in 1970, this bar was a design sensation in its day, with its white leatherette banquettes and walls that are still imprinted with silhouettes of a life-size, frolicking, Twiggy-like model. They call it a *tortilleria*, which means there are 60 or so tortilla variations, alongside a list of kid-friendly dishes and adult-friendly cocktails.

Folquer

C/Torrent de l'Olla 3 (93 217 43 95). Metro Diagonal or Verdaguer. **Open** 1-4pm, 9-11.30pm Mon-Fri; 9-11.30pm Sat. Closed 3wks Aug. **€€€**. **Catalan**. Map p143 D5 ⑫

Filled with an animated, older clientele, it's a welcoming space with daffodil yellow wood panelling and huge splashy artworks. The inventive food is well executed and reasonably priced, never more so than in the lunch deals: the 'Executive' is a sturdy main, such as entrecôte, with a salad, pudding and wine for €14, while the normal menú is cheaper and still creative, with a gourmet hamburger and wild mushrooms, or *suquet de pop* (octopus stew).

Himali

C/Milà i Fontanals 68 (93 285 15 68). Metro Joanic. **Open** noon-4pm, 8pm-midnight Tue-Sun. €€. **Nepalese**. **Map** p143 D4 ⑬

Cocking a snook at the many mediocre Indian restaurants around, Barcelona's first Nepalese eaterie has become a hit. Faced with an alien and impenetrable menu, the set meals seem tempting, but they aren't always the best option: press the waiters for recommendations or try *mugliaco kukhura* (barbecued butter chicken in creamy tomato sauce) or *khasi masala tarkari* (baked spicy lamb). Meat cooked in the tandoori oven (*txulo*) is also worth a try, and there are plenty of vegetarian choices.

Mesopotamia

C/Verdi 65 (93 237 15 63). Metro Fontana. **Open** 8.30pm-midnight Tue-Sat. Closed 2wks Apr. €€. No credit cards. **Map** p143 D3 ⑭

The policy at Barcelona's only Iraqi restaurant is to have everything on the menu at the same price, so the cost won't hold people back from ordering what they want. Best value, though, is the enormous taster menu, which includes great Lebanese wines, a variety of dips for your *riqaq* bread, bulgur wheat with aromatic roast meats and vegetables, sticky baklawa and Arabic teas.

La Nena

NEW C/Ramón y Cajal 36 (93 285 14 76). Metro Fontana or Joanic. **Open** Oct-July 9am-10pm daily. Aug, Sept 9am-2pm, 4-10pm daily. Closed 3wks Aug. €€. No credit cards. **Café**. **Map** p143 D4 ⑮

An oasis at breakfast time, La Nena (the little girl) is as cutesy as its name suggests, and the sweetness carries over into the menu: home-made cakes, biscuits, freshly whipped cream, ice-creams, and chocolate are what this little girl is made of. But the more health-minded can take refuge in home-made yoghurts, a wide range of mueslis, and freshly made juices from orange to papaya.

Noise i Art

C/Topazi 26 (93 217 50 01). Metro Fontana. **Open** 6pm-2.30am Tue-Thur, Sun; 7pm-3am Fri, Sat. Closed 2wks end Aug. No credit cards. **Bar/café**. **Map** p143 D3 ⑯

It's known locally as the 'IKEA bar', which, although some of the plastic fittings do look strangely familiar, doesn't really do justice to the colourful, pop art interior. A chilled and convivial atmosphere is occasionally livened up with a flamenco session, and all the usual Gràcia staples such as houmous and tabbouleh are served along with various salads and pasta dishes.

Octubre

C/Julián Romea 18 (93 218 25 18). FGC Gràcia/metro Diagonal. **Open** 1.30-3.30pm, 9-11pm Mon-Fri; 9-11pm Sat. Closed Aug. €€. **Catalan**. **Map** p142 B4 ⑰

Time stands still in this quiet little spot, with quaint old-fashioned decor, swathes of lace and brown table linen. Time often stands still, in fact, between placing an order and receiving any food, but this is all part of Octubre's sleepy charm, along with a roll-call of reasonably priced and mainly Catalan dishes. The beef in mustard sauce is excellent, and wild mushroom risotto, while not outstanding, is decent enough for the price. The puddings also vary a fair bit, but Octubre is more about atmosphere than anything else.

Puku Café

C/Guilleries 10 (93 368 25 73). Metro Fontana. **Open** 7pm-1.30am Mon-Wed; 7pm-2am Thur; 7pm-3am Fri, Sat. **Bar/café**. **Map** p143 D3 ⑱

The Puku Café has two very different vibes. During the week it's a colourful meeting place, where the casually hip

Get the scoop

If it's ice-cream you're after, few people would disagree that you should immediately look to the red, white and green. Even the Catalans, often reluctant to admit the culinary superiority of other nations, will travel across town to queue for authentic Italian gelati.

One of the most recent gelaterias to open, **Gelaaati!** (C/Llibreteria 7, Barri Gòtic, 93 310 50 45) was rammed within a month, and with good reason. All flavours are made freshly on the premises every day, using natural ingredients – no colourings, no preservatives. Especially good are the hazelnut, pistachio and raspberry, but more unusual flavours include soya bean, celery and avocado. Nearby is the more established **Gelateria Pagliotta** (C/Jaume I 15, 93 310 53 24), another to use only seasonal, natural ingredients and in the hands of the fourth generation of one family. The specialities here include sorbets, frozen yoghurts and ice-cream for diabetics.

Up in the north of the Eixample, **Cremeria Toscana** (p131) is a charming little ice-cream parlour,

where around 20 different flavours are made daily, from tangy mandarin to impossibly creamy coconut. I dopocena ('after dinner') are miniature gourmet sundaes, mixing parmesan and pear flavours; mascarpone and tiramisu; chocolate and pistachio; or liquorice and mint. Beyond here, in a leafy square in Gràcia, is the **Gelateria Caffetteria Italiana** (Plaça Revolució 2, 93 210 2339, closed Mon, Tue & Nov-Feb), run by an Italian mother-and-daughter team and famous for its dark chocolate flavour – of which it runs out every night.

Like pizza, football and gesticulation, however, making ice-cream is one of many habits stolen from the Italians by the Argentines and then bettered. **Fratello** (Passeig Joan de Borbó 15, 93 221 48 39), the Barcelona arm of a Buenos Aires-based chain, is one of the best. Handily located on the main drag up to the beach, its helado is freshly made on the premises every day in a dazzling array of flavours: try the butterscotch-like dulce de leche or zingy zabaglione.

hang out over a bottle of wine and maybe some cactus and lime ice-cream. At weekends, however, the amber walls and deep orange columns prop up a younger, scruffier crowd, nodding along to some of the city's best DJs spinning a varied playlist based around electropop.

Salambó

C/Torrijos 51 (93 218 69 66). Metro Fontana or Joanic. **Open** noon-1am Mon-Thur, Sun; noon-3am Fri, Sat. **Café**. Map p143 D3 ⑲

The time-honoured meeting place for Verdi cinema-goers, Salambó is a large and ever so slightly staid split-level café that serves coffee, teas and filled ciabatta to the *barri*'s more conservative element. At night, those who are planning to eat are given preference when it comes to bagging a table.

Samsara

C/Terol 6 (93 285 36 88). Metro Fontana or Joanic. **Open** *June-Sept* 8.30pm-2am Mon-Thur; 8.30pm-3am Fri; 8.30pm-3am Sat. *Oct-May* 1.30-4pm, 8.30pm-2am Mon-Thur; 1.30-4pm, 8.30pm-3am Fri; 8.30pm-3am Sat. €€€. **Tapas**. Map p143 D4 ⑳

A combination of Moroccan-themed decor and intelligent cooking, Samsara has built up quite a following among Gràcia foodies. Its tapas are diminutive but don't want for flavour or imagination: try monkfish ceviche with mango or watermelon gazpacho with basil oil. Photos line the walls, and a DJ plays lounge and the smoothest of house later in the week.

San Kil

C/Legalitat 22 (93 284 41 79). Metro Fontana or Joanic. **Open** 12.30-4pm, 8pm-midnight Mon-Sat. Closed 2wks Aug. €€. **Korean**. Map p143 E3 ㉑

If you've never eaten Korean before, it pays to gen up before you head to this bright, spartan restaurant. *Panch'an* is the ideal starter: four little dishes containing vegetable appetisers, one of which will be tangy *kimch'i* (fermented cabbage with chilli). Then try mouth-watering *pulgogi* – beef served sizzling at the table and eaten rolled into lettuce

leaves – and maybe *pibimbap* – rice with vegetables (and occasionally meat) topped with a fried egg.

Shojiro

C/Ros de Olano 11 (93 415 65 48). Metro Fontana. **Open** 1.30-3.30pm Mon; 1.30-3.30pm, 9-11.30pm Tue-Sat. Closed 2wks Apr, 2wks Aug. €€€. **Catalan/Japanese**. Map p142 C4 ㉒

A curious but successful mix of Catalan and Japanese applies to the decor as much as the food, with original 'mosaic' flooring and dark green paintwork setting off a clean feng-shui look. There are only set meals, starting with an amuse-bouche, then offering sushi with strips of nori, sticky rice and salad, or courgette soup and pancetta as a starter, with salmon teriyaki or spring chicken confit with potato dauphinois as mains. Puddings might include a wonderfully refreshing own-made apple ice-cream.

Sureny

Plaça de la Revolució 17 (93 213 75 56). Metro Fontana or Joanic. **Open** 8.30pm-midnight Tue-Thur; 8.30pm-1am Fri, Sat; 1-3.30pm, 8pm-midnight Sun. Closed last wk Sept, 1st wk Oct, 2nd wk Apr. €€. **Tapas**. Map p143 D4 ㉓

A well-kept gastronomic secret, Sureny boasts superb tapas and knowledgeable staff. As well as the usual run-of-the-mill tortilla 'n' calamares, look out for tuna marinated in ginger and soy, partridge and venison in season, and a sublime duck foie with redcurrant sauce.

La Tarantella

C/Fraternitat 37 (93 284 98 57). Metro Fontana. **Open** 8.30pm-midnight Tue; 1.30-4pm, 8.30pm-midnight Wed-Sun. €€. **Pizzeria**. Map p143 D5 ㉔

Forge your way through the brightly lit tunnel of a bar into the cosy, low-ceilinged back room, warmed with beams and yellow paintwork. Here you can dine on decent budget Italian grub (salads, pasta and pizzas). Toppings are generous, even a bit much at times: the house pizza comes slathered in mozzarella, ham, mushrooms and onion, while the Extremeño is a mountain of mozzarella, chorizo and egg.

Shopping

Hibernian Books

C/Montseny 17 (93 217 47 96/ www.hibernian-books.com). Metro Fontana. **Open** *Sept-July* 4-8.30pm Mon; 10.30am-8.30pm Tue-Sat. *Aug* 11am-2pm, 5-8.30pm Mon-Sat. No credit cards. **Map** p142 C4 ㉕

Hibernian Books stocks over 30,000 fiction and non-fiction books in English. A kids' corner, armchairs, packed shelves and tea and coffee furnish this bookworm's lair, which operates a part-exchange system for those keen on offloading some suitcase ballast.

Vinus & Brindis

NEW *Torrent de l'Olla 147 (93 218 30 37/www.vinusbrindis.com). Metro Fontana.* **Open** June-Oct 11am-2.15pm, 5-9.15pm Mon-Sat. Nov-May 10.30am-2pm, 5-9pm Mon-Sat. **Map** p143 D3 ㉖

This franchise of approachable wine shops has a young, funky feel. It specialises in young and upcoming wine areas, winemakers and wines. Staff are more than eager to advise, and it always has a good range of easy-drinking wines for under six euros, as well as special monthly offers.

Samsara

Nightlife

Mond Bar

Plaça del Sol 21 (93 272 09 10/www. mondclub.com). Metro Fontana. **Open** 8.30pm-3am daily. **Admission** free. No credit cards. **Map** p142 C4 ㉗

This tiny two-level bar gets sweaty and smoky as the coolest cats in Gràcia pack in for an early drink. Recent problems with the neighbours saw the DJs replaced with a jukebox.

Vinilo

NEW *C/Matilde 2 (mobile 626 464 759/http://vinilus.blogspot.com). Metro Fontana.* **Open** 8pm-2.30am Mon-Thur, Sun; 7pm-3am Fri, Sat. **Admission** free. **No credit cards. Map** p142 C4 ㉘

A venue for grown-ups was long overdue in Gràcia, indeed in Barcelona. Local musician Jordi opened this cosy red-velveted bar/café almost a year ago and he's having rip-roaring success. Doubling as a casual eating place that serves up damn fine crêpes, Vinilo gets a mention in this section simply because of its immaculate music selection – Sparklehorse, Coco Rosie, Rufus Wainwright, Antony and the Johnsons and the Sleepy Jackson all get good runs here, as do the Beatles and Pink Floyd. Some great Japanese animation projections too. A place that comes into its own during the colder months.

Arts & leisure

Verdi

C/Verdi 32 (93 238 79 90/www.cines-verdi.com). Metro Fontana. No credit cards. **Map** p143 D3 ㉙

A long-standing champion of foreign cinema, the original five-screen Verdi, plus its four-screen annexe Verdi Park on the next street over, offer a diverse programme of interesting, accessible cinema from around the world, concentrating on Asia and Europe, as well as some Spanish repertoire. At peak times, chaos reigns; arrive early and make sure you don't mistake the queue of people going in for the queue buying tickets. **Other locations:** Verdi Park, C/Torrijos 49 (93 238 79 90).

Enric Rovira Shop

Other Districts

Sants & Les Corts

For many arriving by bus or train, Estació de Sants is their first sight of Barcelona. Most take one look at the forbidding **Plaça dels Països Catalans**, which looks like it was designed with skateboard tricks in mind, and get the hell out of the area. Over the next few years, however, the station and immediate surroundings are set for a long-overdue facelift as the new high-speed Barcelona–France train terminal is built (due to be finished in 2008, though this looks unlikely).

High-rise streets of mismatching apartment blocks now obscure any trace of the rustic origins of **Les Corts** (literally, 'cowsheds' or 'pigsties'), as the village itself was swallowed up by Barcelona in the late 19th century. One pocket of tranquillity is the **Plaça de la Concòrdia**, a quiet square dominated by a 40-metre (131-foot) bell tower. This is an anachronistic oasis housing the civic centre Can Deu, formerly a farmhouse and now home to a great bar that hosts jazz acts every other Thursday. The area is much better known, though, for what happens every other weekend, when tens of thousands pour in to watch FC Barcelona, whose **Nou Camp** stadium takes up much of the west of the *barrio*.

Sights & museums

Parc de l'Espanya Industrial

Passeig de Antoni (no phone). Metro Sants-Estació. **Open** 10am-sunset daily. A puzzling and futuristic space, with ten otherworldly watchtowers looking over a boating lake with a statue of Neptune in the middle, flanked by a

Shopping

Enric Rovira Shop

Avda Josep Tarradellas 113, Les Corts (93 419 25 47/www.enricrovira.com). Metro Entença. **Open** 10am-2.30pm, 5-8pm Tue-Fri; 10am-2.30pm Sat. Closed Aug.

Perhaps the best place in town for designer chocolates, this is where substance actually keeps up with style. Rovira's Gaudi-esque chocolate tile is an iconic gift for any choc lover, and his pink peppercorn truffles make great after-dinner conversation pieces.

L'Illa

Avda Diagonal 545-55, Les Corts (93 444 00 00/www.lilla.com). Metro Maria Cristina. **Open** 10am-9.30pm Mon-Sat. *Supermarket* 9.30am-9.30pm Mon-Sat.

This monolithic mall features all the usual fashion favourites but also has a good range of Catalan brands such as Camper, Custo and Antonio Miró. It has been gaining a good reputation lately for its food offerings, with specialist gourmet food stalls and interesting eateries such as sushi and oyster bars.

Nightlife

Bikini

C/Déu i Mata 105, Les Corts (93 322 08 00/www.bikinibcn.com). Metro Les Corts or Maria Cristina. **Open** *Club* midnight-5am Wed-Sun. *Gigs* varies. **Admission** (incl 1 drink) €15.

It's not easy to find Bikini in the nondescript, soulless streets behind the L'Illa shopping centre. But it's worth making the effort to seek it out, as you'll find top-flight gigs here by serious musicians of every conceivable stripe, from Femi Kuti to Thievery Corporation, and from Marianne Faithfull to Amp Fiddler. After the gigs, stay for club nights with house, funk and hip hop on the turntables. On Sunday watch Barça football matches on the big screen from 8.30pm, then party on to the latest dance sounds from 10.30pm.

stretch of mud that is used mainly for walking dogs. By the entrance children are encouraged to clamber over Andrés Nagel's *Drac,* a massive and sinister black dragon.

Eating & drinking

Icho

NEW *C/Deu i Mata 69-95, Les Corts (93 444 33 70/www.ichobcnjapones. com).* **Open** 1.30-3.30pm, 9-11.30pm Tue-Sat. Closed 2wks Aug. **Japanese/ Spanish**. €€€€.

In a coolly designed space under the NH Constanza, Icho (in Japanese it means gingko tree – of which three graceful examples sit outside) fuses Japanese with Spanish cooking. This really shouldn't work, but in fact it does, beautifully – perhaps because you can offset the digestive demands of tender suckling pig and pumpkin purée with a stunning platter of sushi, or balance a starter of foie and eel with tuna tartare and creamed tofu with wasabi. The portions aren't especially large, but diners are encouraged to order several and share.

Arts & leisure

Auditori Winterthur

*L'Illa, Avda Diagonal 547, Les Corts
(93 290 11 02/www.winterthur.es).
Metro Maria Cristina.* **Open** *Information*
8.30am-1.30pm, 3-5.30pm Mon-Fri.
Closed Aug.

A charming, intimate venue in the
unlikely setting of L'Illa shopping centre. Though it hosts few concerts,
they're generally of high quality; the
Schubert cycle and series of song
recitals, both annual events, are well
worth catching.

Nou Camp – FC Barcelona

*Nou Camp, Avda Aristides Maillol,
Les Corts (93 496 36 00/08/www.
fcbarcelona.com). Metro Collblanc
or Palau Reial.* **Ticket office** *Sept-
June* 9am-1.30pm, 3.30-6pm Mon-
Thur; 9am-2.30pm Fri; from 11am
match days. Tickets available from
2wks before each match. **Tickets**
€19-€125. **Museum** *Open* 10am-
6.30pm Mon-Sat; 10am-2pm Sun.
Admission €5.30; €3.70 reductions;
free under-5s. *Guided tour* €9.50;
€6.60 reductions. No credit cards.

Everyone agreed (even, grudgingly, at
Real Madrid) that Barça deserved to
pick up the Champions League trophy
last year. Barça's mixture of flair and
professionalism managed to combine
the brawn of Puyol and Márquez with
the outstanding creativity of players
like Xavi and Messi. Having the best
footballer in the world playing at the
top of his game didn't do any harm,
either. But Ronaldinho remains very
much a team player and, unlike a certain other club, Barça's *galácticos*
enjoyed their football and kept themselves focused on common goals. Barça
fans seem to have overcome their natural pessimism, but it has not escaped
their notice that Real Madrid has significantly strengthened its side.

Getting tickets can be something of
a lottery, especially for the big games.
Around 4,000 tickets usually go on sale
on the day of the match: join the queue
an hour or so beforehand. 'Rented out'
seats go on sale from these offices and

can also be bought through Servi-
Caixa ATMs. If there are none left, buy
a *reventa* ticket from touts at the gates.

Tibidabo & Collserola

Tibidabo is the dominant peak
of the Collserola massif, with its
sweeping views of the whole of the
Barcelona conurbation stretching
out to the sea. The ugly, neo-Gothic
Sagrat Cor temple crowning it
has become one of the city's most
recognisable landmarks; thousands
of people head to the top of the hill
at weekends to whoop and scream
their way around the creaky, old-
fashioned **funfair**.

Getting up to the top on the
clanking old **Tramvia Blau** (Blue
Tram) and then the **funicular
railway** is part of the fun; Plaça
Doctor Andreu between the two is
a great place for an alfresco drink.
For the best view of the city, either
take a lift up the needle of Norman
Foster's communications tower,
the **Torre de Collserola**, or up
to the *mirador* at the feet of Christ
atop the Sagrat Cor.

The vast **Parc de Collserola**
is more a series of forested hills
than a park; its shady paths
through holm oaks and pines open
out to spectacular views. It's most
easily reached by FGC train on the
Terrassa–Sabadell line from Plaça
Catalunya or Passeig de Gràcia,
getting off at **Baixador de
Vallvidrera** station.

Sights & museums

Funicular de Tibidabo

*Plaça Doctor Andreu to Plaça Tibidabo
(93 211 79 42). FGC Avda Tibidabo,
then Tramvia Blau.* **Open** As funfair
(see below), but starting 30mins earlier.
Tickets *Single* €2; €1.50 reductions.
Return €3; €2 reductions. No credit
cards.

This art deco vehicle offers occasional
glimpses of the city below as it winds

Danzatoria p155

through the pine forests up to the summit. The service has been running since 1901, but only according to a complicated timetable. For those who are feeling energetic, it's nearly an hour's (mostly pleasant) hike up from Plaça Doctor Andreu.

Tibidabo funfair

Plaça del Tibidabo, Tibidabo (93 211 79 42/www.tibidabo.es). FGC Avda Tibidabo. **Open** *Nov-mid Dec, mid Jan-Feb* noon-6pm Sat, Sun. *Mar, Apr* noon-7pm Sat, Sun. *May, June* noon-8pm Sat, Sun. *July* noon-8pm Wed-Fri; noon-11pm Sat; noon-10pm Sun. *Aug* noon-10pm Mon-Thur; noon-11pm Fri-Sun. *1st 2wks Sept* noon-8pm Wed-Fri; noon-9pm Sat, Sun. *2nd 2wks Sept* noon-9pm Sat, Sun. *Oct* noon-7pm Sat, Sun. Closed mid Dec-mid Jan. **Admission** *Rides* €11. *Unlimited rides* €22; €9-€17 reductions; free children under 90cm.

After years of falling profits, the fair has invested millions and boomed in popularity again – thanks, in part, to a terrifying new freefall ride called the Pendulum and a new hot-air balloon style ride for smaller children. Other attractions includes everything from a house of horrors and bumper cars to the Avió, the world's first popular flight simulator built in 1928. Don't miss the antique mechanical puppets at the Museu d'Autòmats or the hourly puppet shows at the Marionetàrium (from 1pm). At the weekends, there are circus parades and, in the summer, *correfocs* (fire runs) and street theatre.

Torre de Collserola

Ctra de Vallvidrera al Tibidabo (93 406 93 54/www.torredecollserola.com). FGC Peu Funicular, then funicular. **Open** *Apr-June, Sept* 11am-2.30pm, 3.30-7pm Wed-Fri; 11am-7pm Sat, Sun. *July, Aug* 11am-2.30pm, 3.30-8pm Mon-Fri; 11am-8pm Sat, Sun. *Oct-Mar* 11am-2.30pm, 3.30-6pm Mon-Fri; 11am-6pm Sat, Sun. **Admission** €5; €4 reductions; free under-4s.

Norman Foster's communications tower was built in 1992 to transmit images of the Olympics around the world. Visible from just about anywhere in the city and always flashing at night, the tower is loved and hated in almost equal measure, but its extraordinary views of Barcelona and the Mediterranean are unbeatable.

Eating & drinking

Merbeyé

Plaça Doctor Andreu, Tibidabo (93 417 92 79). FGC Avda Tibidabo, then Tramvia Blau/bus 60. **Open** noon-2.30am Mon-Thur; noon-3.30am Fri, Sat; noon-2am Sun. **Bar**.

Merbeyé is a cocktail bar straight from central casting: moodily lit and plush with red velvet. In summer there's also a peaceful, stylish terrace for alfresco fun. The clientele runs from the shabbily genteel to flashy Barça players and their bling-encrusted wives.

La Venta

Plaça Doctor Andreu, Tibidabo (93 212 64 55). FGC Avda Tibidabo, then Tramvia Blau. **Open** 1.30-3.15pm, 9-11.15pm Mon-Sat. €€€. **Mediterranean**.

Monestir de Pedralbes p156

Perched high above the city, La Venta's Moorish-influenced interior plays second fiddle to the terrace for every season: shaded by day and uncovered by night in summer, sealed and warmed with a wood-burning stove in winter. Starters include lentil and spider crab salad; sea urchins au gratin; and langoustine ravioli, filled with leek and foie mousse. Simpler but high-quality mains run from rack of lamb to delicate monkfish in filo pastry with pesto.

Nightlife

Danzatoria

Avda Tibidabo 61, Tibidabo (93 211 62 61/www.danzatoria-barcelona.com). FGC Avda Tibidabo, then 10min walk. **Open** 11pm-2.30am Tue, Wed; 11.30pm-3am Thur-Sat. **Admission** free.

The uptown location attracts an upscale crowd to this spectacular converted manor house on a hill overlooking Barcelona. The hipness factor goes up as you climb the club's glamour-glutted storeys. Preened *pija* flesh is shaken on hot-house dancefloors, or laid across sofas hanging from the ceiling in the chill-out lounges. We've had reports of snotty staff, but who cares when you're lounging in one of the layers of palm-filled gardens, accompanied by some gorgeous creature and some (very expensive) champagne.

Mirablau

Plaça Doctor Andreu 1, Tibidabo (93 418 58 79). FGC Avda Tibidabo, then Tramvia Blau. **Open** 11am-4.30am Mon-Thur; 11am-5.30am Fri-Sun. **Admission** free. **Credit** V.

It doesn't get any more uptown than this, either geographically or socially. Located at the top of Tibidabo, this small bar is packed with the high rollers of Barcelona, from local footballers living on the hill to international businessmen on the company card, as well as young *pijos* stopping by for a drink before heading off to nearby Danzatoria on daddy's ride. Apart from the cheesy Spanish pop, its real attraction is the breathtaking view.

Zona Alta

Zona Alta (the 'upper zone', or 'uptown') is the name given to a series of smart neighbourhoods, including **Sant Gervasi**, **Sarrià**, **Pedralbes** and **Putxet**, that stretch out across the lower reaches of the Collserola hills. The centre of Sarrià and the streets of old Pedralbes around the monastery retain a whiff of the sleepy country towns these once were.

Gaudí fans are rewarded by a trip up to the **Pavellons de la Finca Güell** at Avda Pedralbes 15; its extraordinary wrought-iron gate features a dragon into whose gaping mouth the foolhardy can fit their heads. Once inside the gardens, accessed via the main gate on Avda Diagonal, be sure to look out for a delightful fountain designed by the master himself. Across near Putxet is Gaudí's relatively sober **Col·legi de les Teresianes** (C/Ganduxer 85-105), while up towards Tibidabo, just off Plaça Bonanova, rises his remarkable Gothic-influenced **Torre Figueres** or **Bellesguard**.

Sights & museums

CosmoCaixa

C/Teodor Roviralta 47-51 (93 212 60 50/www.fundacio.lacaixa.es). Bus 60/ FGC Avda Tibidabo, then Tramvia Blau. **Open** 10am-8pm Tue-Sun. **Admission** €3; €2 reductions; free under-3s. *Planetarium* €2; €1.50 reductions; free under-3s.

The long and eagerly awaited revamp of the Fundació La Caixa's science museum and planetarium, to create the biggest in Europe, was only partially successful. First off, its size is a little misleading: apart from a couple of spaces – the Flooded Forest, a reproduction of a bit of Amazonia complete with flora and fauna, and the Geological Wall – the collection has not been proportionally expanded to fit the new building. A glass-enclosed spiral ramp runs down an impressive six floors, but actually represents quite a long walk to reach the main collection five floors down. What's more, for all the fanfare made by the museum about taking exhibits out of glass cases and making scientific theories accessible, many of the displays look very dated.

On the plus side, the installations for children are excellent: the Bubble Planetarium pleases kids aged three to eight, and the wonderful Clik (aimed at ages three to six) and Flash (for ages seven to nine) introduce kids to science through games. Toca Toca! ('Touch! Touch!') educates children about which animals and plants are safe and which should be avoided. One of the real highlights, for kids and adults, remains the hugely entertaining sound telescope, which is situated outside on the Plaça de la Ciència.

Event highlights 'Physics and music: vibrations for the soul' (running until 30 Mar 2008).

Monestir de Pedralbes

Baixada del Monestir 9 (93 203 92 82). FGC Reina Elisenda. **Open** 10am-2pm Tue-Sun. **Admission** €4; €2.50 reductions; free under-12s. Free 1st Sun of mth.

In 1326 the widowed Queen Elisenda of Montcada used her inheritance to buy this land and build a convent for the 'Poor Clare' order of nuns, which she soon joined. The result is a jewel of Gothic architecture, with an understated single-nave church with fine stained-glass windows and a beautiful three-storey 14th-century cloister. The place was out of bounds to the general public until 1983 when the nuns, a closed order, opened it up as a museum in the mornings (they escape to a nearby annexe).

The site offers a fascinating insight into life in a medieval convent, taking you through the kitchens, pharmacy and refectory with its huge vaulted ceiling. To one side is the tiny chapel of Sant Miquel, with murals dating to 1343 by Ferrer Bassa, a Catalan painter and student of Giotto. In the former dormitory next to the cloister is a selection of hitherto undisplayed objects belonging to the nuns. Among them are illuminated books, furniture and objects reflecting the artistic and religious life of the community.

Museu de Ceràmica & Museu de les Arts Decoratives

Palau Reial de Pedralbes, Avda Diagonal 686 (93 280 16 21/ www.museuceramica.bcn.es/www. museuartsdecoratives.bcn.es). Metro Palau Reial. **Open** 10am-6pm Tue-Sat; 10am-3pm Sun. **Admission** *Combined admission with Museu Tèxtil* €3.50; €2 reductions; free under-16s. Free 1st Sun of mth. No credit cards.

These two collections – accessible, along with the Textile Museum, on the same ticket – are housed in the august Palau Reial; originally designed for the family of Eusebi Güell, Gaudí's patron, it was later used as a royal palace. The Museum of Decorative Arts is informative and fun, and looks at the different styles informing the design of artefacts in Europe since the Middle Ages, from Romanesque to art deco and beyond. A second section is devoted to post-war Catalan design of objects as diverse as urinals and man-sized inflatable pens.

The Ceramics Museum is equally fascinating, showing how Moorish ceramic techniques from the 13th century were developed after the Reconquista with the addition of colours (especially blue and yellow) in centres such as Manises (in Valencia) and Barcelona. Two 18th-century murals are of sociological interest: one, La Xocolatada, shows the bourgeoisie at a garden party, while the other, by the same artist, depicts the working classes at a bullfight in the Plaza Mayor in Madrid. Upstairs is a section showing 20th-century ceramics, which includes a room dedicated to Miró and Picasso. The two museums, along with the Textile Museum and several smaller collections, are to be merged in the

Museu de les Art Decoratives

Setting the scene

Director Pedro Almodóvar called Barcelona 'a splendid natural film set'. Indeed, the Old City has become so clogged with cameramen and dolly tracks that the Ajuntament now only allows two shoots a month in certain areas. Here's our pick of the city's finest filmic moments.

■ Woody Allen's latest project, **Midnight in Barcelona**, is based on a series of bilingual romantic entanglements starring Penélope Cruz, Javier Bardem and Allen's new muse, Scarlett Johansson.

■ Tom Tykwer's **Perfume** (2006) converted the old town into 18th-century Paris by covering shop fronts in a mixture of latex batter and mashed potato. Plaça Sant Felip Neri and the Parc del Laberint d'Horta staged two of the murder scenes, while Poble Espanyol was packed, Spencer Tunick-style, with 750 naked extras for the orgy scene.

■ Manuel Huerga's acclaimed **Salvador** (2006) used 1970s-style locations in telling the grim story of Salvador Puig Antich, the last anarchist to be executed by garrotte under Franco.

■ Calista Flockhart starred in Jaume Balagueró's supernatural gore flop **Fragile** (2005). Far more interesting to the local paparazzi was her boyfriend, Harrison Ford, trashing municipal street furniture.

■ Barcelona's industrial suburbs stood in for an anonymous West Coast American backdrop in Brad Anderson's **The Machinist** (2004), starring a famously emaciated Christian Bale.

future in a Museu de Disseny (Design Museum) as part of the cultural over-haul of the Plaça de les Glòries.

Parc de la Creueta del Coll

C/Mare de Déu del Coll (no phone). Metro Penitents. **Open** 10am-sunset daily. **Admission** free.
This park was created from a quarry in 1987 by Josep Martorell and David Mackay, the team that went on to design the Vila Olímpica. It boasts a sizeable swimming pool, complete with its own 'desert island', and an interesting sculpture by Eduardo Chillida: called *In Praise of Water*, it consists of a 50-ton hunk of curled granite sus-pended on cables.

Tramvia Blau (Blue Tram)

Avda Tibidabo (Plaça Kennedy) to Plaça Doctor Andreu (93 318 70 74/www.tramvia.org/tramviablau). FGC Avda Tibidabo. **Open** *Mid June-mid Sept* 10am-8pm daily. *Mid Sept-mid June* 10am-6pm Sat. **Frequency** 20mins. **Tickets** €2.10 single; €3.10 return. No credit cards.
Barcelonins and tourists have been clanking 1,225m (4,000ft) up Avda Tibidabo in the 'blue trams' since 1902. In the winter months, when the tram only operates on weekends, a rather more prosaic bus takes you up (or you can walk it in 15 minutes).

Nightlife

Elephant

Passeig dels Til·lers 1 (93 334 02 58/www.elephantbcn.com). Metro Palau Reial. **Open** 11.30pm-4am Wed, Thur; 11.30pm-5am Fri, Sat. **Admission** free Wed, Thur; €12 Fri, Sat.
If you have a Porsche and a model girl-friend, this is where you meet your peers. Housed in a converted mansion, Elephant is as elegant and high-design as its customers. The big attraction is the outdoor bar and terrace dancefloor, though the low-key and low-volume (due to neighbours' complaints) house music doesn't inspire much hands-in-the-air action.

Otto Zutz

C/Lincoln 15 (93 238 07 22/www. grupo-ottozutz.com). FGC Gràcia. **Open** midnight-5am Tue, Wed; midnight-5.30am Thur-Sat. **Admission** (incl 1 drink) €15.

Run by the same people as City Hall, Otto Zutz was once *the* nightclub in Barcelona. The space hasn't changed much, but the models, film people and poseurs have moved on. It would do well to be a little less wrapped up in its pretentions and a little more concerned with the music. Three floors of an old textile factory feature R&B, hip hop and some electro, but the main focus is on the same old not-so-funky house.

Pacha

Avda Doctor Marañon 17 (93 334 32 33/www.clubpachabcn.com). Metro Zona Universitaria. **Open** 11.30pm-4.30am Mon-Sat; 9pm-3am Sun. **Admission** (incl 1 drink) €15.

When Pacha was set to open in Barcelona a few years back, the queues of potential barstaff were so long that they made the evening news. Such is the power of the global clubbing giant that armies of tourists, out-of-towners and locals continue rolling up for fair sound quality, a so-so venue and heaps of attitude.

Sala BeCool

NEW *Plaça Joan Llongueras (93 362 04 13/www.salabecool.com). Metro Hospital Clínic.* **Open** *Gigs* 10pm Thur-Sat. *Club* midnight-5am Thur-Sat. **Admission** *Gigs* varies. *Club* €10.

The latest minimal electro sounds from Berlin reach Barcelona via this chic uptown concert hall. After the live shows by local rock stars, young urbanites throb to euro techno and electro-pop DJs. In an adjacent red room, DJs provide melodic indie pop alternatives to pounding beats.

Universal

C/Marià Cubí 182 bis-184 (93 201 35 96/www.grupocostaeste.com). FGC Muntaner. **Open** 11pm-3.30am Mon-Thur; 11pm-5am Fri, Sat. **Admission** free.

One of a very few clubs in the city that cater to an older crowd, Universal doesn't charge admission to get in, but the drink prices are steep as a result. As it gets later, the music moves from downtempo to soft house, which works the crowd up to a gentle shimmy.

Poblenou

Poblenou has been many things in its time: a farming community, a fishing port, the site of heavy industry factories and a trendy post-industrial suburb. Now it's also a burgeoning technology and business district, snappily tagged '22@'. The factories around here closed down in the 1960s; these days the buildings that haven't been torn down or converted into office blocks are used as schools, civic centres, workshops or, increasingly, coveted lofts.

On its northern edge **Plaça de les Glòries** holds the area's most striking landmark, French architect Jean Nouvel's hugely phallic **Torre Agbar**. The *plaça* has become the gateway to a new commercial and leisure area on the shoreline, known as the Fòrum after the cultural symposium in 2004 for which it was created. Many critics of the Fòrum felt its real purpose was to regenerate this post-industrial wasteland, and certainly part of its legacy is a slew of enormous conference halls and hotels that it is hoped will draw wealthy business clients into the city.

Eating & drinking

Els Pescadors

Plaça Prim 1 (93 225 20 18/www. elspescadors.com). Metro Poblenou. **Open** 1-3.45pm, 8.30pm-midnight daily. **€€€. Catalan.**

In a forgotten, almost rustic square lies this first-rate fish restaurant, with tables under the canopy formed by two huge and ancient *ombú* trees. Suspend your disbelief with the crunchy sardine skeletons that arrive as an aperitif (trust us, they're delicious), and move on to tasty fried *chipirones,* followed by cod and pepper paella or creamy rice with prawns and smoked cheese. Desserts include strawberry gelatine 'spaghetti' in a citric soup, and the waiters are exceptionally professional and friendly.

Shopping

Barcelona Glòries

Avda Diagonal 208 (93 486 04 04/ www.lesglories.com). Metro Glòries. **Open** *Shops* 10am-10pm Mon-Sat.
This mall, office and leisure centre has a seven-screen cinema (films are mostly dubbed into Spanish) and over 220 shops, including a Carrefour supermarket, an H&M, a Mango and a Disney Store, facing on to a large, café-filled square decorated with jets of coloured water. Family-orientated attractions include play areas and entertainment such as bouncy castles and trampolines.

Diagonal Mar

Avda Diagonal 3 (902 53 03 00/ www.diagonalmar.com). Metro El Maresme-Forum. **Open** *Shops* 10 am-10pm Mon-Sat. *Food court & entertainment* 10am-midnight Mon-Thur; 10am-2am Fri, Sat; 11am-midnight Sun.
This three-level mall has an airy marine theme and a sea-facing roof terrace filled with cafés and restaurants of the fast-food variety. Business is a little slow (except at the giant Alcampo supermarket), so it's a good queue-free option. Other anchor stores here include Zara, Mango and FNAC. There are also a bowling alley, exhibitions, concerts and, every Sunday at 12.30pm, children's entertainment.

Els Encants

C/Dos de Maig 177-187, Plaça de la Glòries (93 246 30 30). Metro Glòries. **Open** 9am-6pm Mon, Wed, Fri, Sat. *Auctions* 7.30-9am Mon, Wed, Fri. No credit cards.

It's increasingly hard to find a bargain at Barcelona's old flea market, but it's a diverting way to pass the time: the buyers and sellers are as varied and curious as the bric-a-brac, big pants, Barça memorabilia, cheap electrical gadgets, religious relics and ancient Spanish school books that make up the majority of the stalls' booty. If you want to buy furniture at a decent price come to the auctions at 7am with the commercial buyers or at noon, when unsold stuff drops in price.

Nightlife

Oven

C/Ramon Turró 126 (93 221 06 02). Metro Poblenou. **Open** 1-4pm Mon-Wed; 1-4pm, 9pm-3am Thur-Sat. **Admission** free.
The slickest outfit in the newly hip Poblenou, Oven is a bit tiresome to get to but worth the effort, especially if you make a night of it by having some fine cocktails and dinner here first. The industrial interior segues into grown-up clubland come midnight, when the tables are cleared to make way for dancing, and Barcelona's best-known DJ, Professor Angel Dust, hits the decks with his own mix of house and Afro-Latin tunes.

Razzmatazz

C/Almogàvers 122 (93 320 82 00/ www.salarazzmatazz.com). Metro Bogatell or Marina. **Open** 1-5am Fri, Sat. **Admission** (incl 1 drink) €12.
Skinny jeans, battered Converse and a heavy dose of party-rock dominate this warehouse superclub, and while some of the punters are a bit young and the toilets a bit vile, line-ups are on the ball, diverse and international. As it's essentially five clubs in one, if you're tired of 2manydjs or Miss Kittin in the main Razz Room, you can head upstairs to check out Queens of Noize, Four Tet or Tiga playing the Loft. Razzmatazz is also one of the city's best venues for live music, with acts from the Arctic Monkeys to Queens of the Stone Age to, er, Bananarama.

Essentials

Hotel Omm p175

Hotels

Dozens of new hotels have been springing up over the last few years, and the trend shows no sign of slowing down. While this has certainly made it easier to find accommodation in a city with year-round high occupancy, most new places are at least of four-star standard. There is still a real dearth of more modest hotels that offer fewer frills but provide all the facilities most travellers need.

There is now quite a good range of boutique hotels, but again, they are mostly at the upper end of the scale. If you look hard enough, however, there is plenty of charm at the budget end too, as many *hostales* are situated in fabulous old buildings with elaborate doorways, grand staircases and beautiful tiled floors. A new generation of hoteliers is transforming gloomy old-style *hostales* into bright and friendly establishments with en-suite bathrooms, internet access and other 21st-century essentials.

Booking in advance is strongly recommended, though many of the cheaper hotels won't accept reservations. Hotels often require you to guarantee your booking with credit card details or a cash deposit; whether or not you've provided either, it's always worth calling a few days before your arrival to reconfirm the booking (get it in writing if you can; many readers have reported problems), and check the cancellation policy too. Often you will lose at least the first night.

To be sure of getting a room with natural light or a view, ask for an outside room (*habitació/habitación exterior*), which will usually face

SHORTLIST

Best new
- AC Miramar (p167)
- Petit Palace Opera Garden (p166)
- Hostal HMB (p176)
- Hotel Granados 83 (p175)

Best restaurants
- Hotel Condes de Barcelona (p175)
- Hotel Majestic (p175)
- Hotel Omm (p175)

Cut-price chic
- Banys Orientals (p166)
- Hostal d'Uxelles (p173)
- Market Hotel (p176)
- the5rooms (p176)

Best for romance
- Hostal Girona (p174)
- Hotel Axel (p174)
- Hotel Neri (p166)
- the5rooms (p176)

Best bars
- Hotel Arts (p173)
- Hotel Axel (p174)
- Hotel Omm (p175)
- Hotel Pulitzer (p176)

Best views
- AC Miramar (p167)
- Grand Hotel Central (p169)
- Gran Hotel La Florida (p176)
- Hotel Arts (p173)

Best for a dip
- AC Miramar (p167)
- Gran Hotel La Florida (p176)
- Grand Hotel Central (p169)
- Hotel Arts (p173)

Best on a budget
- Hostal Gat Raval (p169)
- Hostal Gat Xino (p170)
- Hostal Girona (p174)
- Pensió 2000 (p167)

the street. Many of Barcelona's buildings are built around a central airshaft or patio, and the inside rooms (*habitació/habitación interior*) around them can be quite dark, albeit quieter. In some cases, though, these inward-facing rooms are blessed with a view over gardens or open-air patios.

Barri Gòtic & La Rambla

H10 Racó del Pi

C/Pi 7 (93 342 61 90/fax 93 342 61 91/ www. h10hotels.es). Metro Liceu. €€€. Part of the H10 chain, the Racó del Pi offers spacious rooms with parquet floors, handsome terracotta-tiled bathrooms and an elegant glass conservatory on the ground floor. It can be a bargain out of season.

H1898

La Rambla 109 (93 552 95 52/fax 93 552 95 50/www.nnhotels.es). Metro Catalunya or Liceu. €€€€.

ESSENTIALS

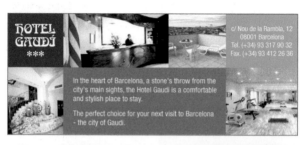

Hostal Rembrandt

There is a rather institutional feel about both rooms and lobby, but the location is excellent, overlooking a pretty square; it is only really worth staying here if you get one of the rooms with a balcony. Some rooms are dark, but all have en-suite bathrooms, and the place is sparkling clean. Book well in advance.

Hostal Lausanne
Portal de l'Àngel 24, 1º 1ª (tel/fax 93 302 11 39/www.hostallausanne.com). Metro Catalunya .€. No credit cards.
This *hostal* feels spacious, with light pouring in from both ends of the building. Of the 17 basic rooms, four have en-suite bathrooms and some have balconies. It may be a bit dated, but it's a friendly and safe place, with a fun backpacker vibe. The street is as quiet at night as it is busy during the day.

Hostal Noya
La Rambla 133, 1º (93 301 48 31). Metro Catalunya. €. No credit cards.
Cheap and cheerful, the Noya is at the top of three flights of stairs. Rooms are basic to say the least, but some have balconies looking out on to La Rambla and there are handsome old tiles on the floor. The lone bathroom is weathered and worn, and it can get busy since it's shared between 12 rooms (there is a separate WC), but all bedrooms do have their own washbasins.

Hostal Rembrandt
C/Portaferrissa 23, pral 1ª (tel/fax 93 318 10 11/www.hostalrembrandt.com). Metro Liceu. €.
A charming 28-room *hostal*: fairly stylish (for the price) with lots of wood panelling, soft lighting and a lift. The pretty interior courtyard makes for a pleasant chill-out zone/eating area. Rooms out front can be a little noisy.

Hotel Colón
Avda Catedral 7 (93 301 14 04/fax 93 317 29 15/www.hotelcolon.es). Metro Jaume I. €€€.
If you have had it with minimalism, stay here. With thick carpets and walls bedecked in bright floral prints, the

A luxury hotel in a splendid 19th-century building right on La Rambla. Rooms are subject to Henley Regatta-type colour schemes; one floor is all perky green-and-white stripes. The more expensive rooms have sizeable wooden-decked terraces, while some of the suites have plunge pools.

Hostal Fontanella
Via Laietana 71, 2º (tel/fax 93 317 59 43/www.hostalfontanella.com). Metro Urquinaona. €€.
The splendid Modernista lift lends an aura of grandeur to this 11-room *hostal*, where devotees of Laura Ashley will feel at home amid the chintz. The downside of the Fontanella's central location is that outward-facing rooms are abuzz with the sound of traffic. But it's clean and comfortable, and double-glazing has recently been installed.

Hostal Jardí
Plaça Sant Josep Oriol 1 (93 301 59 00/ fax 93 342 57 33). Metro Liceu. €€.

ESSENTIALS

Colón is all about making guests feel comfortable. The best rooms are those overlooking the cathedral, some of which have balconies.

Hotel Le Meridien Barcelona

La Rambla 111 (93 318 62 00/fax 93 301 77 76/www.barcelona.lemeridien. com). Metro Liceu. €€€€.

Le Meridien is a great place for spotting celebrities. It has revamped its genteel image with wood floors and leather furnishings, along with rain showers and plasma-screen TVs. Despite its size (it has 233 rooms), it manages to retain an air of intimacy thanks to its helpful, friendly staff.

Hotel Neri

C/Sant Sever 5 (93 304 06 55/fax 93 304 03 37/www.hotelneri.com). Metro Jaume I. €€€€.

A sumptuous boutique hotel, located in an 18th-century palace. After the lobby, which teams flagstone floors and wooden beams with funky designer fixtures, red velvet and gold leaf, the 22 rooms can seem a little serious, with neutral tones, natural materials and rustic finishes, sharp design and high-tech perks (hi-fis, plasma-screen TVs).

Hotel Oriente

La Rambla 45 (93 302 25 58/fax 93 412 38 19/www.husa.es). Metro Liceu. €€€.

Barcelona's first-ever 'grand hotel' was built in 1842. All bedrooms now have pale wood floors, minimalist design and sleek electrical gadgetry, in striking contrast to the ritzy ballroom and dining room. Sadly, no amount of renovation can do away with the noise from La Rambla; light sleepers should ask for a room at the back of the hotel.

Hotel Petit Palace Opera Garden

WC/Boqueria 10 (93 302 00 92/fax 93 302 15 66/www.hthoteles.com). Metro Liceu. €€€.

A private mansion was thoroughly gutted to create this new minimalist haven. The 61 rooms are white and futuristic, with a different zingy colour on each floor and opera scores printed on the walls above the beds. Lamps and chairs lend a swinging '60s air. Some bathrooms have massage showers, others jacuzzi baths. The best thing, perhaps, is the secret (though public) garden at the back.

Pensió Alamar

C/Comtessa de Sobradiel 1, 1º 2ª (93 302 50 12/www.pensioalamar.com). Metro Jaume I or Liceu. €.

Eight of the basic, yet tasteful, rooms at this family-run *hostal* have plant-filled balconies overlooking the street. Beds are new and excellent quality, with crisp cotton sheets, and windows are double-glazed to keep noise to a happy minimum. The downside is that the 12 rooms share two bathrooms. There are good discounts for longer stays, use of a kitchen, and larger rooms for families.

Pensión Hostal Mari-Luz

C/Palau 4 (tel/fax 93 317 34 63/www. pension mariluz.com). Metro Jaume I or Liceu. €.

The entrance and staircase of this 18th-century stone building are certainly imposing, but the downside is the several flights of stairs. The effort is well worth it, however, for the smiling service and homey atmosphere. Stripped wood doors and old floor tiles add character to the 15 otherwise plain but quiet rooms, some of which face a plant-filled inner courtyard. No.4 and No.6 have good en-suite bathrooms.

Born & Sant Pere

Banys Orientals

C/Argenteria 37 (93 268 84 60/ fax 93 268 84 61/www.hotelbanys orientals.com). Metro Jaume I. €€.

Banys Orientals exudes cool with the deeply stylish shades-of-grey minimalism of its rooms, along with nice touches such as complimentary mineral water placed on the landings. The only drawback is the smallish size of some of the rooms. Plans to create a

The height of luxury

Miramar Palace

There was outrage when plans were announced to turn the Miramar Palace on Montjüic into a hotel. For a start, there was the bastardisation of the building itself, a villa built for the 1929 world fair, which many felt should have been preserved. Then there was the rumour that the work would disturb the medieval Jewish burial ground believed to be on the mountain. The plan to complete the AC group's flagship hotel went ahead regardless, and the results, while still contentious in some circles – the original palace façade has been extended considerably on either side – are impressive.

Perched above the recently spruced up cactus gardens of Jardins Mossèn Costa i Llobera, the hotel has great views of the port and the city itself. It has acres of lawn laid out in formal Victorian style, an orange-tree patio and a fine swimming pool: an H-shaped, jade-green affair inset with fibre-optics, which make swimming here at night like floating through the Milky Way.

The Forestier restaurant serves excellent Mediterranean food, while a full-service spa with sauna, steam rooms and indoor swimming pool helps take the edge off travel. Local architect Oscar Tusquet's adaptation of the space is sexy but sympathetic: all champagne-coloured marble and chocolate sofas. The centrepiece is a huge chandelier inspired by Gaudí's models for the Sagrada Familia.

The only downside is the cost, with doubles hovering around the €300 mark, but it's worth asking about promotional offers when booking. The smallest rooms may not have space on their side, but they are at the top of the building, with large private terraces and a hot tub. Many of the deluxe rooms and suites do not, although they do have adorable Lavasca egg-shaped baths: something to bear in mind if travelling mid-winter.

■ AC Miramar Plaza Carlos Ibáñez 3, Passeig de Miramar, Montjuïc (93 281 16 00/www.ac-hotels. com). Metro Paral·lel/Funicular Montjuïc. €€€€.

luxurious new service by tapping into the eponymous thermal baths that lie underneath the hotel are in the pipeline.

Chic&basic

NEW C/Princesa 50 (93 295 46 52/fax 93 295 46 53/www.chicandbasic.com). Metro Arc de Triomf or Jaume I. €€€.
A monochrome space-age theatrical vibe reigns supreme here: if you've ever dreamed of entering your room through a shimmering curtain of transparent plastic twirls, as if you were walking into a waterfall, then welcome home. The building retains its original grand staircase, now attractively furnished with oversized chairs and sofas. A chill-out room contains tea- and coffee-making facilities, a fridge and a microwave, as well as sofas and pouffes.

Ciutat Barcelona

NEW C/Princesa 35 (93 269 74 75/fax 93 269 74 76/www.ciutathotels.com.) Metro Jaume I. €€€.
The Ciutat Barcelona opened in 2006 and has gone over big on the colour co-ordination – even the plastic cups in the chic bathrooms match the red, blue or green colour-scheme of the rooms. Retro shapes prevail in the stylish furnishings and decoration, disguising the fact that rooms are small. There is a great roof terrace with a plunge pool. The Colors restaurant on the ground floor is popular with non-guests.

Grand Hotel Central

Via Laietana 30 (93 295 79 00/ fax 93 268 12 15/www.grandhotel central.com). Metro Jaume I. €€€.
The Grand Hotel Central is another of the recent wave of Barcelona hotels to adhere to the unwritten rule that grey is the new black. The Central's shadowy corridors open up on to sleekly appointed rooms that come with flat-screen TVs, DVD players and Molton Brown toiletries. The real charm of the hotel lies on its roof. Here you can sip a cocktail and admire the fabulous views while floating comfortably in the vertiginous infinity pool.

Pensió 2000

C/Sant Pere Més Alt 6, 1º (93 310 74 66/fax 93 319 42 52/www.pension 2000.com). Metro Urquinaona. €€.
One of Barcelona's best-value pensiones in a charming old building opposite the Palau de la Música. Only two of its six bright and airy rooms are en suite, but the communal facilities are sparkling. Its tall windows, buttercup-yellow walls and a lounge peppered with books and toys make it a cheery place, with a warm, relaxed atmosphere. The large rooms also make it a good bet for holidaying families.

Raval

Abba Rambla Hotel

NEW C/Rambla del Raval 4 (93 505 54 00/fax 93 505 54 01/www.abba hoteles.com). Metro Liceu or Sant Antoni. €€€.
Overlooking the Rambla del Raval, an open space flanked by bars and restaurants, the Abba Rambla is a comfortable and friendly base for nightlife and sightseeing, although rooms are a bit bland. More stylish are the ground-floor lounge and breakfast bar, where you eat perched on high stools.

Casa Camper

C/Elisabets 11 (93 342 62 80/fax 93 342 75 63/www.casacamper.com). Metro Catalunya. €€€€.
Devised by the Mallorcan footwear giant, this is a holistic concept-fest of a boutique hotel where Mediterranean simplicity meets contemporary cool. You get a pair of plastic Camper clogs to shuffle around in and your own personal lounge across the corridor, complete with extra TV and a hammock. There is nothing as naff as a minibar, but you can help yourself to free snacks and refreshments in the café whenever the fancy takes you.

Hostal Gat Raval

C/Joaquín Costa 44, 2º (93 481 66 70/fax 93 342 66 97/www. gataccommodation.com). Metro Universitat. €€.

Flat rates

Renting a flat can be a great way of experiencing the city, but it pays to do your research. Most short-stay apartments are in the Old City. This is handy for sights and nightlife, but many buildings here are at least a couple of hundred years old, so it's worth finding out what condition they are in. Many places have been tastefully restored, but do check what the entrance and staircase are like – they are decidedly unsavoury in some buildings.

A more common problem, however, is noise. With such a density of population, features such as soundproofing and air-conditioning are worth noting.

Holiday apartments are often designed to sleep lots of people in a small space. If you intend to be out all day and most of the night, you could end up saving money. In Barceloneta flats are particularly small, but this need not be a problem if they have been well converted, and the proximity to the beach is a big advantage in summer.

There is no shortage of horror stories, and it pays to use a little common sense. Check the small print (payment, deposits, cancellation fees, and so on) and exactly what is included before booking.

The following offer apartments: www.inside-bcn.com, www.oh-barcelona.com, www.rentaflatin barcelona.com, www.barcelona living.com, www.friendlyrentals. com, www.1st-barcelona.com, www.rentthesun.com, www.apart mentsbcn.net, www.flatsbydays. com. There is also gay-operated www.outlet4spain.com.

Gat Raval embodies everything that 21st-century budget accommodation should be: smart, clean and funky, with bright, sunshiny rooms. Each boasts a work by a local artist, and some have balconies. The only downsides are that nearly all the bathrooms are communal (though very clean) and there is no lift.

Hostal Gat Xino

C/Hospital 155 (93 324 88 33/fax 93 324 88 34/www.gataccommodation. com). Metro Sant Antoni. €€.
This 'Gat' has a bright and breezy breakfast room complete with apple-green polka-dot walls, a wood-decked patio and a roof terrace with black beanbags for chilling out. There's more bright green in the rooms, all of which are en suite, with good-quality beds, crisp white linen and the regulation flat-screen TVs. The best have their own small terraces.

Hosteria Grau

C/Ramelleres 27 (93 301 81 35/fax 93 317 68 25/www.hostalgrau.com). Metro Catalunya. €€.
This charming, family-run *hostal* oozes character, with a tiled spiral staircase and fabulous 1970s-style communal areas, including a funky café next door. The open fireplace is a luxury if you visit in the winter. Rooms are basic, comfortable and fairly quiet. There are also some apartments available on the top floor. Book well in advance.

Hotel Ambassador

C/Pintor Fortuny 13 (93 342 61 80/fax 93 302 79 77/www. rivolihotels.com). Metro Catalunya. €€€€.
The Ambassador has been refurbished, and now boasts a heady blend of water features, gold paint and smoked glass, a colossus of a chandelier and a freestanding Modernista bar that dominates the lounge area. Rooms are straightforwardly decorated, with no scary designer features, and there's also a pool and a jacuzzi on the rooftop.

Hotel España

C/Sant Pau 9-11 (93 318 17 58/fax 93 317 11 34/www.hotelespanya.com). Metro Liceu. €€€.

The lower floors at this Modernista landmark were designed by Domènech i Montaner in 1902. The main restaurant is decorated with floral tiling and elaborate woodwork, while the larger dining room beyond it features dreamy murals of mermaids by Ramon Casas, and the bar boasts a sculpted marble fireplace. After all this grandeur, the bedrooms are unexciting.

Hotel Mesón Castilla

C/Valldonzella 5 (93 318 21 82/fax 93 412 40 20/www.mesoncastilla.com). Metro Universitat. €€€.

If you want a change from contemporary design, check into this chocolate-box hotel, which opened in 1952. Before then, it was a private house belonging to an aristocratic family. Public areas are full of antiques, while the rooms are all different and decorated with hand-painted furniture, with tiled floors. The best have tranquil terraces, with a delightful plant-packed one off the breakfast room.

Hotel Principal

C/Junta de Comerç 8 (93 318 89 74/fax 93 412 08 19/www.hotelprincipal.es). Metro Liceu. €€€.

After an impressive revamp, the Principal offers rooms of a good standard, with flat-screen TVs, original artworks and marble bathrooms. Guests can relax on loungers on the roof, where there is also a suite with a private terrace. The buffet breakfast is served in a pleasant, light room.

Hotel Sant Agustí

Plaça Sant Agustí 3 (93 318 16 58/ fax 93 317 29 28/www.hotelsa.com). Metro Liceu. €€€.

With its sandstone walls and huge, arched windows looking on to the *plaça*, not to mention the pink marble lobby filled with forest-green furniture, this imposing hotel is the oldest in Barcelona. Housed in the former convent of St Augustine, it was converted into a hotel in 1840. Rooms are spacious and comfortable, but there's no soundproofing. Good buffet breakfast.

Casa Camper p169

Barceloneta & the Ports

Hostal Poblenou

C/Taulat 30, pral (93 221 26 01/ www.hostalpoblenou.com). Metro Poblenou. €€.

Poblenou is a delightful *hostal* in an elegant restored building a short walk from the beach. The five rooms are all light and airy, with their own bathrooms, and breakfast is served on a sunny terrace. There is wireless internet as well as a shared terminal, and guests can help themselves to tea, coffee and mineral water.

Hotel Arts

C/Marina 19-21 (93 221 10 00/fax 93 221 10 70/www.ritzcarlton.com). Metro Ciutadella-Vila Olímpica. €€€€.

The 44-storey, Ritz-Carlton-run Arts has redesigned all its rooms, and scores top marks for exemplary service. CD players, interactive TV, sea and city views and a 'Club' floor for VIPs are just some of the hedonistic perks awaiting guests. Outdoors, the beachfront pool overlooks Frank Gehry's bronze fish sculpture, and there is a range of bars and restaurants. The spectacular duplex apartments have butlering round-the-clock and chef services. The luxurious Six Senses Spa has fabulous views and is open to non-guests.

Hotel Duquesa de Cardona

Passeig Colom 12 (93 268 90 90/fax 93 268 29 31/www.hduquesade cardona.com). Metro Drassanes or Jaume I. €€€€.

This elegantly restored 16th-century palace retains lots of original features and is furnished with natural materials complemented by a soft colour scheme. The cosy bedrooms make it ideal for a romantic stay, particularly the deluxe rooms and junior suites on the higher floors with views out across the harbour. The beach is a ten-minute walk away, but guests can sunbathe on the decked roof terrace and then cool off afterwards in the plunge pool.

Hotel Medinaceli

NEW *Plaça del Duc de Medinaceli 8 (93 481 77 25/fax 93 481 77 27/ www.gargallo-hotels.com). Metro Drassanes.* €€€€.

The 44 rooms in this restored palace near the harbour are done out in soothing rusty shades. Some of the bathrooms have jacuzzi baths, while others come with massage showers. Repro versions of the sofa Dalí created inspired by Mae West's lips decorate the lobby, to match the crimson velvet thrones in the first-floor courtyard.

Montjuïc

Hostal BCN Port

NEW *Avda Paral·lel 15, entl (93 324 95 00/fax 93 324 93 53/www. hostalbcnport.com). Metro Drassanes or Paral·lel.* €€.

A smart new *hostal* near the ferry port, the BCN Port has rooms that are furnished in a chic contemporary style with not a hint of the kitsch decor prevalent in more traditional budget places. All the 19 rooms have en-suite bathrooms, as well as televisions and air-conditioning. Check the website for last-minute discounts.

Eixample

Hostal Central Barcelona

C/Diputació 346, pral 2ª (93 245 19 81/fax 93 270 07 54/www.hostal centralbarcelona.com). Metro Tetuán. €€.

Lodging at the Central, spread across two floors of an old Modernista building, is like staying in a rambling flat rather than a *hostal*. Rooms have kept their original tiling and high ceilings, but are kitted out with air-conditioning and double glazing; walls painted in a wide palette, from duck-egg blue to daffodil yellow, jolly things up.

Hostal d'Uxelles

Gran Via de les Corts Catalanes 688, pral (93 265 25 60/fax 93 232 85 67/ www.hotelduxelles.com). Metro Tetuán. €€.

A tastefully decorated *hostal*, with pretty tiles and antique furnishings. Pastel colours rule, and drapes hang romantically above the bedsteads. The best rooms have plant-filled balconies with tables and chairs, where you can have breakfast. It's a bargain, and staff are friendly too.

Hostal Eden

C/Balmes 55, pral 1ª (93 454 66 20/ fax 93 452 66 21/www.hostaleden.net). Metro Passeig de Gràcia. €€.

Located on three floors, this warm and relaxed *hostal* with friendly, helpful staff offers free internet access and has a sunny patio with a shower. The best rooms have marble bathrooms with corner baths, and Nos.114 and 115, at the rear, are quiet and have large windows overlooking the patio. Room 103 is dark but good-sized and quirky, with a sprawling bathroom.

Hostal Girona

C/Girona 24, 1º 1ª (tel/fax 93 265 02 59/www.hostalgirona.com). Metro Urquinaona. €€.

This gem of a *hostal* is filled with antiques, chandeliers and oriental rugs. The rooms may be on the simple side, but they all have charm. Outward-facing rooms have small balconies overlooking C/Girona; darker rooms with bigger balconies face on to a quiet patio. Gorgeous and good value.

Hostal Goya

C/Pau Claris 74, 1º (93 302 25 65/fax 93 412 04 35/www.hostalgoya.com). Metro Urquinaona. €€.

Located in a typical Eixample building with fabulous tiled floors, the bedrooms are done out in chocolates and creams, with comfy beds, chunky duvets and cushions; the bathrooms are equally luxurious. The best rooms either give out on to the street or the terrace at the back. The Goya is excellent value for money and a real gem of a place to stay.

Hostal Palacios

Rambla de Catalunya 27, 1º (93 301 30 79/fax 93 301 37 92/www.hostal palacios.com). Metro Catalunya. €€.

Situated in a sumptuous building, the 11 rooms at the Palacios are well equipped and decorated in a tasteful style, more typical of a four-star, with good bathrooms, air-con, digital TV and internet connection. Rates may seem high for a *hostal*, but the standard of the rooms, together with the location, make it good value.

Hostal San Remo

C/Ausiàs Marc 19, 1º 2ª (93 302 19 89/www.hostalsanremo.com). Metro Urquinaona. €.

The friendly owner Rosa and her fluffy white dog live on site and take good care of their guests. All seven of the rooms are equipped with air-con, blue-and-white striped bedspreads and modern wooden furniture; five out of seven have en-suite bathrooms, and most of them have a little balcony and double glazing. A good place to stay.

Hotel Axel

C/Aribau 33 (93 323 93 93/fax 93 323 93 94/www.axelhotels.com). Metro Universitat. €€€.

The buzzy Axel is a cornerstone of the 'Gaixample', as the area around the hotel is known. Good-looking staff sport T-shirts with the logo 'heterofriendly', and certainly everyone is made welcome at this funky boutique hotel. Huge beds come as standard, as does free mineral water. 'Superior' rooms have stained-glass gallery balconies and hydro-massage bathtubs. The Sky Bar on the rooftop is where it all happens, with a little pool, jacuzzi, sun deck, sauna and steam room.

Hotel Claris

C/Pau Claris 150 (93 487 62 62/fax 93 215 79 70/www.derbyhotels.es). Metro Passeig de Gràcia. €€€€.

Antiques and contemporary design merge together behind the neoclassical exterior of the Claris, which contains the largest private collection of Egyptian art in Spain. Some bedrooms are on the small side, while others are duplex, but all have Chesterfield sofas and plenty of art. The rooftop has a small pool, a cocktail bar and DJ.

Hostal Goya

Hotel Condes de Barcelona

Passeig de Gràcia 73-75 (93 445 00 00/fax 93 445 32 32/www.condesde barcelona.com). Metro Passeig de Gràcia. €€€€.
Renowned for its good service, the Condes is made up of two buildings that face each other across C/Mallorca. The building on the north side occupies a 19th-century palace and has a plunge pool on the roof. In the newer building, rooms on the seventh floor have terraces and a view of La Pedrera.

Hotel Constanza

C/Bruc 33 (93 270 19 10/fax 93 317 40 24/www.hotelconstanza.com). Metro Urquinaona. €€€.
The lobby has boxy, white sofas, lots of dark wood and Japanese silk screens painted with giant white lilies. Upstairs, wine-coloured corridors lead to sumptuous bedrooms with dark wood and leather furnishings, huge pillows and quality cotton sheets. Those at the back are quietest, and some of them have their own private terraces.

Hotel Granados 83

NEW *C/Enric Granados 83 (93 492 96 70/fax 93 492 96 90/www.derby hotels.es). Metro Diagonal.* €€€.
The original ironwork structure of this former hospital lends an unexpectedly industrial feel to the Granados 83. The 77 rooms, with brickwork walls, include duplex and triplex versions, some with their own terraces and plunge pools. For those mere mortals inhabiting the standard rooms, there is a rooftop pool and sun deck.

Hotel Jazz

C/Pelai 3 (93 552 96 96/fax 93 552 96 97/www.nnhotels.es). Metro Catalunya. €€€.
Rooms at the Hotel Jazz are super-stylish in calming tones of grey, beige and black, softened with parquet floors and spiced up with dapper pinstripe cushions. The beds are larger than usual for hotels, and bathrooms feature polished black tiles. A rooftop pool and sun deck top things off.

Hotel Majestic

Passeig de Gràcia 68 (93 488 17 17/ fax 93 488 18 80/www.hotelmajestic.es). Metro Passeig de Gràcia. €€€€.
The Majestic has long been one of Barcelona's grandest hotels. Behind a neoclassical façade lies a panoply of perks, such as a service that allows you to print a selection of the day's news-papers from all over the world. Rooms are suitably opulent, decorated with classical flair. The Drolma restaurant is one of the finest in the city.

Hotel Omm

C/Rosselló 265 (93 445 40 00/fax 93 445 40 04/www.hotelomm.es). Metro Diagonal. €€€€.
Feng shui goes space age at the drop-dead cool Omm. Bedrooms are sooth-ingly stylish, with lacquer screens and every gadget imaginable. Get a corner room and spend all day watching the urban scene below, before heading down to the Spaciomm spa for a Japanese massage. Up on the roof, the plunge pool offers fabulous views of Gaudí's landmark buildings.

Hotel Pulitzer

C/Bergara 8 (93 481 67 67/fax 93 481 64 64/www.hotelpulitzer.es). Metro Catalunya. €€€.

A discreet façade reveals an impressive lobby that's stuffed with comfortable white leather sofas, a reading area and a swanky bar and restaurant. The rooftop terrace is a fabulous spot for a cocktail, with tropical plants and views across the city. The rooms are small, but sumptuously decorated with cool elephant-grey marble and leather trim.

Market Hotel

Passatge Sant Antoni Abat 10 (93 325 12 05/fax 93 424 29 65/www.market hotel.com.es). Metro Sant Antoni. €€€.

The people who brought us the wildly successful Quinze Nits chain of restaurants apply their low-budget, high-design approach to this hotel, although prices have crept up in the year since it opened. The monochrome rooms are comfortable and stylish and downstairs is a keenly priced restaurant.

Prestige Paseo de Gràcia

Passeig de Gràcia 62 (93 272 41 80/ fax 93 272 41/81/www.prestige hotels.com). Metro Passeig de Gràcia. €€€€.

A 1930s building, revamped with a pleasing minimalist design scheme and Japanese gardens. The rooms are equipped with plasma-screen TVs, intelligent lighting systems, free minibars and even umbrellas. Outside their rooms, the hotel's guests hang out in the cool Zeroom lounge-bar-library, where expert concierges (of the funky rather than fusty variety) are constantly on hand.

the5rooms

C/Pau Claris 72 (93 342 78 80/fax 93 342 78 81/www.thefiverooms.com). Metro Catalunya or Urquinaona. €€€.

A chic and comfortable B&B in a handsome building, where the delightful Jessica Delgado makes every effort to ensure guests feel at home. Books and magazines are dotted around the stylish sitting areas and bedrooms, and breakfast is served at any time of day.

Casa Fuster

Passeig de Gràcia 132 (93 255 30 00/fax 93 255 30 02/www.hotelcasa fuster.com). Metro Diagonal. €€€€.

Designed by the illustrious Modernista architect Lluís Domènech i Montaner as a family home, this has regained its former glory as a swanky hotel with both art nouveau and art deco features. The 96 opulent rooms have original architectural details, along with flat-screen TVs and remote-controlled lighting. The bathrooms have period tiling alongside hydro-massage bathtubs and power showers.

Hostal HMB

NEW *C/Bonavista 21, 1° (93 368 20 13/www.hostalhmb.com). Metro Diagonal.* €€.

An excellent addition to Barcelona's budget hotel scene, the HMB opened in 2006 and it feels every bit as crisp, clean and airy as you might hope. Situated on the first floor with a lift, it has 12 rooms, which have high ceilings and are tastefully decorated in tones of blue and green with wood floors, flat-screen TVs and good lighting. All have private marble bathrooms with good showers. Bright contemporary artwork adorns the lobby and corridors.

Gran Hotel La Florida

Carretera de Vallvidrera al Tibidabo 83-93 (93 259 30 00/fax 93 259 30 01/www.hotellaflorida.com). €€€€.

From 1925 through to the 1950s, this was Barcelona's grandest hotel, frequented by an impressive roster of royals and film stars. It has lavish suites designed by artists, private terraces and gardens, a summer outdoor nightclub, breathtaking views from its infinity pool, and a luxury spa. A good choice if you want to relax in opulent style and spend most evenings in the hotel, but getting a cab from town at night can be tricky.

Getting Around

Arriving & leaving

By air

Aeroport de Barcelona

902 40 47 04/www.aena.es.

Barcelona's airport is at El Prat, just south-west of the city. Each airline works from one of the three main terminals (A, B or C) for all arrivals and departures. There are tourist information desks and currency exchanges in terminals A and B.

Aerobús

The airport bus (information 93 415 60 20) runs from each terminal to Plaça Catalunya, with stops at Plaça d'Espanya, C/Urgell and Plaça Universitat. Buses to the airport go from Plaça Catalunya (in front of El Corte Inglés), stopping at Sants station and Plaça d'Espanya. Buses run every 12-13mins, leaving the airport from 6am-midnight Mon-Fri and 6.30am-midnight at weekends, returning from Plaça Catalunya 5.30am-11.15pm Mon-Fri and 6am-11.15pm at weekends. The trip takes 35-45mins; a single is €3.75, a return (valid one week) €6.45. At night the N17 runs every hour, on the hour, between the airport (from 10pm) and Plaça Catalunya (from 11pm), with several stops on the way, including Plaça d'Espanya and Plaça Universitat. Last departures are at 5am. Journey time is 45 mins; the cost is a single metro fare.

Airport trains

A long overhead walkway between the terminals leads to the airport train station. Trains stop at Sants, Plaça Catalunya, Arc de Triomf and Clot-Aragó, all of which are also metro stops. Trains leave the airport at 13mins and 43mins past the hour, 6.13am-11.43pm Mon-Fri. Trains to the airport leave Plaça Catalunya at 8mins and 38mins past the hour, 5.38am-10.08pm Mon-Fri (5mins later from Sants). Weekend times vary slightly, but there are still usually trains every 30mins, mostly leaving Plaça Catalunya at 11mins and 41mins past the hour. The journey takes 17-30mins and costs €2.40 one way (there are no return tickets). Be aware that tickets are only valid for 2hrs after purchase. A little-publicised fact is that the T-10 metro pass can also be used.

Taxis from the airport

The basic taxi fare from the airport to central Barcelona should be €18-€26, including a €3 airport supplement. Fares are about 15% higher after 9pm and at weekends. There is a 90¢ supplement for each large piece of luggage placed in the car boot. All licensed cab drivers use the ranks outside the terminals.

By bus

Most long-distance coaches (both national and international) stop or terminate at **Estació d'Autobusos Barcelona-Nord** (C/Ali Bei 80, 902 26 06 06, www.barcelonanord.com). The **Estació d'Autobusos Barcelona-Sants** at C/Viriat, between Sants rail station and Sants-Estació metro stop, is only a secondary stop for many coaches, though some international Eurolines services (information 93 490 40 00, www.eurolines.es) begin and end journeys at Sants.

By train

Most long-distance services operated by the Spanish state railway company **RENFE** run from **Barcelona-Sants** station, easily reached by metro. A few services

ESSENTIALS

from the French border or south to Tarragona stop at the **Estació de França** in the Born, near the Barceloneta metro, but it's otherwise sparsely served. Many trains stop at **Passeig de Gràcia**, which can be the handiest for the city centre and also has a metro stop.

RENFE

National 902 24 02 02/international 902 24 34 02/www.renfe.es. **Open** *National* 5am-10pm daily. *International* 7am-midnight daily.

RENFE tickets can be bought at train stations, travel agents or reserved over the phone and delivered to an address or hotel for a small extra fee. They have some English-speaking phone operators.

Public transport

Although it's run by different organisations, Barcelona public transport is now highly integrated, with the same tickets valid for up to four changes of transport on bus, tram, local train and metro lines as long as you do it within 75 minutes. The **metro** is generally the quickest and easiest way of getting around the city. All metro lines operate from 5am to midnight Monday to Thursday, Sunday and public holidays; 5am to 2am Friday, and all through Saturday night as a pilot project. Depending on the success of this pilot, trains may also run all night on Friday from October 2007. **Buses** run throughout the night and to areas not covered by the metro system. Local buses and the metro are run by the city transport authority (**TMB**). Two underground train lines connect with the metro but are run by Catalan government railways, the **FGC**. One runs north from Plaça Catalunya; the other runs west from Plaça d'Espanya to Cornellà. Two tramlines are of limited use to visitors.

FGC information

Vestibule, Plaça Catalunya FGC station (93 205 15 15/www.fgc.net). **Open** 7am-9pm Mon-Fri.
Other locations: FGC Provença (open 9am-7pm Mon-Fri, closed Aug); FGC Plaça d'Espanya (open 9am-2pm, 4-7pm Mon-Fri).

TMB information

Main vestibule, Metro Universitat, Eixample (93 318 70 74/www.tmb.net). **Open** 8am-8pm Mon-Fri.
Other locations: vestibule, Metro Sants Estació & Sagrada Família (both 7am-9pm Mon-Fri; Sants also opens 9am-7pm Sat, 9am-2pm Sun); vestibule, Metro Diagonal (8am-8pm Mon-Fri).

Buses

Many city bus routes originate in or pass through the city centre, at Plaça Catalunya, Plaça Universitat and Plaça Urquinaona. However, they often run along different parallel streets, due to the city's one-way system. Not all stops are labelled and street signs are not always easy to locate. Most routes run 6am-10.30pm daily except Sundays. There's usually a bus every 10-15mins, but they're less frequent before 8am, after 9pm and on Saturdays. On Sundays, buses are less frequent still; a few do not run at all.

Board at the front and disembark through the middle or rear doors. Only single tickets can be bought from the driver; if you have a *targeta,* insert it into the machine behind the driver as you board.

Fares and tickets

Travel in the Barcelona urban area has a flat fare of €1.20 per journey, but multi-journey tickets or *targetes* are better value. The basic ten-trip *targeta* is the **T-10** (Catalan *Te-Deu*, Spanish *Te-Diez*) for €6.90, which can be shared by any number of people travelling simultaneously; the ticket is validated in the machines on the